THE
ANNALS

of the American Academy of
Political and Social Science

VOLUME 682 | MARCH 2019

Attitudes about Work: How They are Formed and Why They Matter

SPECIAL EDITORS:

Gerbert Kraaykamp
Radboud University, Nijmegen

Zeynep Cemalcılar
Koç University, Istanbul

Jale Tosun
Heidelberg University

Los Angeles | London | New Delhi
Singapore | Washington DC | Melbourne

Origin and Purpose. The Academy was organized December 14, 1889, to promote the progress of political and social science, especially through publications and meetings. The Academy does not take sides in controverted questions, but seeks to gather and present reliable information to assist the public in forming an intelligent and accurate judgment.

Meetings. The Academy occasionally holds a meeting in the spring extending over two days.

Publications. THE ANNALS of The American Academy of Political and Social Science is the bimonthly publication of the Academy. Each issue contains articles on some prominent social or political problem, written at the invitation of the editors. These volumes constitute important reference works on the topics with which they deal, and they are extensively cited by authorities throughout the United States and abroad.

Subscriptions. THE ANNALS of The American Academy of Political and Social Science (ISSN 0002-7162) (J295) is published bimonthly—in January, March, May, July, September, and November—by SAGE Publishing, 2455 Teller Road, Thousand Oaks, CA 91320. Periodicals postage paid at Thousand Oaks, California, and at additional mailing offices. POSTMASTER: Send address changes to The Annals of The American Academy of Political and Social Science, c/o SAGE Publishing, 2455 Teller Road, Thousand Oaks, CA 91320. Institutions may subscribe to THE ANNALS at the annual rate: $1191 (clothbound, $1345). Individuals may subscribe to the ANNALS at the annual rate: $130 (clothbound, $191). Single issues of THE ANNALS may be obtained by individuals for $40 each (clothbound, $56). Single issues of THE ANNALS have proven to be excellent supplementary texts for classroom use. Direct inquiries regarding adoptions to THE ANNALS c/o SAGE Publishing (address below).

All correspondence concerning membership in the Academy, dues renewals, inquiries about membership status, and/or purchase of single issues of THE ANNALS should be sent to THE ANNALS c/o SAGE Publishing, 2455 Teller Road, Thousand Oaks, CA 91320. Telephone: (800) 818-SAGE (7243) and (805) 499-0721; Fax/Order line: (805) 375-1700; e-mail: journals@sagepub.com. *Please note that orders under $30 must be prepaid.* For all customers outside the Americas, please visit http://www.sagepub.co.uk/customerCare.nav for information.

Printed on acid-free paper

THE ANNALS

© 2019 by The American Academy of Political and Social Science

Editorial Office: 202 S. 36th Street, Philadelphia, PA 19104-3806
For information about individual and institutional subscriptions address:
SAGE Publishing
2455 Teller Road
Thousand Oaks, CA 91320

For SAGE Publishing: Peter Geraghty (Production) and Mimi Nguyen (Marketing)

From India and South Asia, write to:
SAGE PUBLICATIONS INDIA Pvt Ltd
B-42 Panchsheel Enclave, P.O. Box 4109
New Delhi 110 017
INDIA

From Europe, the Middle East, and Africa, write to:
SAGE PUBLICATIONS LTD
1 Oliver's Yard, 55 City Road
London EC1Y 1SP
UNITED KINGDOM

International Standard Serial Number ISSN 0002-7162
ISBN 978-1-5443-7700-1 (Vol. 682, 2019) paper
ISBN 978-1-5443-7701-8 (Vol. 682, 2019) cloth
Manufactured in the United States of America. First printing, March 2019

Information about membership rates, institutional subscriptions, and back issue prices may be found on the facing page.

Advertising. Current rates and specifications may be obtained by writing to The Annals Advertising and Promotion Manager at the Thousand Oaks office (address above). Acceptance of advertising in this journal in no way implies endorsement of the advertised product or service by SAGE or the journal's affiliated society(ies) or the journal editor(s). No endorsement is intended or implied. SAGE reserves the right to reject any advertising it deems as inappropriate for this journal.

Claims. Claims for undelivered copies must be made no later than six months following month of publication. The publisher will supply replacement issues when losses have been sustained in transit and when the reserve stock will permit.

Change of Address. Six weeks' advance notice must be given when notifying of change of address. Please send the old address label along with the new address to the SAGE office address above to ensure proper identification. Please specify the name of the journal.

THE
ANNALS

of the American Academy of Political and Social Science

VOLUME 682 | MARCH 2019

IN THIS ISSUE:

Attitudes about Work: How They are Formed and Why They Matter

Special Editors: GERBERT KRAAYKAMP, ZEYNEP CEMALCILAR, and JALE TOSUN

Introduction

Conceptual Clarifications on Work Attitudes

How are Work Values Formed?

What are the Effects of Attitudes Toward Work?

Reflections

FORTHCOMING

The Future of Educational Assessment
Special Editors: MICHAEL FEUER, JAMES PELLEGRINO,
and AMY BERMAN

Mexican Migration Project
Special Editors: DOUGLAS S. MASSEY and JORGE DURAND

Introduction

Transmission of Work Attitudes and Values: Comparisons, Consequences, and Implications

By
GERBERT KRAAYKAMP,
ZEYNEP CEMALCILAR,
and
JALE TOSUN

Are attitudes toward work and perceptions of the benefits of work transmitted from parents to youth similarly across a variety of cultural contexts? What determines the centrality of work to one's life? How are intrinsic work values (intangible rewards such as autonomy, learning opportunities, and self-fulfillment) and extrinsic work values (such as status, income, and financial safety) shaped; and how do these work attitudes have consequences in the political, economic, and well-being domains? Are the determinants of work values robust across countries, and do the consequences of having certain work values differ by country? These research questions guide this issue of *The ANNALS*. This introductory article clarifies key concepts underlying the volume and provides an overview of the data sources and analytic approaches addressed in the individual contributions. Most importantly, we provide a broad theoretical framework with notions from various disciplines aimed at giving readers a fuller grasp of the multifaceted significance of work values.

Keywords: comparative analysis; transmission; work attitudes and values

Next to the importance that people attach to their family, work is one of the most valued qualities of life. In European countries, more than 80 percent of the population indicates that work is of major importance (World Value Survey wave 6; authors' calculations

Gerbert Kraaykamp is a professor of empirical sociology in the Department of Sociology at Radboud University, in the Netherlands. His major research interests include educational inequality, intergenerational transmission, and health inequality. He has published widely on these subjects in international scientific journals.

Zeynep Cemalcılar is an associate professor of social psychology at Koc University, Istanbul, Turkey. Her most recent research focuses on youth autonomy and self-sufficiency, subjective socioeconomic status, brief social psychological interventions, and technology in the social life.

Correspondence: g.kraaykamp@ru.nl

DOI: 10.1177/0002716219831947

based on Inglehart et al. 2014). This may not come as a surprise because most people, after leaving full-time education, face a lengthy period of being active in paid work, self-employment, or civil service. Daily activities are centered on work, and work provides financial security; most importantly, though, work relates to feelings of self-worth and self-identification (Rosso, Dekas, and Wrzesniewski 2010). Because work is perceived as exceptionally important by most people, several studies also underscore that qualities of work are strongly related to feelings of individual well-being and subjective health (Gallie et al. 2016). It is, therefore, often a major life event when people lose their work: the resulting financial restraints can impair the acquisition of basic necessities and luxury goods; but most importantly, losing employment can result in a loss of self-worth.

Building Research Questions

Attitudes toward work are the principles that guide individuals' vocational aspirations, career choices, and job satisfaction, and they also influence personal well-being (Kalleberg 1977; Gallie 2007; Gallie, Felstead, and Green 2012). These attitudes, work beliefs, or work ethic may also have implications for satisfaction with politico-administrative institutions and political participation (Shore and Tosun 2019a, 2019b). From an institutional perspective, employees' attitudes toward work are important since they likely affect the performance of businesses and the management of work tasks in modern competitive organizations (Robertson, Birch, and Cooper 2012). Work attitudes are regarded as even more important with the emergence of "new" forms of employment, which are characterized by more flexible working arrangements, temporary contracts, and enhanced responsibility for the employees (Bureau and Corsani 2016). It is unclear, however, whether working in more insecure labor arrangements increases or decreases intrinsic or extrinsic work values.

Aside from the effects for the individual, attitudes about working are also fundamental for general social welfare and the functioning of modern societies. Max Weber (1905/2013) pointed at the consequences of work ethics grounded in Protestant faith for economic growth in Western countries, and modernization theory (Inglehart and Baker 2000) implies that values related to work are

Jale Tosun is professor at the Institute of Political Science at Heidelberg University, Germany. Her research focuses on comparative public policy, international political economy, and public administration.

NOTE: This issue benefited from financial support by the project Cultural Pathways to Economic Self-Sufficiency and Entrepreneurship (CUPESSE; Seventh Framework Programme; Grant Agreement No. 61325), the Field of Focus 3 "Cultural Dynamics in Globalised Worlds," and the Field of Focus 4 "Self-Regulation and Regulation: Individuals and Organisations" at Heidelberg University. We further acknowledge helpful comments on this article by Julia Weiss. Dominic Afscharian, Marcel Katzlinger, Lucas Leopold, Julian Rossello, and Paul Thalmann provided valuable research assistance to the entire volume.

FIGURE 1
Conceptual Model

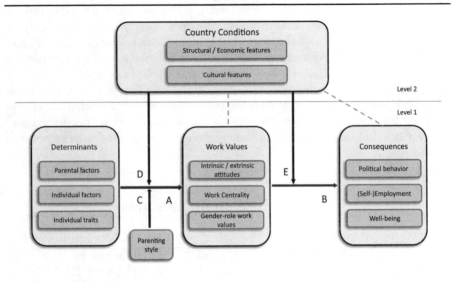

meaningful to explain the differences in cultural modernity and economic development between and within countries.

From this, it follows that the topic of work values is of great interest to the social sciences and that social scientific approaches to employment need to address more than the typical questions that preoccupy labor economists (e.g., labor supply, wage growth, skills mismatch, for example). Acknowledging the widespread interest in work values that cuts across disciplinary borders, in this volume we bring together theoretically informed and methodologically rigorous empirical investigations, seeking to further the state of research on the importance of work values and attitudes in the social sciences and the use of this scientific knowledge to improve development of public policy. To deal with this challenge, we aim to answer three main research questions. Figure 1 provides a schematic overview of this volume in terms of questions and relationships.

Several contributions deal with the first question, in which we focus on factors that possibly explain individual differences in work values and attitudes. Our main interest lies with studying processes of intergenerational transmission. So how do parents affect the work values of their children? Moreover, individual explanations dealing with personality traits and educational and occupational resources are taken into account (Figure 1, arrow A). The first question reads, *To what extent are parental qualities, individual traits, and individual resources relevant for the explanation of a person's work values?*

Work values may also have consequences in other domains of people's lives. By means of long-lasting socialization processes in a work context, individuals may develop work attitudes that consequentially lead to more motivation to be politically active, to become self-employed and report more well-being (arrow B). The second general question thus is, *To what extent do work values have consequences in the political, economic, and well-being domain?*

Last, this volume acknowledges that work values may not be similarly constituted and consequential in all contexts. Contexts are expected to affect people in various ways. Our collection of research is unique because we aim to point to the conditional effects of parental socialization in the transmission of values and resources across generations (arrow C). Additionally, we investigate the intergenerational transmission and possible consequences of work values in a number of countries. By doing so, we offer the opportunity to investigate whether transmission processes are differently affected by a country's economic and cultural constellation (arrow D) and whether having certain work values leads to different consequences in economically and culturally different countries (Figure 1, arrow E). This leads to the third research question: *To what extent do economic and cultural qualities of countries condition (1) the impact of determinants of work values and (2) the impact of work values on self-employment, political engagement, and well-being?*

To answer these research questions, contributing authors make use of several cross-national data sources with abundant information on both determinants of work values, on intrinsic and extrinsic work values and work ethics, and on several possible consequences of work values. We further combine theoretical insights from different branches of social and behavioral research to arrive at a more complete understanding of the causes and consequences of people's work values in varying contexts.

Work Values and Attitudes: Clarification of the Concepts

Values may be observed as internalized representations of moral beliefs that function as guiding principles for people's actions (Cemalcilar, Secinti, and Sumer 2018). A person's attitudes most often relate to a specific theme or situation and reflect personal opinions (Rokeach 1973). Values and attitudes are closely aligned, and research suggests that they are the products of cultural, institutional, and personal forces acting upon the individual (Brief and Nord 1990). Consequently, values and attitudes regarding work are shaped by interpersonal interactions, by social norms, and by experiences in the domain of work and in personal life. They mostly refer to goals people desire and would like to achieve through working. In this issue, the terms *work values* and *work attitudes* are used rather interchangeably. All contributions to this issue conceive extrinsic, and/or intrinsic work values, and/or work centrality as main dependent or independent characteristics of work attitudes (see Figure 1).

First, from Maslow's (1954) notion of a hierarchy of needs, it follows that some rewards from work are more basic than others (Kalleberg and Marsden, this volume). Basic needs generally refer to income resulting from work and the long-term security that work may offer. *Extrinsic work values* relate to these basic needs and emphasize the consequences of work in the sense of tangible rewards external to the individual, including status, income, and financial safety (Deci and Ryan 2000). Thus, people who aim to earn a lot of money, or obtain social status, or gain power and prestige in social networks are expected to be driven by extrinsic values (Van den Broek et al., this volume). Inherently, extrinsic values are not related to the work itself, the way one (has to) works, or the content of the work. Halman and Müller (2006) even stress that extrinsic rewards may be seen as a compensation for the general obligatory, unpleasant character of work.

Second, people generally come to value meaningful, self-actualizing work after fundamental needs regarding income and security have been fulfilled (Kalleberg and Marsden, this volume). Hence, these *intrinsic work values* focus on the process of work, that is, the intangible rewards that reflect the inherent interest in and motivation from work such as the job's potential to offer learning experience or working creatively (Deci and Ryan 2000). Likewise, others describe intrinsic work values in terms of the desire or strive for personal development, community contribution, and self-fulfillment (Van den Broek et al., this volume). Another aspect of intrinsic work values relates to people's value of the relative freedom to arrange their own work, decide on working hours, and decide on cooperation with others. It is important to acknowledge that prior research has demonstrated that extrinsic and intrinsic work values are not opposing phenomena but often go together within a worker (Gesthuizen and Verbakel 2011).

Third, we are interested in *work centrality*, which has its roots in Max Weber's work on the Protestant work ethic. A strong work ethic would have led to economic prosperity in Protestant countries in the eighteenth century (M. Weber 1905/2013). Work ethics may be described as the degree to which individuals place work at the center of their lives and regard hard work as intrinsically good (Cemalcilar, Secinti, and Sumer 2018). We conceive work centrality to correspond to individuals' perception of how important work is in their lives (Paullay, Alliger, and Stone-Romero 1994). We expect work ethics to vary across countries, since they are closely related to traditionalism and modernity of societal norms in different societies (Inglehart and Baker 2000).

Transmission of Work Values: Various Mechanisms

As an overarching and comprehensive theoretical guiding line to study transmission of work values, we employ Bronfenbrenner's (1979) socio-ecological framework. A focal point of this socio-ecological model is the relationship of individuals with their direct environment. Bronfenbrenner assumes that an individual's behavior and beliefs are affected by the social settings in which a person is situated and is developing (family, neighborhood, country). More specifically, Bronfenbrenner distinguishes micro, meso, exo, and macro systems that all are influential for the (lifelong) socialization and learning of individuals.

According to Bronfenbrenner (1979), these different systems may be observed as overarching layers, which may be described as a series of Russian dolls; the innermost level represents the individual (ego). An individual is accordingly sur-rounded and affected by different environmental forces. For instance, features of environments and experiences in a person's youth are directly associated with the family (micro-system), whereas growing up in lower- or higher-status families indirectly relates to the resource position of parents in comparison with their direct social environment (exo-system). Meso-systems refer to the school and work environments in which people are socialized and are affected through social and ideological learning (Grusec and Hastings 2014). Country characteristics affecting a person's development relate to macro-system features in Bronfenbrenner's terminology. The socio-ecological model closely aligns with Bourdieu's (1986) idea of the social space. Bourdieu argues that a person's life-style—attitudes and behaviors—is affected by a person's position in a so-called social space and by the distribution of scarce resources in that space.

From these theoretical insights, it follows that people may differ in their work values because they reside in different social settings (Kalleberg and Marsden, this volume). Therefore, all contributions emphasize that transmission of work values will be affected and conditioned by characteristics of the social environ-ments in which people are living. This may refer to the families from which individuals originate (e.g., Schönpflug 2008), the schooling they have experi-enced (e.g., Chapoulie 2017), and the workplaces in which they worked (e.g., B. Weber et al. 2017), but also to the country in which they are living (e.g., Hofstede 1984). Public policy is directed at the modification of these contexts in which people live, identifying specific target groups and designing policy measures to bring about behavioral changes (Tosun and Treib 2018). Growing up in a society, people also acquire cultural norms and values of their close surroundings via enculturation (Inglehart and Baker 2000). Consequently, a unique key feature of this volume is its country-comparative focus. We expect to provide novel insights into and a better understanding of how contexts matter for individuals' work attitudes and work ethics.

To explain the transmission of work values in this volume, we presume that the development of work-related opinions and values within individuals takes place during interactions with the social environment of people. First, we discuss how work values are nurtured in the process of socialization in families, schools, and work (Figure 1, arrows A and C). Second, we address how work values transfer to other domains and environments (arrow B). Third, we consider the larger country context. We study how causes and consequences of works values are conditioned by the structural and cultural constellation of various countries (arrows D and E).

Determinants of work values: Three socializing environments

A main issue that is addressed in this volume is how work values are formed and shaped within the individual (Gallie, this volume; Kalleberg and Marsden, this volume). In our research, we distinguish three levels of socialization or ideo-logical learning—in the family home, in education at schools, and at the work-place—to explain a person's work values. We thereby acknowledge that work values are shaped by experiences inside and outside the workforce (Kalleberg and Marsden, this volume). This is relevant because socialization in a family with intrinsic or extrinsic work values probably also predetermines children for certain schooling tracks and levels and also for a career in specific occupations (see, e.g., Chapoulie 2017). Hence, socialization environments are interrelated, and selection may be seen as a serious drawback. Therefore, to gain a complete picture of transmission processes with regard to work values, we account for all three major socialization domains (arrow A).

First, during childhood, the family provides the primary socialization ground, and it is expected to affect a person's work values (Kohn 1969). Especially in behavioral sciences and sociology, values and attitudes toward work are observed as being the outcome of a long-lasting process of upbringing and socialization in the family home (Schönpflug 2001). Socialization then is seen as "the acceptance of values, standards, and customs of a society as well as the ability to function in an adaptive way in the larger social context" (Grusec and Davidov 2007, 284). Parents convey their values and beliefs to their children directly (e.g., through active education), as well as indirectly through everyday routines (e.g., modeling desired behavior, norm-setting), and through the opportunities they provide to their children (Bryant, Zvonkovic, and Reynolds 2006; Döring et al. 2017). Opinions, activities, and instructions related to work in parental socialization likely result in (adult) attitudes on how to participate in a market economy, on how to value work, and what in work is meaningful and relevant. For instance, parents may exemplify in their upbringing a vast interest in earning money, thereby cultivating their children with more extrinsic work values; whereas other parents may emphasize self-development and independence, socializing their children with intrinsic work values (Wyrwich 2015). Parent-child value similarity as a result of socialization in the family may be observed as important for social adaptation and cultural continuity (Trommsdorff 2008). Yet there is no consensus on the degree of value similarity (Barni et al. 2013).

Second, education affects and nurtures people's attitudes (Kalmijn and Kraaykamp 2007). Through various experiences and learning processes, especially related to enrollment in higher education, children are expected to develop liberal and modern attitudes (Pascarella and Terenzini 1991). It may be that institutions of higher education transmit these values to students directly (by instruction), but likely having more education advances a person's breadth of perspective, which for instance leads to support for postmaterialistic (Inglehart and Baker 2000) and intrinsic work values (Gallie, this volume). It may also be that cognitive abilities of the higher educated affect their work attitudes directly, but it seems more likely that people with more cognitive abilities are better able to deal with complex issues and therefore express more balanced normative opinions (Kalmijn and Kraaykamp 2007).

Third, socialization in work-related values likely takes place at the workplace and will be affected by work circumstances and a person's work history. Kalleberg (1977) has stated that variation in work values are connected to differences in the nature of the jobs people perform and mentions organizational structure, job content, social factors, promotion opportunities, and hours of work as possible relevant factors. In this type of explanation of value differentiation, attitudes of workers are seen as a direct, one-to-one reflection of the structure of their workplace.

In this special issue of *The ANNALS*, we aim to advance our knowledge by investigating what socialization processes and qualities of parents, schools, and workplaces are important in the development of work attitudes (Figure 1, arrow A) (Aydinli et al. 2015; Jaramillo et al. 2017). Additionally, we study whether the quality of parenting is related to the transmission of work values in the family (arrow C). As a general expectation on the determinants of work values, we assume that parental socialization will nurture values with children that resemble parental values (parent-child similarity). Further, we expect, from the theoretical notions of Maslow (1954) and Inglehart and Baker (2000), that higher-income groups and those with higher education will more often support intrinsic work values and assign less value to the centrality of work in their lives. Finally, uncertain circumstances in a person's daily work probably lead to support for extrinsic work values more often. In this volume, we seek to identify the magnitude of the various socializing conditions that intervene in these value transmission processes.

Consequences of work values: How do they transfer in other domains?

We presume that the various ways people relate to their work, in terms of extrinsic or intrinsic values, or work commitment, may affect other domains of human life. First, in social psychology, self-determination theory (Deci and Ryan 2000) assumes that the incorporation of specific types of values (intrinsic or extrinsic) matters when looking at individual well-being. From this perspective, extrinsic work values are less satisfying for a person, because they are not associated with self-development and self-worth; there is a major focus on externalities. In contrast, self-actualization lies at the base of developing intrinsic work values. Thus, we expect that extrinsically motivated workers will be less satisfied with their life, experience less positive and more negative emotions, and have a negative self-image (Van den Broek et al., this volume). Indeed, meta-analytic evidence on single countries shows that people pursuing extrinsic rather than intrinsic values suffer from lower psychological and physical health (Dittmar et al. 2014). Based on prior research, we may also expect that intrinsically motivated workers with a high work ethic will more often start their work careers as self-employed than those who are extrinsically motivated (Lukeš et al., this volume).

Second, because work values are developed in various workplaces under various conditions, it is likely that parallel specific knowledge and capabilities will be produced. In the workplace, people also obtain the civic skills, mindset, and social networks they need to politically and socially participate. From this so-called spillover model (Visser et al., this volume), we may assume that work offers opportunities to learn how to participate in politics and how to start as self-employed. Moreover, work values may provide the ideological position and motivation required for political participation (Sobel 1993; Shore and Tosun 2019b).

Third, work values may be expressions of underlying moral and political positions (Visser et al., this volume). Such ideological positions will be (partly) developed at the workplace and may be important when looking at other behaviors and attitudes in the economic, political, and personal well-being domains (Inglehart and Baker 2000). This especially seems relevant because the work domain is important in politics; wage systems, company regulations, and labor market laws are directly affected by political decision-making.

In this volume, we thus aim to investigate what consequences intrinsic and extrinsic work values and work centrality have for individual nonelectoral political participation, for self-employment prospects, and for overall well-being (Figure 1, arrow B). As a general expectation, we assume that intrinsic work values go together with ideological learning and with interest in expanding capabilities. Thus, it is likely that intrinsically motivated workers with a high work ethic are also more politically active, more often self-employed, and score higher on well-being. On the other hand, extrinsically motivated people will be less often self-employed and more often will suffer from lower levels of well-being (see Lukeš et al., this volume).

Country comparisons: Are causes and consequences of work values affected differently by contexts?

One of the major contributions of this volume is that we consider work values in a cross-national comparative perspective. As Bronfenbrenner (1979) and Coleman (1988) presume, people may act and develop differently because of the social settings they are in. With regard to work values and attitudes, we expect that countries differ in the number of people who express support for intrinsic and extrinsic values. Indeed, earlier studies have shown that macroeconomic conditions affect support for extrinsic and intrinsic work values (Gallie 2007; Gesthuizen and Verbakel 2011). Such main effects are displayed in Figure 1 with dotted lines. However, in this volume, we actually are more interested in so-called conditioning factors (arrows D and E). By conditioning factors, we are referring to structural and cultural features of countries that affect the magnitude of the associations of various determinants of work values (arrow D) and of the associations between work values and their consequences (arrow E). Earlier comparative research on conditional effects of work values is generally lacking, and therefore our expectations are to some extent speculative.

First, we expect structural macroeconomic conditions to affect the transmission of work values between parents and children (Kittel et al., this volume). We further assume that the relationship between the individual determinants (education, workplace) and work values may be differently affected by a country's economic progress and wealth (arrow D). In general, we expect that transmission will be more difficult in times of economic crises and high unemployment, and that parents are more likely to transmit extrinsic work values that exemplify stable income and security. It may also be that macroeconomic circumstances affect the association between work values and becoming self-employed, nonelectoral participation, and personal well-being (arrow E). Perhaps economic adversity leads workers with extrinsic work values to express even lower well-being and to refrain from taking part in nonelectoral political action.

Second, based on the eminent works of Hofstede (1984) and Inglehart et al. (2014), we expect that the transmission of work values is affected by the cultural make-up (i.e., cultural values and norms) of a country (Figure 1, arrow D). Culturally, countries may be distinguished by their level of individualism or by their normative constellation (in family norms or gender norms). The transmission of work values by parents is more likely in collectivistic and family-orientated countries (Cemalcilar et al., this volume; Sümer et al., this volume). People are more bound to collective norms in such countries where there is larger attention to the family and social support. In contrast, individual determinants of educational attainment and workplace characteristics could be more relevant in individualistic countries. It is also likely that cultural features of a country affect the impact of work values for various consequences (arrow E). For instance, the Person-Environment fit perspective (Kristof-Brown, Zimmerman, and Johnson 2005) argues that the potential benefits of having a certain value is dependent on the values that are stressed in a person's larger environment. Consequently, we expect people with extrinsic values to experience more well-being in countries with an individualistic nature. Likewise, intrinsically motivated people will be more politically active in a collectivistic surrounding (Visser et al., this volume).

Data Sources

The contributions to this volume rely on six datasets, which vary with regard to the number of countries covered and to whether the data are longitudinal or cross-sectional. By using different databases, we seek to offer a rigorous test of our hypotheses that (country) contexts matter for how work values are being formed and what consequences they have. Of the six datasets used for the empirical analyses, five are well established and frequently used in social sciences.

First, the Cultural Pathways to Economic Self-Sufficiency (CUPESSE) data explicitly explore the role of the family setting for shaping the attitudes of the millennial generation in eleven countries: Austria, Czech Republic, Denmark, Germany, Greece, Hungary, Italy, Spain, Switzerland, Turkey, and the United Kingdom (for details, see Tosun et al. 2018). The CUPESSE dataset is novel and unique in its cross-national two-generation design. The sample was restricted to young adults between the ages of 18 and 35. Next to primary respondents, fathers and mothers were questioned, which underscores CUPESSE's unique qualities and makes it complementary to the other data sources. The CUPESSE dataset consists of 20,008 observations (with 5,945 observations with information on at least one parent).

Second, Kalleberg and Marsden as well as Gesthuizen et al. draw on data produced by the International Social Survey Programme (ISSP), which was established in 1984 and conducts annual surveys on diverse topics relevant to social sciences (see Scholz et al. 2017). What makes the ISSP data unique is that they cover a vast number of countries around the globe at different levels of socioeconomic development. Together with its design as a repeated survey, the ISSP data allow for comparisons across countries and over time.

Third, Van den Broeck et al. utilize data from the World Values Survey (WVS), which is also a repeated survey that is administered every five years (see Inglehart et al. 2014). The survey started in 1981 and consists of nationally representative surveys conducted in almost one hundred countries, which makes the WVS comparable to the ISSP. The current seventh wave of the WVS started in January 2017 and is expected to be completed in December 2019 with about seventy to eighty countries joining the program.

Fourth, Gesthuizen et al. employ the European Values Study (EVS) in their equivalence study. The EVS is a large-scale, cross-national, and longitudinal survey research program on basic human values, with the last wave taking place in 2017 in forty-seven European countries (see Bréchon and Gonthier 2017). Topics addressed in the EVS are values related to life, family, work, religion, politics, and society. The 2017 wave of the EVS places great emphasis on the Euro crisis and processes of disintegration in the European Union and how these developments have affected the identity of "Europeans." The current wave of the EVS is also interesting since it is based on a collaboration with the WVS.

Fifth, the European Social Survey (ESS) data are used by Lukeš et al. and Visser et al. in their contributions. ESS was established in 2001 and has been fielded biennially since 2002. The latest wave for which data are already available is the eighth wave (see, e.g., Breen 2017). The ninth wave is currently being fielded in twenty-five European countries. There is an overlap between the ESS and the EVS with their measurement of human values, which makes these two datasets complementary.

Last, Kalleberg and Marsden use single-country data originating from the General Social Survey (GSS), which is a continuing survey of adults in the United States stressing over-time replication of social indicators (see Smith et al. 2017). The GSS was first launched in 1972. While this database contains data for U.S. respondents only, its main strength lies in its longitudinal data that allow for rigorous testing of hypotheses.

Overview of the Contributions

This issue consists of eleven substantive empirical-analytical contributions that concentrate on the causes and consequences of work values and two reflection pieces that aim to distill the broader practical and scientific implications of the cumulative body of research.

To start, Duncan Gallie gives a comprehensive overview of how research on work values has developed over time. In his review, he identifies four phases in the pertinent literature on work values, with the first one starting in the late 1960s and early 1970s. This phase focused on the impact of economic development on work values. The second phase identified by Gallie corresponds to research in the early 1980s, which was concerned with the role of work values in accounting for unemployment. In the late 1980s, the third phase of research started and extended the focus to the implications of changing work values for women's increasing participation in the labor market. Since the 1990s, there has been increased interest in the intensity of role attachment to one's job and organization, which constitutes the fourth and final phase.

The contribution by Arne Kalleberg and Peter Marsden poses the following question: Are the work values of the millennial generation distinctive from those of other generations? In the past, scholars have raised similar questions about the distinctiveness of generations, but finding any compelling explanations for differences between generations has been complicated by aging effects, cohort or generational differences, and period effects. Using GSS and ISSP data, the authors assess the importance of life course differences and conclude that there are few differences in work values among members of different generations. They also find that people from less advantaged social origins are more likely to value extrinsic work values than those from more advantaged backgrounds.

Maurice Gesthuizen, Daniel Kovarek, and Carolin Rapp are interested in learning whether individuals in different cultural contexts place different emphasis on the items constructing either the extrinsic or the intrinsic work values scale. The authors show that there is a difference in the comparability of the data that tap into extrinsic and intrinsic work values: the latter are comparable in much fewer countries (namely, eight) than the first. Yet even with extrinsic work values, the data are comparable only for twenty-two of the forty-seven countries examined. The findings suggest that there is a trade-off between the number of items on the scale and the number of countries to include in an analysis. The findings presented add to the general methodological discussion of how many items are needed to measure a construct when aiming to produce data suitable for cross-national comparisons. While extrinsic and intrinsic work values are multidimensional concepts and require multiple items to capture different aspects of the individual dimensions, a greater number of items results in data that are less comparable across countries. In other words, the authors provide a methodological justification for scaling down the number of items used in cross-national survey studies.

Nebi Sümer, Daniela Pauknerová, Mihaela Vancea, and Elif Manuoğlu examine in detail the intergenerational transmission of work values in the Czech Republic, Spain, and Turkey. Relying on data produced in the CUPESSE project, the authors concentrate on parent-child similarities and the moderating role of parenting behaviors on work values. Of all contributions to this volume, this research perspective most directly captures processes of socialization in families and the mechanisms of the intergenerational transmission of work values in different cultural contexts. While there are differences in the parent-child similarity in work values (with respondents in Turkey having the highest and in the Czech Republic the lowest scores), the mechanisms of how work values are transmitted are remarkably similar across the countries examined. Parents that grant autonomy to their children, exert low levels of psychological control, and give their children emotional warmth increase the chances that their children have stronger moral and redistributive work values and weaker gender role–based work values.

Zeynep Cemalcilar, Carsten Jensen, and Jale Tosun examine both the extent to which work values of young people are determined by the work values of their parents and the extent to which the transmission of work values is conditioned by gender. Drawing from CUPESSE data for Denmark, Germany, Turkey, and the United Kingdom, they show that there is an unconditional and robust effect of socialization within families on work values. In other words, neither gender nor country idiosyncrasies, such as welfare regimes, condition the effect of the inter-generational transmission of work values.

The analyses of Bernhard Kittel, Panos Tsakloglou, and Fabian Kalleitner show that the transmission of work values within the family is a more fundamental determinant of work centrality in adolescents than individual and contextual factors. However, variation across regions does independently affect work values as well. The authors find that parental influence is the most robust determinant of adolescent work centrality, but individual-level variation is also affected by regional-level factors such as the female labor force participation rate.

Similarly drawing on the CUPESSE data and making use of the two-genera-tional structure of the data, Bettina Schuck and Jennifer Shore investigate whether the social mobility that young people have experienced (see Torche 2015) and the future mobility that they expect have an impact on their attitudes toward work and welfare. Results of logistic regression analyses suggest that the relationship between upward/downward mobility and an individual's views on work and welfare varies depending on the dimension of mobility, with expected future mobility exerting a stronger effect on attitudes toward work and welfare than past mobility experiences.

Martin Lukeš, Federico Vegetti, and Manuel Feldmann examine how work values impact different forms of labor market participation of young adults across Europe. The authors use both CUPESSE and ESS data to address their research question. The findings confirm the importance of intrinsic work values for self-employment and show that extrinsic values are more important to employees than to self-employed young people. The authors also find that work centrality does not differ between the employed and self-employed, which is a rather surprising finding considering the additional workload for self-employed people.

Emily Rainsford, William Maloney, and Sebastian Popa ask whether experiences of unemployment and low-quality work conditions have an impact on young adult's work values. Using CUPESSE data for young people in eleven European countries, the authors observe a positive effect on extrinsic work values for overqualification. In addition, their empirical investigation shows that unemployment and low-quality work conditions have a larger impact on the "younger" workers in their sample than their "older" counterparts. The latter finding underlines the importance of treating young people not as one coherent group and the need to look into how exactly age and work values are causally linked. In other words, among the young people, the "youngest" ones are the most vulnerable ones in terms of the "scarring effects" (Brandt and Hank 2014) of unemployment and underemployment. Consequently, policies aiming to promote the employment of young people should give this group priority and attempt to prevent them from experiencing unemployment or having to work in low-quality jobs (Tosun et al., this volume).

Mark Visser, Maurice Gesthuizen, and Gerbert Kraaykamp examine to what extent extrinsic and intrinsic work values are associated with nonelectoral political participation. The authors apply multilevel analysis to data from two rounds of the ESS covering thirty-one countries. The results show that people who are extrinsically motivated are less politically active while people who are intrinsically motivated are more politically active. Findings also show that people who highly value extrinsic job rewards are even less politically active in individualist countries, whereas people who highly value intrinsic job aspects are even more engaged politically in those countries. Lower levels of wealth, higher unemployment rates, and greater income inequality all weaken the relationship between work values and political action.

Anja Van den Broeck, Arne Vanderstukken, Karin Proost, and Bert Schreurs assess the health-enhancing effects of work values, which offers valuable insights into the effects of work values and how these depend on or are affected by contexts. Using data originating from the WVS, this contribution contrasts both perspectives in predicting life satisfaction, happiness, and health of young adults ($N = 10,430$) across the world. Results of multilevel analyses generally suggest that the type of values held by young adults and the type of values prevailing in one's environment matter more than their fit in the prediction of their life satisfaction, happiness, and health, as predicted by self-determination theory.

A final group of contributions offers a practical and academic reflection on the findings of the individual contributions to this volume. With a background in Greek and European Union politics, Anna Diamantopoulou and Kyriakos Pierrakakis show that work values were at the center of both the political and public debate on the causes of the so-called Eurozone debt crisis, which unfolded in 2009 (see also Tosun, Wetzel, and Zapryanova 2014). Most importantly, the Greek population—which was particularly heavily affected by the crisis—was perceived to be responsible for its economic hardship due to its low work values. Such claims were expressed by mass media as well as politicians of the other EU member states and became internalized by the general public in these countries as indicated by public opinion data.

In the last article, Jale Tosun, Gerbert Kraaykamp, and Zeynep Cemalcilar summarize the main findings of the volume. Furthermore, the editors reflect on the findings by adopting interdisciplinary perspectives from psychology, public policy, and sociology. Most importantly, this piece highlights the main takeaway for the general public, social scientific scholars, and policy-makers.

References

Aydinli, Arzu, Michael Bender, Athanasios Chasiotis, Fons J. R. van de Vijver, Zeynep Cemalcilar, Alice Chong, and Xiandong Yue. 2015. Implicit and explicit prosocial motivation as antecedents of volunteering: The moderating role of parenthood. *Personality and Individual Differences* 74 (2): 127–32.

Barni, Daniela, Sara Alfieri, Elena Marta, and Rosa Rosnat. 2013. Overall and unique similarities between parents' values and adolescent or emerging adult children's values. *Journal of Adolescence* 36 (6): 1135–41.

Bourdieu, Pierre. 1986. The forms of capital. In *Handbook of theory and research for the sociology of education*, ed. John G. Richardson, 241–58. New York, NY: Greenwood Press.

Brandt, Martina, and Karsten Hank. 2014. Scars that will not disappear: Long-term associations between early and later life unemployment under different welfare regimes. *Journal of Social Policy* 43 (4): 727–43.

Bréchon, Pierre, and Frédéric Gonthier, eds. 2017. *European values. Trends and divides over thirty years*. Leiden: Brill Publishers.

Breen, Michael J., ed. 2017. *Values and identities in Europe: Evidence from the European Social Survey*. New York, NY: Taylor & Francis.

Brief, Arthur P., and Walter R. Nord, eds. 1990. *Meanings of occupational work: A collection of essays*. Lexington, MA: Lexington Books.

Bronfenbrenner, U. 1979. *The ecology of human developments: Experiments by nature and design*. London: Harvard University Press.

Bryant, Brenda K., Anisa M. Zvonkovic, and Paula Reynolds. 2006. Parenting in relation to child and adolescent vocational development. *Journal of Vocational Behavior* 69 (1): 149–75.

Bureau, Marie-Christine, and Antonella Corsani. 2016. New forms of employment in a 24lobalized world: Three figures of knowledge workers. *Work Organisation, Labour and Globalisation* 10 (2): 101–12.

Cemalcilar, Zeynep, Ekin Secinti, and Nebi Sumer. 2018. Intergenerational transmission of work values: A meta-analytic review. *Journal of Youth and Adolescence* 47 (8): 1559–79.

Chapoulie, Jean-Michel. 2017. Schooling in France: From organizational to informal inequality. *The ANNALS of the American Academy of Political and Social Science* 673:235–50.

Coleman, James S. 1988. Social capital in the creation of human capital. *American Journal of Sociology* 94:95–120.

Deci, Edward L., and Richard M. Ryan. 2000. The "what" and "why" of goal pursuits: Human needs and the self-determination of human behavior. *Psychological Inquiry* 11 (4): 227–68.

Dittmar, Helga, Rod Bond, Megan Hurst, and Tim Kasser. 2014. The relationship between materialism and personal well-being: A meta-analysis. *Journal of Personality and Social Psychology* 107 (5): 879–924.

Döring, Anna K., Elena Makarova, Walter Herzog, and Anat Bardi. 2017. Parent-child value similarity in families with young children: The predictive power of prosocial educational goals. *British Journal of Psychology* 108 (4): 737–56.

Gallie, Duncan. 2007. Welfare regimes, employment systems and job preference orientations. *European Sociological Review* 23 (3): 279–93.

Gallie, Duncan, Alan Felstead, and Francis Green. 2012. Job preferences and the intrinsic quality of work: The changing attitudes of British employees 1992–2006. *Work, Employment and Society* 26 (5): 806–21.

Gallie, Duncan, Michael Gebel, Johannes Giesecke, Karin Halldén, Peter Van der Meer, and Rudi Wielers. 2016. Quality of work and job satisfaction: Comparing female part-time work in four European countries. *International Review of Sociology* 26 (3): 457–81.

Gesthuizen, Maurice, and Ellen Verbakel. 2011. Job preferences in Europe: Tests for scale invariance and examining cross-national variation using EVS. *European Societies* 13 (5): 663–86.

Grusec, Joan E., and Maayan Davidov. 2007. Socialization in the family: The roles of parents. In *Handbook of socialization theory and research*, eds. Joan E. Grusec and Paul D. Hastings, 284–308. New York, NY: Guilford Publications.

Grusec, Joan E., and Paul D. Hastings, eds. 2014. *Handbook of socialization: Theory and research*. New York, NY: Guilford Publications.

Halman, Loek, and Hans Müller. 2006. Contemporary work values in Africa and Europe: Comparing orientations to work in African and European societies. *International Journal of Comparative Sociology* 47 (2): 117–43.

Hofstede, Geert. 1984. *Culture's consequences: International differences in work-related values*. Thousand Oaks, CA: Sage Publications.

Inglehart, Ronald, and Wayn E. Baker. 2000. Modernization, cultural change, and the persistence of traditional values. *American Sociological Review* 65 (1): 19–51.

Inglehart, Ronald, Christian Haerpfer, Alejandro Moreno, Christian Welzel, Kseniya Kizilova, Jaime Diez-Medrano, Marta Lagos, Pippa Norris, Eduard Ponarin, and Bi Puranen, eds. 2014. World Values Survey: Round Six – Country-pooled datafile version. Available from http://www.worldvaluessurvey.org/.

Jaramillo, Jorge M., María I. Rendón, Lorenza Muñoz, Mirjam Weis, and Gisela Trommsdorff. 2017. Children's self-regulation in cultural contexts: The role of parental socialization theories, goals, and practices. *Frontiers in Psychology* 8 (923): 1–21.

Kalleberg, Arne L. 1977. Work values and job rewards: A theory of job satisfaction. *American Sociological Review* 42 (1): 124–43.

Kalmijn, Matthijs, and Gerbert Kraaykamp. 2007. Social stratification and attitudes: A comparative analysis of the effects of class and education in Europe 1. *British Journal of Sociology* 58 (4): 547–76.

Kohn, Melvin L. 1969. *Class and conformity: A study in values*. Homewood, IL: Dorsey Press.

Kristof-Brown, Amy L., Ryan D. Zimmerman, and Erin C. Johnson. 2005. Consequences of individuals' fit at work: A meta-analysis of person-job, person-organization, person-group, and person-supervisor fit. *Personnel Psychology* 58 (2): 281–342.

Maslow, Abraham H. 1954. *Motivation and personality*. New York, NY: Harper.

Pascarella, Ernest T., and Patrick T. Terenzini. 1991. *How college affects students*. San Francisco, CA: Jossey-Bass.

Paullay, Irina M., George M. Alliger, and Eugene F. Stone-Romero. 1994. Construct validation of two instruments designed to measure job involvement and work centrality. *Journal of Applied Psychology* 79 (2): 224–28.

Robertson, Ivan T., Alex Jansen Birch, and Cary L. Cooper. 2012. Job and work attitudes, engagement and employee performance: Where does psychological well-being fit in? *Leadership & Organization Development Journal* 33 (3): 224–32.

Rokeach, Milton. 1973. *The nature of human values*. New York, NY: Free Press.

Rosso, Brent D., Kathryn H. Dekas, and Amy Wrzesniewski. 2010. On the meaning of work: A theoretical integration and review. *Research in Organizational Behavior* 30:91–127.

Scholz, Evi, Regina Jutz, Jon H. Pammett, and Markus Hadler. 2017. ISSP and the ISSP 2014 Citizenship II Module: An introduction. *International Journal of Sociology* 47 (1): 1–9.

Schönpflug, Ute. 2001. Intergenerational transmission of values: The role of transmission belts. *Journal of Cross-Cultural Psychology* 32 (2): 174–85.

Schönpflug, Ute, ed. 2008. *Cultural transmission: Psychological, developmental, social, and methodological aspects*. Cambridge: Cambridge University Press.

Shore, Jennifer, and Jale Tosun. 2019a. Assessing youth labour market services: Young people's perceptions and evaluations of service delivery in Germany. *Public Policy and Administration* 34 (1): 22–41.

Shore, Jennifer, and Jale Tosun. 2019b. Personally affected, politically disaffected? How experiences with public employment services impact young people's political efficacy. *Social Policy & Administration*. DOI: 10.1111/spol.12496.

Smith, Tom W., Michael Davern, Jeremy Freese, and Michael Hout. 2017. *General Social Surveys, 1972–2016*. Chicago, IL: NORC.

Sobel, Richard. 1993. From occupational involvement to political participation: An exploratory analysis. *Political Behavior* 15 (4): 339–53.

Torche, Florencia. 2015. Analyses of intergenerational mobility: An interdisciplinary review. *The ANNALS of the American Academy of Political and Social Science* 657 (1): 37–62.

Tosun, Jale, Jose L. Arco-Tirado, Maurizio Caserta, Zeynep Cemalcilar, Markus Freitag, Felix Hörisch, Carsten Jensen, Bernhard Kittel, Levente Littvay, Martin Lukes, et al. 2018. Perceived economic self-sufficiency: A country- and generation-comparative approach. *European Political Science*. doi:10.1057/s41304-018-0186-3.

Tosun, Jale, and Oliver Treib. 2018. Linking policy design and implementation styles. In *The Routledge handbook of policy design*, eds. Michael Howlett and Ishani Mukherjee, 316–30. London: Routledge.

Tosun, Jale, Anne Wetzel, and Galina Zapryanova. 2014. The EU in crisis: Advancing the debate. *Journal of European Integration* 36 (3): 195–211.

Trommsdorff, Gisela. 2008. Intergenerational relations and cultural transmission. In *Cultural transmission: Psychological, developmental, social, and methodological aspects*, ed. Ute Schönpflug, 126–60. Cambridge: Cambridge University Press.

Weber, Bruce A., J. Matthew Fannin, Sam M. Cordes, and Thomas G. Johnson. 2017. Upward mobility of low-income youth in metropolitan, micropolitan, and rural America. *The ANNALS of the American Academy of Political and Social Science* 672:103–22.

Weber, Max. 1905/2013. *The Protestant ethic and the spirit of capitalism*. New York, NY: Routledge.

Wyrwich, Michael. 2015. Entrepreneurship and the intergenerational transmission of values. *Small Business Economics* 45 (1): 191–213.

Conceptual Clarifications on Work Attitudes

Research on Work Values in a Changing Economic and Social Context

By
DUNCAN GALLIE

This article examines the agenda of research on work values that has been developing since the late 1960s. It distinguishes four phases, which successively broadened the scope of research on work values. The first phase focused on the likely impact of economic development and rising incomes on work values. The second interrogated the role of work values for those experiencing unemployment. The third extended the focus to gendered work values related to women's increasing participation in the labor market. Finally, there has been increased interest in the strength of role attachment to a job and organization. In each area of research, the growth over time of cross-national comparative studies has revealed variations in work values across countries that point to the importance of understanding differences in institutional structures and cultural values.

Keywords: work values; orientations to work; postmaterialism; unemployment; gender attitudes; knowledge economy; high performance management

Work values have been central to debates over the last 50 years about the implications of the changing nature of work for personal well-being. There have been strongly contrasting views, however, about their nature, the factors that influence them, and their stability or change over time. These arguments have been shaped by the changing economic and social context across the globe, which has influenced particular value structures and their determinants.

A developing research literature has revealed the importance of accounting for the multidimensionality of work values. At the most

Duncan Gallie is an emeritus fellow of Nuffield College, Oxford. His research has focused on the quality of work and on unemployment. He has advised the French government on psychosocial risks at work and the OECD on guidelines to national governments for monitoring the quality of work.

Correspondence: duncan.gallie@nuffield.ox.ac.uk

DOI: 10.1177/0002716219826038

general level, they can be conceived as relatively enduring ideals that provide personal goals, motivate behavior, and give standards for judging the desirability of situations and actions (Hitlin and Piliavin 2004).

They can refer, however, to quite different facets of people's relationship to work (Mercure and Vultur 2010). They may relate to the importance or centrality that people attach to work as part of their overall life preoccupations (Dubin 1956). This may be the absolute level of importance of work to people's lives (often referred to as employment commitment) or its relative importance in relation to other life values. Work values also can refer to the rewards that people want from work—for instance whether they are primarily attached to intrinsic values such as autonomy, self-realization through the use of their skills, and personal development, or whether they are primarily concerned with extrinsic values, such as pay and hours—that help them to achieve goals outside work. Last, work values may concern the value that people attach to their roles as members of a specific organization or as practitioners of a particular type of job.

The relative importance of these dimensions in discussions of work values has varied over time. Underlying such shifts of emphasis has been change in the principal concerns of academics and policy-makers about the broader social implications of work values. This has reflected both the structural transformations and the cyclical phases of advanced capitalist societies over the period.

The aim of this article is to chart the main contours of this evolving research agenda, and to highlight the very different types of work values that need to be taken into account and some of the key lessons that have been learned about the factors that determine them. Very broadly, it is possible to distinguish four phases in the literature, characterized by progressive extension of the scope of research themes. The first, starting in the late 1960s and early 1970s, focused on the likely impact on work values of economic development—providing strongly contrasting scenarios of increasing instrumentalism and rising post-materialist values. The second, stimulated by the economic crisis of the early 1980s, was concerned with the role of work values in accounting for unemployment. The third, increasingly important from the late 1980s on, extended the focus to the implications for changing work values of women's increasing participation in the labor market. Finally, in the last two decades, in a context of theoretical interest in the growth of a knowledge economy and its presumed affinity with high performance systems of management, there has been increased interest in the intensity of role attachment to a job and organization.

Economic Development, Instrumentalism and Post-Materialist Values

The emergence of sociological debates about work values, in the late 1960s and early 1970s, developed in reaction to an earlier intellectual environment in which work values were commonly viewed as an expression of relatively constant human needs. The most direct challenge to the assumptions of these earlier traditions was raised by the Affluent Worker study (Goldthorpe et al. 1968). The authors' point of departure was that "wants and expectations are culturally determined *variables*, not psychological constants" (p. 178). More specifically, they argued that work values were in the process of transformation, with structural changes leading to a more privatized social life and a growing importance of conjugal family life. This was associated with an increased concern with consumption and, hence, with a definition of work as largely instrumental, a means to ends, which were extrinsic to the work situation. The shift involved then both a change in the centrality of work to people's lives and in the values that they attached to work. Goldthorpe et al. (1968, 1969) argued that these new orientations to work were likely to be prototypical and would develop more widely in the future among both manual workers in manufacturing and lower white collar workers involved in routine administrative work.

The study initiated a debate that informed research over many years. Some critics suggested that withdrawal of interest from work might reflect the lack of opportunities for self-realization in work (Daniel 1969). The conditions of work in the automobile assembly lines that Goldthorpe and his colleagues had studied could be seen as the quintessence of the type of alienating work environment that Marx had thought likely to lead to a harmful suppression of the inner human need for self-realization through work. Other critical contributions questioned whether there was a need to distinguish instrumental from economic orientations (Ingham 1970), whether orientations were in fact relatively stable over time (Blackburn and Mann 1979), and whether diverse and complex empirical patterns of work values can be captured adequately by relatively simple typologies (Bennett 1974, 1978; Mercure and Vultur 2010).

In the early 1970s, however, a strongly contrasting prediction emerged about the consequences of economic and social change for work values. Inglehart (1971, 1977) argued that unprecedented prosperity and the absence of total warfare had provided people with a level of security that was conducive to an upward shift in aspirations away from "materialist" toward "post-materialist" values, which gave primacy to values of self-actualization. Such value shifts, he argued, occur through generational change, since values are acquired primarily in early socialization and remain relatively stable through adult life. Although this line of research was initially concerned with the implication of value shifts for people's political priorities, the growth of post-materialist values became relevant for various institutional spheres, including work (Inglehart 1977).

Empirical research in the following decades led to a considerably more complex picture of the pattern of change in work values than suggested by either of these conflicting scenarios. A cross-national study in the mid-1980s of the relative importance of work and other life domains concluded that work, followed closely by the home and family, remained the most central life domain for adults (Super and Šverko 1995). The same study showed that, in terms of specific reward values, personal development, ability utilization, and achievement were ranked highest in all countries. The measure most frequently used by research into employment commitment focused on nonfinancial (or intrinsic) employment commitment—whether people would wish to continue to work, even if they had enough money to live as comfortably as they would like for the rest of their lives. Studies in the United States show that employment commitment was very high in the 1970s—approximately 72 percent wanted to continue to work, even without the need for money (Quinn and Staines 1979). However, there was a downward trend in employment commitment in the United States from the mid-1970s through to approximately 1993, which then leveled off between 1994 and 2006, at which time 68 percent wanted to continue in work irrespective of financial need (Highhouse et al. 2010). A British study in 1981, using the same measure, found that 69 percent of all employed men and 65 percent of women would want to continue to work even without financial necessity (Warr 1982). Subsequent research suggested that employment commitment in Britain remained very stable over the period 1981 to 1992 (Gallie et al. 1998).

A comparison of work values in European countries between the early 1990s and the mid-2000s (Hajdu and Sik 2015) concluded that, while work had become less central relative to other life spheres for people in the EU (especially in the postsocialist countries), there was only a very marginal decline in employment commitment. Moreover, there was no evidence that this reflected differences in specific birth cohorts, contrary to the view that there had been changes in the importance attached to work due to changes in patterns of early socialization.

With respect to work reward values, Esser and Lindh (2018), in a study of nineteen OECD countries, found, in general, a picture of relative stability in extrinsic and intrinsic job preferences, with, in some countries, a tendency toward an increase in the importance of intrinsic values. A picture of intergenerational stability in intrinsic work values emerges from studies in the United States (Twenge 2010). The influence of family background on work values is one factor that can help to explain this continuity (Lindsay and Knox 1984). Further, since in many cross-national studies, education has been found to be strongly related to levels of employment commitment and to expressive and self-development values, the general rise in education levels may partially explain the continuing (and possibly increasing) importance of intrinsic values (MOW 1987; Harding, Phillips, and Forgarty 1986; Hult and Svallfors 2002).

The principal conclusion, however, that emerged from comparative studies was that there was substantial variation among countries in work centrality, employment commitment, and work reward values. This was shown for work centrality in the 1980s by a cross-national study involving eight countries (MOW 1987). Others studies have found considerable differences in employment commitment. Hult and Svallfors (2002) noted the higher level of employment commitment in Norway and Sweden than in liberal countries—such as Britain, New Zealand, and the United States—with their much weaker forms of employment and labor market regulation. They saw this as evidence of a "production regime" effect, whereby a stronger emphasis on skill-oriented work in coordinated market economies led to work practices that were more conducive to high commitment than those in more rule-oriented systems. Taking a broader range of countries, Esser (2005) concluded that both strong welfare systems and skills-focused production systems favored higher employment commitment. Steiber (2013) found employment commitment highest in the continental and Scandinavian countries, and lowest in the southern and in the transition (or formerly state socialist) European countries. She accounted for this in terms of variations in both the level of economic development and in the quality of jobs.

There were also important country variations with respect to the importance of reward values. Gallie (2007) found that intrinsic values were significantly stronger in Denmark, Finland, and Sweden than in either Germany or Britain, and attributed this in particular to the higher education level of employees and the better quality of working conditions in the former countries. In their study of OECD countries, Esser and Lindh (2018) concluded that extrinsic and "collective" intrinsic values (such as work useful for society or that helps others) differ mainly across countries rather than period, although valuations of job autonomy were more similar.

In short, the comparative studies point to three broad conclusions. There is no necessary logic of economic development that leads to a decline in commitment to employment and to higher instrumentalism; rather, the evidence points to a high stability of work values over time. Second, institutional factors make a substantial difference to employment commitment even among more economically developed countries. Finally, while early socialization and education were generally important determinants of employment commitment and intrinsic reward values, differences in job quality also help to account for country differences.

Unemployment and Employment Commitment

The sharp rise in unemployment, and particularly long-term unemployment, in almost all OECD countries in the early 1980s led to the emergence of a new agenda, focusing on the role of work values in accounting for the behavior of the unemployed. For neo-liberal economists, the growth of long-term unemployment was accentuated by a low level of work motivation among those who had lost their jobs, partly resulting from the financial safety net provided by the welfare state. In this perspective, relatively high levels of benefit relative to potential wages led people to prefer to remain unemployed rather than actively seek work. It is a view informed by the assumption that work is a "disutility" for people, so that there will be a general preference for leisure over work, as long as it is possible to afford what is required to meet basic needs. This may be reinforced by a tendency of people to adapt to their situation over time by finding other activities that fill their time and give a sense to their everyday lives.

The main approach for testing these assumptions was to examine the relationship between the replacement rate (the ratio of unemployment benefit to earnings from employment) and the duration of unemployment. The empirical results, however, did not provide impressive evidence in support of the theory. In a review of over a decade of research, Spiezia (2000) concluded that even those studies that had detected an effect of benefits on unemployment duration found that it was rather small. On average, the estimates implied that a 10 percent increase in the replacement rate would be associated with an increase of only one to one and a half weeks in unemployment duration.

The view that the unemployed are work shy and that unemployment durations are an indicator of low commitment to employment came under sustained criticism from both psychologists and sociologists. An influential paper by Peter Warr (1982), drawing on a national survey in Britain, showed that a majority of unemployed men (62 percent) wanted employment even if there was no financial necessity for it, although the figure was notably lower for women. A British study, carried out in 1986 when unemployment reached its highest level in that decade, found that the commitment of the unemployed was even higher than that of the employed—77 percent compared with 66 percent (Gallie and Vogler 1994). The difference in employment commitment between unemployed men and women had virtually disappeared. The same study showed that the unemployed were also not characterized by any high level of inflexibility with respect to the pay they were hoping to receive or their openness to retraining, although only a minority (40 percent) were willing to move from the area they lived in to find a job.

In the 1990s, with the increased availability of cross-national data, research on the unemployed expanded into the comparison of European countries. The results proved very consistent across countries in the EU-15:[1] a study in 1996 found that in all countries the unemployed had higher employment commitment than the employed (Gallie and Alm 2000). The extent of difference varied, however, between countries. It was greatest in the Netherlands, Great Britain, Greece, and France and lowest in Finland, Sweden, and Denmark. Steiber (2013), drawing on data for nineteen European countries in 2010, also found that the unemployed were more committed than those in paid work. Although the commitment scores for the unemployed were higher than for the employed in each region (other the Scandinavian countries where they were the same), the difference was only statistically significant in the southern and transition (or Eastern European) countries. The relatively higher employment commitment of the unemployed in those two regions did not reflect greater commitment of the unemployed themselves in those regions, but the markedly lower commitment of those in work.

Even if there is little evidence that the unemployed overall have lower commitment to employment, it could be that there are particular subgroups—such as the long-term unemployed or the young—that are likely to develop cultures antithetical to the work ethic. However, the empirical evidence suggested that the employment commitment of those with longer experiences of unemployment (12 months or more) was very similar to that of those who had shorter-term experiences of job loss (Gallie and Alm 2000). Steiber (2013), examining data a decade later, also found little impact of duration of unemployment on employment commitment. Similarly, there was no evidence that the young unemployed had a weaker attachment to work. Indeed, the evidence showed higher levels of commitment among younger British unemployed people (16–24) than those in all other age groups (Warr 1982), while, in a wider set of European countries, Steiber (2013) found that the unemployed in their twenties had significantly higher levels of employment commitment than their equivalents in work.

The issue of whether unemployment benefits undermined employment motivation had implications for views about the welfare state. Those who thought that replacement rates were demotivating favored a minimalist welfare state that emphasized cutting benefits to increase financial pressure on the unemployed. Esser (2005) addressed this issue by comparing the employment commitment of those who were in countries with relatively generous welfare regimes and those who were in countries that had low benefit (primarily means tested) provision. Focussing on twelve countries—Canada, Denmark, Germany, Italy, Japan, the Netherlands, New Zealand, Norway, Sweden, Switzerland, the United Kingdom, and the United States—she brought together attitudinal data with detailed comparative information on the level of a variety of welfare benefits. This showed that higher benefit provision was related to higher, not lower, employment commitment both for those in work, and also, even more strongly, for the unemployed. This positive effect was reinforced by institutional systems in which production was organized in a way that led to high quality jobs.

The overall picture then is that the unemployed are at least as committed to employment as those in work, and that generous welfare provision encourages higher motivation. The principal measures used, however, capture general attitudes toward employment rather than views about particular types of jobs. As Warr (1982) has shown, a commitment to work, even among the employed, does not necessarily imply that people would want their current job. It seems reasonable to assume that people respond using the reference point of a desirable or decent job. A recent British study found that, despite the consistent evidence of a positive attitude toward employment, the unemployed may not necessarily think that taking "any job" would be an improvement on the state of unemployment (Dunn, Grasso, and Saunders 2014). Indeed, perhaps reflecting greater familiarity with the characteristics of poor jobs, they were more likely to disagree that this would be the case. The quality of proposed job offers may then be an important factor moderating the implications of employment commitment for labor market behavior. This would again point to the higher capacity for the integration of the unemployed in countries that foster the conditions for better job quality.

Gender Differences in Work Values

In the early phase of the expansion of women's employment participation, the prevailing view was that women were entering the labor market largely as secondary workers, with rather different work attitudes than men—particularly with respect to lower work centrality, weaker commitment to employment, and lower attachment to the intrinsic rewards of work. The subsequent sharp rise in female employment rates placed a new central issue on the research agenda: whether women have continued to have distinctive patterns of work attitudes despite their growing participation in the labor force or whether there has been a convergence in work values between men and women.

Studies in the 1980s generally confirmed that women were less likely to regard paid employment as a central life interest. The Meaning of Work (MOW 1987) comparative study of eight countries, examining data from 1980 to 1982, found that work centrality was significantly higher for men than for women. Comparing the United States, West Germany, and Israel, Agassi (1982) concluded that women were notably less likely to have a self-image as a basic earner, although there was much less difference with respect to employment commitment. For Britain, Dex (1988) showed that, as late as the 1980s, there was a strong norm among women of working age that women with pre-school-age children should stay at home. The evidence was more mixed for work reward values. De Vaus and McAllister (1991), in a study of nine European countries from the early 1980s, concluded that women were less attached to intrinsic values than men. However, both Agassi (1982) and Dex (1988) found that women's work reward values had much in common with those of men, although women attached more importance to social relationships at work and less importance to career advancement. Both authors considered that the distinctiveness of women's attitudes reflected primarily the structural constraints they faced, with respect to the poor quality of their jobs (Agassi 1982) or the availability of suitable childcare (Dex 1988), rather than any essential differences between men and women. They reached a similar conclusion that there was likely to be growing convergence in the work values of men and women.

Hakim (1991, 1996, 2000) was highly sceptical about the likelihood of convergence. She emphasized the role of choice in women's selection of jobs, and interpreted their diverse labor market outcomes as arising from relatively stable differences in work values. These differences underlie both the choice between full-time or part-time work, and the decision to participate in the labor market. A substantial proportion of women in western industrial societies have markedly lower work commitment than men, and this helps to account for their higher job satisfaction, despite having poorer jobs (Hakim 1991). The argument that women's preferences are based on "genuine choice," are "qualitatively different" to those of men, and reflect "conflicting interests" (Hakim 2000) suggests that differences in work values are relatively stable across time and rooted in life-style choices that form part of self-identity, making rapid convergence unlikely.

The empirical evidence from Britain, which, together with the United States, had provided the principal evidence for Hakim's thesis, was not altogether supportive of this. The period between 1981 and 1992 witnessed the disappearance of the earlier sharp differentials in employment commitment not only between male and female employees overall, but, most crucially, between female full-time and part-time employees (Hakim 1996). Moreover, from at least the early 1990s, there was no evidence that British men and women overall differed in their attachment to intrinsic work values (Gallie, Felstead, and Green 2012), although female part-time workers placed a lower importance on intrinsic values than fulltimers of either sex (Zou 2015). Research also showed a very substantial decline over the 1990s, both in the general population and among mothers of pre-school children, in the belief that maternal employment was damaging for young children, a development attributable both to personal experiences in the labor market and to the observed behavior of other mothers (Himmelweit and Sigal 2004).

The cross-national evidence of a decline of traditional views about sex roles in the 1980s and early 1990s also appeared to give support to the view that there was a general trend toward convergence in men's and women's views about work values. Scott, Alwin, and Braun (1996) found that more of the shift toward liberal values occurred within cohorts than through the process of cohort succession. This suggested that the experience of labor market participation was an important factor in changing values. Longitudinal studies confirmed that, although both play a role, the responsiveness of women's work values to the experience of employment was more common than an effect of values on mother's employment decisions (Himmelweit and Sigal 2004; Steiber and Haas 2012).

Moreover, by the end of the 2000s, there was no evidence that women in European countries had lower levels of employment commitment or intrinsic reward values than men. Steiber (2013) found that women reported significantly higher commitment than men in nine countries (Norway, Sweden, Finland, Germany, France, Poland, Estonia, Slovenia, and the UK), the same level of commitment in eight other countries, and lower commitment only in Greece and Portugal. In their study of nineteen OECD countries, Esser and Lindh (2018) found that women, on average, expressed stronger intrinsic preferences and were more concerned with job autonomy than men.

A number of researchers noted that the pace of change in women's sex-role attitudes declined markedly in the 1990s, raising the possibility that the gender revolution had stalled (Cotter, Hermsen, and Vanneman 2011). But more recent analyses conclude that egalitarian change has continued, although in a more diverse way than foreseen in scenarios of convergence. Traditional role norms have continued to change, but are being replaced, not just by liberal egalitarian values, favoring similar roles for men and women, but also by other types of egalitarianism in which both work and family are central life priorities (Charles and Grusky 2004; Cotter, Hermsen, and Vanneman 2011; Knight and Brinton 2017; Wall 2007). In this view, there is (possibly growing) heterogeneity in women's work values, but within the context of a general transition away from traditionalism.

It is clear from the evidence that the centrality of work for women varies substantially across countries in which macro-social factors are important determinants of work values. Alwin, Braun, and Scott (1992) noted the marked differences between the egalitarian values of women in the United States and the strong traditionalism of German women, particularly with respect to the appropriateness of working when there were pre-school children in the household. British women were intermediate, with a greater favorability toward part-time work as a way of reconciling the conflicted priorities of work and family values. In an eight country comparative study, drawing on data from 1988, Haller and Hoellinger (1994) found that British, American, and Dutch women were the most likely to support egalitarian views about gender roles; the Germans, Irish, and Italians were intermediate; and the Austrians and, most particularly, the Hungarians were the most traditional. Knight and Brinton (2017) concluded that Eastern European countries were distinctive in the relatively high prevalence of "egalitarian familism," which gives high value to both work and family, while the

Northern European countries were closer to the United States in the prevalence of liberal egalitarian values. They rejected the view that there is any long-term process convergence in sex role values between countries; while traditional values have been declining in most countries, there has been country divergence in the types of egalitarian values that are replacing them.

Scholars have differed in their views about the factors that account for country differences. Some have emphasized the importance of institutional differences, while others have stressed primarily the role of differences in gender and family cultures (Pfau-Effinger 2012). Institutional explanations focus primarily on national differences in the availability of public childcare and parental leave provision (Steiber and Haas 2009, 2012) or the opportunities for part-time work (Alwin, Braun, and Scott 1992). Cultural explanations have included the influence of the religious heritages of different countries—in particular the role of the Catholic Church in upholding traditional conceptions of the family in Austria, Italy, and Ireland or of the persistence of a paternalistic authority culture in Germany (Haller and Hoellinger 1994). Knight and Brinton (2017) note the distinctiveness of the current values of women living in countries that were previously state socialist regimes. The relative importance of institutional and cultural determinants, however, is inherently difficult to resolve given their likely reciprocal effects over time (Pfau-Effinger 2005) and the empirical difficulties of disentangling the influence of different macro-structural factors with a small number of country cases (Steiber and Haas 2012).

Overall, while there seems to have been a general trend away from traditional role values among women, there still appear to be significant differences in the centrality of work in the life priorities of men and women, reflecting greater heterogeneity in women's values. A more polycentric structure of central life goals, however, proves to be compatible with a commitment to employment and to intrinsic reward values similar to men's.

New Forms of Management and Work Role Values in a Post-Fordist Era

The most recent scholarly discussion about the nature of work values was stimulated by analyses of the changing nature of the production processes in advanced societies. Already in the 1980s, Walton (1985) and Lawler (1986) had argued that traditional forms of work organization, which had relied on a highly developed division of labor, close supervision, and top-down directive forms of management, were no longer adequate to meet the demands of emerging technologies and market conditions. In the conditions of a more competitive international economy, firms would need to compete in terms of quality as well as cost and this would require being able to draw on the skills and ideas of the workforce. New forms of "high involvement or high commitment" management would involve a shift from "control" to "commitment," by enhancing the discretion that employees could exercise over their work tasks and their participation in organizational decisions. In the

1990s, this line of thinking was reinforced by a growing literature on high performance management systems (Appelbaum et al. 2000) and, in the 2000s, by theories of "discretionary/learning" organizations. While the former emphasized the benefits of higher involvement for productivity, the latter underlined its importance for meeting increasing rates of change and demand for innovation in an economy driven by information technology (Lundvall and Nielsen 2007; Valeyre et al. 2009; Lundvall and Lorenz 2011). These analyses revealed the importance of long-term commitment of workers to their firm and of the high levels of work engagement that are needed among workers to ensure that they take initiative and are creative at work. In contrast to the issues of work centrality and the relative importance of work reward values, this perspective placed the focus on the values people attach to their roles in their specific organizations and jobs.

There have been two influential bodies of empirical research relating to such values: research on organizational commitment and research on work engagement. Organizational commitment has a long history in scholarly research (Mowday et al. 1982), but it came to have a more central place in research on work values in the 1990s, particularly through the work of Meyer and Alan (1991, 1997; Meyer, Allen, and Gellatly 1990). Meyer and Alan drew a distinction between affective commitment (emotional attachment to, identification with, and involvement in the organization); continuance commitment (based on an evaluation of the costs of leaving the organization); and normative commitment (sense of obligation to continue in employment with the current employer). Research has focused predominantly on affective commitment.

The evidence available suggests that levels of organizational commitment in the workforce are relatively modest. A British national study of employees in 1998 (Cully et al. 1999) found that only 8 percent of employees strongly agreed that they shared many of their organization's values, only 15 percent felt loyal to their organization, and 16 percent felt proud to tell people where they worked. On the basis of a summary scale derived from the three items, only 11 percent of employees could be classified as highly committed. A study based on the British Skills and Employment surveys (Zhou 2009) found somewhat higher figures for 2001: 12 percent for similar values; 19 percent for pride in the organization; and 32 percent for loyalty. But, in both studies, the most common response indicated moderate commitment, with less than a quarter of employees selecting responses indicating a lack of commitment. There may be some evidence that commitment has been growing more recently. While Zhou (2009) found no change in overall organizational commitment between 1992 and 2001, van Wanrooy et al. (2013) found an increase in commitment between 2004 and 2011.

Work engagement research, which focuses particularly on the work tasks involved in the job, can also trace its roots back to earlier decades (under the term "job involvement"), but it gained a new dynamic in the 2000s with the emergence of researchers arguing for an increased emphasis on the strength of workers' expressive attachment to their work role. Work engagement is indicated by a psychological state involving a "positive, fulfilling, work-related state of mind," manifested by high levels of energy (vigor) and identification with/dedication to work (Shaufeli, Bakker, and Salanova 2006). In earlier versions, the concept also included a third dimension, absorption in the job, but it remains controversial whether this is best understood as an outcome of energy and identification or as an independent dimension of work engagement (Bakker et al. 2008; Bakker, Albrecht, and Leiter 2011; Schaufeli and Salanova 2011).

Given its relative recentness in the research field, representative statistics on work engagement are scarce; research involving the full set of indicators has been carried out primarily on samples of employees in particular occupations or workplaces. However, a British study (van Wanrooy et al. 2013), that used a proxy measure of whether people use their own initiative to carry out tasks that were not required as part of their work, found employees' level of job "engagement" was a little higher than their level of "organizational commitment" as expressed through similarity of values or pride in the organization.

Research points to the importance of work experience as a primary determinant of values about one's role at work—both with respect to the organization and to the job. Both Lincoln and Kalleberg (1990) and Zhou (2009) emphasize the significance of diverse mechanisms of participation in decision-making for organizational commitment. In a review of 155 published and unpublished studies, Meyer et al. (2002) found that the strongest correlations with affective organizational commitment were those relating to work experience factors, with organizational or personal characteristics having weaker effects. More recently, Boyd et al. (2011), in an Australian longitudinal study, showed that job autonomy and procedural fairness predicted workers' future organizational commitment.

Similarly, the work environment plays a central role in work engagement. Bakker, Albrecht, and Leiter (2011) underline two key drivers of engagement: job and personal resources. Job resources include factors such as skill variety, decision latitude (autonomy), opportunities to learn, and social support. Personal resources relate to factors such as self-efficacy and resilience. A meta-analysis by Halbesleben (2010) found a relationship between job resources and work engagement with respect both to measures of overall job resources and of specific resources, in particular job control. There is also some support for this from longitudinal research. A study by Shaufeli, Bakker, and Van Rhenen (2009) showed that higher job resources predicted higher work engagement in the subsequent year, while a Finnish longitudinal study (Mauno, Kinnunen, and Ruokolainen 2007) showed that job control was the most robust predictor of future work engagement.

Good comparative data are still relatively rare and are restricted to organizational commitment. A large-scale study carried out in manufacturing industries in Indiana in the United States and in the Atsugi region in Japan in the 1980s (Near 1989; Lincoln and Kalleberg 1990) showed that, contrary to expectation, organizational commitment was higher in the United States than in Japan. A study drawing on International Social Survey Programme (ISSP) data for 1997 similarly found that the United States stood out as highest in organizational commitment compared with countries as diverse as Britain, Norway, Sweden, West Germany, and New Zealand (Hult and Svallfors 2002). This contrasted sharply with the pattern for employment commitment, for which the Scandinavian countries had the highest levels of commitment. Given that evidence points very consistently to the significance of work experiences in affecting organizational commitment, it is unexpected that the Nordic countries, which are often found to have the best working conditions, do not also have the highest levels of organizational commitment. Hult and Svallfors (2002) suggest that a factor that may help to account for this is the high level of union organization in these countries. Where unions are influential, they may actively counter too strong an identification with management objectives and views, thereby undercutting organizational commitment. It is notable that Sweden, where organizational commitment was lowest, also had the largest class differences in organizational commitment.

Conclusion

The four substantive areas of research on work values that I have discussed here differ in their core debates, but highlight a number of issues that are of general importance for the study of work values. The first is the need to distinguish between different value dimensions, in particular, work centrality, employment commitment, work reward values, and work role values. Researchers sometimes assume that one can infer the nature of other types of work values—for instance employment commitment or the importance of intrinsic reward values—from evidence about work centrality—for instance, employment commitment or the importance of intrinsic reward values. But this is not the case. The different dimensions can be combined in diverse ways, leading to varied patterns of overall work values. Further, there are grounds for thinking that different types of factors help to best account for the diverse value dimensions. For instance, early socialization and education were clearly major influences on work centrality and employment commitment, while the nature of the work environment is the primary factor with respect to work role values.

At the start of the period that we reviewed—late 1960s and early 1970s—the literature was characterized by bold predictions about the direction of change in work values. These varied however between scenarios of the declining importance of work for people's self-identity and life priorities, to arguments of the growing centrality of work as a source of self-expression. Research has revealed, however, that the trends are considerably more complex. The centrality of work may have declined partly because male workers attach more importance than in the past to their family and leisure lives and partly because female workers, with more diverse life priorities, have become an increasingly important component of the workforce. But this does not imply that workers are any less committed to having a job or that they attach less importance to the intrinsic rewards that work can provide. Rather, the overall importance of both employment commitment and intrinsic job reward values has been remarkably stable over time and there is no evidence of generational change. Moreover, research on the unemployed has clearly shown the persisting importance attached to having a job, irrespective of the financial pressures to do so, even in a situation where intrinsic rewards may be hard to come by.

Further, in each area of research, the growth over time of cross-national comparative studies has revealed national variations in work values that point to the inadequacy of earlier explanations of work values in terms of levels of economic growth or change in industrial structures. The workforces of different countries differ significantly in their overall levels of employment commitment, the strength of commitment to work of the unemployed, the relative value that women attach to work and the family, and the extent to which people feel committed to their organizations. This underlines the importance of understanding national differences in institutional structures—in particular the system of employment regulation, the strength of trade union organization, and the level of support for employment offered by the welfare state—and in cultural values, in particular the values attached to equality and the role of the family.

The themes covered in this article will doubtless be supplemented soon by yet another major issue—the future of work values in an age of digital transformation. Some predictions of the effects of technological change on job loss in the next decades suggest that it will be so precipitous, particularly for those in lower skilled positions, that significant sectors of those of working age will be faced with indefinite exclusion from the labor market. Such predictions of the effects of a technological revolution are not entirely new. There was a similar discussion in the early 1960s with the introduction of continuous-process technologies, and in the 1980s when the introduction of computers began to change the nature of work. Moreover, it is notable that, in the longer term, previous technological revolutions did not have catastrophic effects on the overall employment rate. But the past is not a certain guide to the future, and it will be surely important to extend the research agenda to monitor how values about work are affected by what will probably be a period of unusually rapid and widespread technical and social change.

Note

1. The EU-15 countries include Austria, Belgium, Denmark, Finland, France, Germany, Greece, Ireland, Italy, Luxembourg, Netherlands, Portugal, Spain, Sweden, and the United Kingdom.

References

Agassi, Judith. B. 1982. *Comparing the work attitudes of women and men*. Lexington, MA: Heath and Company.

Alwin, Duane F., Michael Braun, and Jacqueline Scott. 1992. The separation of work and the family: Attitudes towards women's labour force participation in Germany, Britain and the United States. *European Sociological Review* 8:13–37.

Appelbaum, Eileen, Thomas Bailey, Peter Berg, and Arne L. Kalleberg. 2000. *Manufacturing advantage: Why high performance work systems pay off*. Ithaca, NY: Cornell University.

Bakker, Arnold B., Wilmar B. Schaufeli, Michael P. Leiter, and Toon W. Taris. 2008. Work engagement: An emerging concept in occupational health psychology. *Work and Stress* 22:187–200.

Bakker, Arnold B., Simon L. Albrecht, and Michael P. Leiter. 2011. Key questions regarding work engagement. *European Journal of Work and Organizational Psychology* 20:4–28.

Bennett, Roger. 1974. Orientations to work and some implications for management. *Journal of Management Studies* 11:149–62.

Bennett, Roger. 1978. Orientation to work and organizational analysis: a conceptual analysis, integration and suggested application. *Journal of Management Studies* 15:187–210.

Blackburn, Robert M., and Michael Mann. 1979. *The working class in the labour market*. London: Macmillan.

Boyd, Carolyn M., Arnold B. Bakker, Silvia Pignata, Anthony H. Winefield, Nicole Gillespie, and Con Stough. 2011. A longitudinal test of the job demands-resources model among Australian University Academics. *Applied Psychology: An International Review* 60:112–40.

Charles, Maria, and David B. Grusky. 2004. *Occupational ghettoes: The worldwide segregation of men and women*. Stanford, CA: Stanford University Press.

Cotter, David, Joan M. Hermsen, and Reeve Vanneman. 2011. The end of the gender revolution? Gender role attitudes from 1977 to 2008. *American Journal of Sociology* 117:258–89.

Cully, Mark, Stephen Woodland, Andrew O'Reilly, and Gill Dix. 1999. *Britain at work*. London: Routledge.

Daniel, William W. 1969. Industrial behaviour and orientation to work—A critique. *Journal of Management Studies* 6:366–75.

De Vaus, David, and Ian Mcallister. 1991. Gender and work orientation: Values and satisfaction in Western Europe. *Work and Occupations* 18:72–93.

Dex, Shirley. 1988. *Women's attitudes towards work*. London: Macmillan.

Dubin, Robert. 1956. Industrial workers' worlds: A study of the "central life interest" of industrial workers. *Social Problems* 3:131–42.

Dunn, Andrew, Maria T. Grasso, and Clare Saunders. 2014. Unemployment and attitudes to work: Asking the "right" question. *Work, employment and society* 28:904–25.

Esser, Ingrid. 2005. *Why work? Comparative studies on welfare regimes and individual's work orientations*. Stockholm: Swedish Institute for Social Research.

Esser, Ingrid and Arvid Lindh. 2018. Job preferences in comparative perspective 1989–2015: A multidimensional evaluation of individual and contextual influences. *International Journal of Sociology* 48:142–69.

Gallie, Duncan, and Carolyn Vogler. 1994. Unemployment and attitudes to work. In *Social change and the experience of unemployment*, eds. Duncan Gallie, Catherine Marsh, and Carolyn Vogler, 1–30. Oxford: Oxford University Press.

Gallie, Duncan, Michael White, Yuan Cheng, and Mark Tomlinson. 1998. *Restructuring the employment relationship*. Oxford: Clarendon Press.

Gallie, Duncan, and Susanne Alm. 2000. Unemployment, gender and attitudes to work. In *Welfare regimes and the experience of unemployment in Europe*, eds. Duncan Gallie and Serge Paugam, 109–33. Oxford: Oxford University Press.

Gallie, Duncan. 2007. Welfare regimes, employment systems and job preference orientations. *European Sociological Review* 23:279–93.

Gallie, Duncan, Alan Felstead, and Francis Green. 2012. Job preferences and the intrinsic quality of work: The changing attitudes of British employees 1992–2006. *Work, Employment and Society* 26:806–21.

Goldthorpe, John H., David Lockwood, Frank Bechhofer, and Jennifer Platt. 1968. *The affluent worker: Industrial attitudes and behaviour*. Cambridge: Cambridge University Press.

Goldthorpe, John H., David Lockwood, Frank Bechhofer, and Jennifer Platt. 1969. *The affluent worker in the class structure*. Cambridge: Cambridge University Press.

Hajdu, Gábor, and Endre Sik. 2015. Searching for gaps: Are work values of the younger generations changing? STYLE Working Papers. WP9.1 CROME. University of Brighton.

Hakim, Catherine. 1991. Grateful slaves and self-made women: fact and fantasy in women's work orientations. *European Sociological Review* 7:101–21.

Hakim, Catherine. 1996. *Key issues in women's work*. London: The Athlone Press.

Hakim, Catherine. 2000. *Work-lifestyle choices in the 21st century: Preference theory*. Oxford: Oxford University Press.

Halbesleben, Jonathon R. B. 2010. A meta-analysis of work engagement: Relationships with burnout, demands, resources, and consequences. In *Work engagement: A handbook of essential theory and research*, eds. Arnold B. Bakker and Michael P. Leiter, 102–17. New York, NY: Psychology Press.

Haller, Max, and Franz Hoellinger. 1994. Female employment and the change of gender roles: The conflictual relationship between participation and attitudes in international comparison. *International Sociology* 9:87–112.

Harding, Stephen D., David R. Phillips, and Michael P. Forgarty. 1986. *Contrasting values in Western Europe. Unity, diversity & change.* Basingstoke: Macmillan.

Highhouse, Scott, Michael J. Zickar, and Maya Yankelevich. 2010. Would you work if you won the lottery? Tracking changes in the American work ethic. *Journal of Applied Psychology* 95 (2):349–57.

Himmelweit, Susan, and Maria Sigala. 2004. Choice and the relationship between identities and behaviour for mothers with pre-school children: Some implications for policy from a UK Study. *Journal of Social Policy* 33:455–78.

Hitlin, Steven, and Jane A. Piliavin. 2004. Values: Reviving a dormant concept. *Annual review of Sociology* 30:359–93.

Hult, Carl, and Stefan Svallfors. 2002. Production regimes and work orientations: A comparison of six western countries. *European Sociological Review* 18:315–31.

Ingham, Geoffrey K. 1970. *Size of industrial organization and worker behaviour.* Cambridge: Cambridge University Press.

Inglehart, Ronald. 1971. The silent revolution in Europe: Intergenerational change in post- industrial societies. *The American Political Science Review* 65:991–1017.

Inglehart, Ronald. 1977. *The silent revolution: Changing values and political styles among western publics.* Princeton, NJ: Princeton University Press.

Knight, Carly R., and Mary C. Brinton. 2017. One egalitarianism or several? Two decades of gender-role attitude change in Europe. *American Journal of Sociology* 122:1485–1532.

Lawler, Edward E. 1986. *High-involvement management. Participative strategies for improving organizational performance.* New York, NY: Jossey-Bass Inc.

Lincoln, James R., and Arne L. Kalleberg. 1990. *Culture, control, and commitment: A study of work organization and work attitudes in the United States and Japan.* Cambridge: Cambridge University Press.

Lindsay, Paul, and William E. Knox. 1984. Continuity and change in work values among young adults: A longitudinal study. *American Journal of Sociology* 89 (4): 818–931.

Lundvall, Bengt-Åke, and Edward Lorenz. 2011. Social investment in the globalising learning economy: A European perspective. *Towards a Social Investment Welfare State?: Ideas, Policies, Challenges,* eds. Nathalie Morel, Bruno Palier, and Joakim Paime, 235–260. Oxford: Oxford University Press.

Lundvall, Bengt-Åke, and Peter Nielsen. 2007. Knowledge Management and Innovation Performance. *International Journal of Manpower* 28:207–23.

Mauno, Saija, Ulla Kinnunen, and Mervi Ruokolainen. 2007. Job demands and resources as antecedents of work engagement: A longitudinal study. *Journal of Vocational Behavior* 70:149–71.

Mercure, Daniel, and Mircea Vultur. 2010. *La signification du travail: Nouveau modèle productif et ethos du travail Au Québec.* Québec: Presses de l'Université Laval.

Meyer, John P., and Natalie J. Allen. 1991. A three-component conceptualization of organizational commitment. *Human Resource Management Review* 1:61–89.

Meyer, John. P., Natalie J. Allen, and I.R. Gellatly. 1990. Affective and continuance commitment to the organization: Evaluation of measures and analysis of concurrent and time-lagged relations. *Journal of Applied Psychology* 75 (6):710–20.

Meyer, John P., David J. Stanley, Lynne Herscovitch, and Laryassa Topolnytsky. 2002. Affective, continuance, and normative commitment to the organization: A meta-analysis of antecedents, correlates, and consequences. *Journal of Vocational Behavior* 61:20–52.

Meyer, John. P., and Natalie J. Allen 1997. *Commitment in the workplace. Theory, research and application,* London: Sage.

MOW. 1987. *The meaning of work.* London: Academic Press.

Mowday, Richard T., Lyman W. Porter, Richard M. Steers, and Peter G. Warr. 1982. *Employee-organization linkages: The psychology of commitment, absenteeism, and turnover.* St. Louis, MO: Elsevier Science.

Near, Janet P. 1989. Organizational commitment among Japanese and U.S. workers. *Organization Studies* 10 (3):281–300.

Pfau-Effinger, Birgit. 2005. Welfare state policies and the development of care arrangements. *European Societies* 7:321–47.

Pfau-Effinger, Birgit. 2012. Women's employment in the institutional and cultural context. *International Journal of Sociology and Social Policy* 32:530–43.

Quinn, Robert P., and Graham L. Staines. 1979. *The 1977 quality of employment survey: Descriptive statistics, with comparison data from the 1969–70 and the 1972–73 surveys*. Ann Arbor, MI: Institute for Social Research, University of Michigan.

Schaufeli, Wilmar B., Arnold B. Bakker, and Marisa Salanova. 2006. The measurement of work engagement with a short questionnaire: A cross-national study. *Educational and Psychological Measurement* 66:701–16.

Schaufeli, Wilmar B., Arnold B. Bakker, and Willem Van Rhenen. 2009. How changes in job demands and resources predict burnout, work engagement, and sickness absenteeism. *Journal of Organizational Behavior* 30:893–917.

Schaufeli, Wilmar, and Marisa Salanova. 2011. Work engagement: On how to better catch a slippery concept. *European Journal of Work and Organizational Psychology* 20:39–46.

Scott, Jacqueline, Duane F. Alwin, and Michael Braun. 1996. Generational changes in gender-role attitudes: Britain in a cross-national perspective. *Sociology* 30:471–92.

Spiezia, Vincenzo. 2000. The effects of benefits on unemployment and wages: A comparison of unemployment compensation schemes. *International Labour Review* 139:73–87.

Steiber, Nadia, and Barbara Haas. 2009. *Ideals or compromises? The attitude-behaviour relationship in mothers' employment*. Rochester, NY: Social Science Research Network.

Steiber, Nadia, and Barbara Haas. 2012. Advances in explaining women's employment patterns. *Socio-Economic Review* 10:343–67.

Steiber, Nadia. 2013. Economic downturn and work motivation. In *Economic crisis, quality of work, & social integration*, ed. Duncan Gallie, 195–228. Oxford: Oxford University Press.

Super, Donald E., and Branimir Šverko. 1995. *Life roles, values, and careers: International Findings of the work importance study*. San Francisco, CA: Jossey-Bass.

Twenge, Jean M. 2010. A review of the empirical evidence on generational differences in work attitudes. *Journal of Business Psychology* 25:201–10.

Valeyre, Antoine, Edward Lorenz, Damien Cartron, Peter Csizmadia, Michel Gollac, Miklós Illéssy, and Csaba Makó. 2009. *Working conditions in the European Union: Work organization*. Luxembourg: Office for Official Publications of the European Communities.

van Wanrooy, Brigid, Helen Bewley, Alex Bryson, John Forth, Stephanie Freeth, Lucy Stokes, and Stephen Wood. 2013. *Employment relations in the shadow of recession: Findings from the 2011 workplace employment relations study*. Basingstoke: Palgrave Macmillan.

Wall, Karin 2007. Main patterns in attitudes to the articulation between work and family life: A cross-national analysis. In: *Women, men, work and family in Europe*, eds. Rosemary Crompton, Suzan Lewis and Clare Lyonette, 86–115. Basingstoke, UK: Palgrave Macmillan.

Walton, Richard E. 1985. From control to commitment in the workplace. *Harvard Business Review* 63:77–84.

Warr, Peter. 1982. A national study of non-financial employment commitment. *Journal of Occupational Psychology* 55:297–312.

Zhou, Ying. 2009. *British employees' organizational participation. Trends, determinants and impact*. Berlin: VDM Verlag Dr Muller.

Zou, Min. 2015. Gender, work orientations and job satisfaction. *Work, Employment & Society* 29:13–22.

Work Values in the United States: Age, Period, and Generational Differences

This article examines how processes of aging, generational shifts, and changes over historical time periods shape differences in work values in the United States. Our analyses of data from the General Social Survey and the International Social Survey Program show that changes over historical time periods are most consistently responsible for differences in work values. In particular, during recent periods, Americans tend to place greater importance on jobs that provide security, high income, and opportunities for advancement; this is consistent with a narrative that these job rewards have become more difficult to attain recently and are thus more problematic for workers. Some differences in work values are also attributable to aging or life course processes, especially the greater importance placed on high income during the mid-life years when family responsibilities are generally greatest. By contrast, we find few differences in work values among members of different generations or cohorts. We also find that people from less advantaged social origins and those with greater labor market resources are more likely to value economic rewards.

Keywords: work values; age, period and cohort effects; central life interest

By
ARNE L. KALLEBERG
and
PETER V. MARSDEN

Work values reflect the importance people place on work and its various facets. They are central to theories of work motivation that highlight reasons that people work and the kinds of rewards and benefits that influence their job satisfaction (Kalleberg 1977). Work values also provide insights into workers' goals

Arne L. Kalleberg is a Kenan Distinguished Professor of Sociology at the University of North Carolina at Chapel Hill. He served as the president of the American Sociological Association in 2007–8 and is currently the editor of Social Forces, an international journal of social research.

Peter V. Marsden is the Edith and Benjamin Geisinger Professor of Sociology at Harvard University. He is an expert in organizations and social networks who has served as editor of Sociological Methodology and as a co-principal investigator of the General Social Survey.

Correspondence: arnekal@email.unc.edu

DOI: 10.1177/0002716218822291

and aspirations (e.g., Goldthorpe et al. 1968). Americans, for example, traditionally place great importance on the search for job security and the belief in opportunity (Bernstein 1997).

A key research question is how work values differ over time and among people of different ages or generations. Such temporal differences shed light on social transformations in the conceptions and ideologies of work that characterize a society, as well as on changes that individuals undergo during their life courses. These questions are complex: at a given point in time, age- and generation-related differences in work values cannot be distinguished from one another, while over-time differences may be due to cohorts or generations, aging, time periods, or some mixture of the three sources.[1]

First, ever since Mannheim highlighted the "problem of generations" (1927/1952), social scientists have sought to identify generationally or cohort-distinctive values that reflect the shared experiences of people who are born at the same time and mature together. Recent speculation about the distinctive work values of Millennials (e.g., Pfau 2016; Quiggin 2018) is reminiscent of similar questions raised by scholars about previous generations such as Generation X, the Baby Boomers, the Greatest and Silent Generations, and so on (see e.g., Howe and Strauss 1991; Lorence 1987).

Second, variations in work values may be due to experiences linked to aging, such as developmental or situational life course dynamics that recur over time periods and across generations. During their life courses, people of different ages vary in their psychological adjustments to work and other social roles, producing dissimilarities in their needs from—and attachments to—work and what they feel is important to obtain from jobs (e.g., Kalleberg and Loscocco 1983).

Third, differences in work values could also be due to the specific social, economic, and cultural features of the time periods in which people live. Different historical periods are characterized by particular society-wide ideals about work, and by differential opportunities to obtain intrinsic and extrinsic job rewards due to varying economic conditions and the ways in which work is structured; these characteristics of an historical period are also likely to affect what people come to see as important about work.

This complexity underlying temporal differences in work values helps to explain important gaps and inconsistencies in our understanding of how these work-related attitudes come about. For example, in contrast to widespread speculation about generational differences in work values, a meta-analysis of twenty published and unpublished studies concluded that few differences among generations exist, and those that do are as likely to be attributable to life course stage as to generation (Costanza et al. 2012).

Our overarching research question, then, is about the extent to which processes of aging, generational shifts, and changes across time periods are responsible for observed differences in work values in the United States. A second research question is whether inequality in social origins and labor market resources help to account for differences in work values. Our analyses are based on data from the General Social Survey and the International Social Survey Program.

We begin with an overview of general theoretical approaches to explaining temporal differences in work values, and then state hypotheses related to cohort/ generational, aging/life course, and time period differences, as well as to some mechanisms related to social class, resources, and origins. We adopt a multi-dimensional view of work values, considering the importance people place on work generally, as well as their emphasis on specific work facets such as earnings, security, advancement, and intrinsic qualities that make working meaningful (e.g., opportunities to exercise autonomy and to help others and society). Thereafter, we discuss our data and methods, present and summarize our findings, and discuss their implications for theory and research.

Explaining Temporal Differences in Work Values

People differ in their work values because they reside in diverse social settings and have different individual needs and dispositions (see Salancik and Pfeffer 1977). Sociological theories of work values emphasize the significant influences of social contexts in shaping and altering preferences. Their explanations of time-related differences in work values are rooted in two sets of theories. Roughly, these can be distinguished by whether the locus of mechanisms shaping work values lies *outside* of and/or prior to work lives, or *inside* work contexts, reflecting experience acquired during work careers.[2]

Theories that emphasize the importance of a person's experiences *outside the work context* for work values focus on socialization in the family of origin, learning while in school, and other factors arising before labor force entry. Social backgrounds shape the importance people place on work, while both human and social capital help people to obtain work that is consistent with these work values. Such theories point to group affiliations, circumstances, and experiences outside of work that influence the importance people assign to job facets and prompt them to try to select jobs with particular attributes (and employers to select workers who hold certain values).

The significance attached to particular aspects of jobs and work itself differs among social classes (Kohn 1969), reflecting variations in social norms and cultures as well as in the opportunities people have to realize economic and noneconomic rewards from jobs. Work values shaped by these early influences become increasingly stable in the years after high school (Johnson 2001). Several other articles in this volume of *The ANNALS* (e.g., Sümer, Pauknerova, and Vancea; Schuck and Shore) rely on this account of work values in explaining how parental resources affect the values of their children.

The second set of theories focuses on how experiences *within work contexts* during one's work career may change the importance people place on various job facets. Such theories highlight how job incumbency, other workplace events, and labor force experiences affect the aspects of jobs that workers come to see as more or less important. There are two different psychological mechanisms by which work experiences might shape work values: *reinforcement* (prompting people to value what they already have); and *problematic rewards* (emphasizing job rewards that people are less certain of obtaining, while taking what they have for granted).

A reinforcement explanation posits that workers adapt to the realities of their jobs by either bolstering the work values that initially led them to choose particular jobs (Gruenberg 1980; Johnson 2001), causing them to assign greater importance to things they have already achieved or believe to be achievable, and/or prompting them to devalue job attributes that they believe to be unattainable. Such an account is consistent with a Marxian approach, asserting that alienated workers whose jobs lack challenge or intrinsic meaning may come to see work instrumentally, regarding it as a means to satisfy nonwork needs, as in Goldthorpe et al.'s (1968) study of affluent workers.

An alternative psychological mechanism, "problematic rewards," posits that people may come to value job rewards that they feel least certain about obtaining at a given time. While all workers may have similar basic needs in principle, they are unequally successful in the labor market and vary in their circumstances and capacities to realize particular job rewards. Hence, people differ in what they deem important to obtain from work. This problematic rewards explanation is closely related to Maslow's (1954) notion of a "hierarchy of needs," which holds that some needs (e.g., for survival, security) are more basic than others and must be satisfied before workers become oriented toward "higher order" needs such as self-actualization. Satisfied needs, however, are not primary motivators of behavior. Applied to work values, this theory suggests that workers generally come to value meaningful, self-actualizing work only after more fundamental needs for income and security have been fulfilled.

These general explanations of temporal differences in work values underlie theories of each of the three components of temporal differences: cohort/generation, age/life course, and historical time period. We briefly discuss the rationale for anticipating differences in these three respects and provide an exemplary hypothesis about each.

Cohort/generational differences

Different generations may come to see work differently due to their collective socialization, such as changing ideologies about child rearing and the gender division of labor. Likewise, experiencing either scarcity (e.g., the Great Depression of the 1930s or the Great Recession of 2007–09) or abundance at a crucial juncture such as labor market entry may leave a lasting imprint on a cohort's values. Some have argued that the Millennial generation, for example, is self-absorbed and narcissistic, lazy, and impatient (Twenge 2006). Others view this cohort as less concerned with career advancement or meaningful work than with achieving greater work–life balance (Jenkins 2018).

H1. Millennials are more likely than members of other generations to value having flexible work schedules, given their emphasis on balancing work and family.

Aging/life course differences

Aging or life course explanations maintain that the relative importance of particular job facets changes as people experience different life events such as marriage, childbirth and childrearing, mid-life crises, retirement, and so on. Values formed prior to entry into the labor force may subsequently be altered by the situational demands of different life-course stages, such as family responsibilities that pose greater or lesser needs to realize economic rewards from work. Johnson (2005), for example, showed how marriage and parenthood influence the importance husbands and wives place on aspects of jobs.

> H2. People in their prime working ages will place greatest importance on economic rewards, as this is when economic pressures to support a family are generally highest.

Historical time period differences

Opportunities to obtain good, high-paying, and secure jobs vary across economic cycles associated with different periods, highlighting the differential availability or achievability of job rewards and calling attention to those that are problematic. Similarly, sociocultural valuations placed on aspects of work (e.g., the "Greed is Good" mantra of the 1980s) vary over time in ways that may influence everyone, not just those in particular generations or age groups. The period since the mid-1970s in the United States has been called the "age of precarious work," during which the transformation of employment relations has produced greater insecurity and uncertainty for workers, and reduced opportunities for economic rewards and career advancement (Kalleberg 2009).

> H3. Americans are more apt to value greater security, economic rewards, and opportunities for advancement in recent years, as these have become increasingly problematic to attain given the rise of precarious work.

Structural Mechanisms

We also examine several specific structural explanations of differences in work values that are rooted in experiences both *outside* the labor market and *within* work contexts.

One prominent theory (e.g., Kohn 1969) stresses the impacts on work values of social origins and parental influences during early childhood socialization. It holds that middle-class parents tend to accentuate the importance of autonomy and self-direction, since they have found such capacities to be most useful and rewarding during their working lives. On the other hand, working-class parents are more apt to encourage obedience and conformity, again reflecting the qualities that have proved valuable to them.

H4. People from more advantaged social origins are more apt to value intrinsic
rewards such as having interesting work, since they are more likely to take
extrinsic rewards for granted. Economic rewards are valued more by people
from less advantaged origins.

Within the labor market, people with more resources (such as human and
social capital) are better able to obtain good paying, relatively secure jobs. The
problematic rewards perspective anticipates that such workers will be less apt to
stress extrinsic rewards and more likely to value intrinsic ones. By contrast, those
who are unemployed or lack marketable skills are more likely to place higher
value on jobs that pay adequately and are relatively secure (Martin and Tuch
1993; Kalleberg and Marsden 2013).

H5. People who have more resources in the labor market (e.g., men, whites,
the better educated) are more likely to value intrinsic rewards as opposed
to extrinsic rewards such as security and advancement (which are apt to be
valued more by women, blacks, and the less educated).

Data, Measures, and Methods

Our analyses draw on data assembled by the General Social Survey (GSS) project,
a continuing survey of U.S. adults stressing over-time replication of social indicators.
The GSS has been conducted every year or two since 1972. Each round draws a new
sample representative of Americans aged 18 and above, and gathers information on
numerous sociodemographic variables together with many behaviors and attitudes,
including work values. The GSS also collects International Social Survey Program
(ISSP) data for the United States. By measuring the same indicators repeatedly over
time, its design enables both the tracking of trends and the separation of age-related
from cohort-related differences. We use the 1973–2016 GSSs, especially data from
ISSP modules on "work orientations" collected in 1989, 1998, 2006, and 2016.[3]

Work values measures

We briefly describe the eight distinct indicators of work values in our analyses;
Appendix A in the online appendix presents the specific wording for each of
these. The first is about work as a "central life interest," asking whether someone
would continue to work or stop working if they were to become sufficiently
wealthy to have the option. In 2016, nearly three-quarters of those questioned
(71.4 percent) stated that they would continue working.

For the other seven indicators, respondents rate different features of jobs,
including both extrinsic aspects (security, high income, potential for advancement) and intrinsic ones (interesting work, opportunity to help others, opportunity to help society); we also study ratings of flexible hours, but do not classify it
as either extrinsic or intrinsic.

Ratings range from "not at all important" to "very important." In 2016, most respondents assigned high importance to all seven features: more than half rated each as "very important" or "important." Security was most often rated as "very important" (by 73.6 percent of respondents), followed by interesting work (51.6 percent), advancement (49.6 percent), helping society (47.5 percent), helping others (42.1 percent), high income (29.0 percent), and flexible hours (16.7 percent). Ratings of extrinsic values are moderately correlated with one another, as are those of intrinsic ones; correlations between extrinsic and intrinsic rewards are weaker. Our analyses focus on factors that distinguish people who rate a given facet as "very important" as opposed to those who rate it less highly.

Explanatory variables

Our explanatory variables include indicators of temporal differences (age, period, and cohort), variations in social origins, and current respondent characteristics. We describe these briefly here; Appendix B provides summary statistics for them in 2016.

Temporal variables. The GSS measures date of birth (and hence birth cohort) directly and calculates age as the difference between the survey date and date of birth; the survey year defines period. Consistent with general practice, we construct twelve age groups spanning approximately five-year intervals (from 18–25 to greater than 75). We also use five-year groups to distinguish generations, ranging from those born before 1900 to those born after 1995. For work as a central life interest, we categorize periods into five-year intervals (from 1972–75 through 2011–16); We have only one measure per decade for the seven ISSP ratings, however, so there the periods refer to years 1989, 1998, 2006, and 2016.

Social origins. We tap differences in the class-related socialization to which respondents are exposed via retrospective reports about the family of origin when a respondent was 16 years old. We rely primarily on reports about the years of education completed by the respondent's parents.[4] Parents' education is closely linked to all three types of resources that parents might convey to children: cultural; social; and economic/financial.

Respondent characteristics. To represent variations in ascribed characteristics, we use indicator variables identifying black and male respondents. Years of education and the socioeconomic index (SEI) score for a respondent's primary occupation measure differences in achieved status.[5] We also incorporate life-course variations by including an indicator variable for marital status and a measure of the number of children (age 17 or younger) who live in the respondent's household.

Analytic methods

We assess our hypotheses using hierarchical logistic regression analyses (Yang and Land 2013), in which period and cohort differences are modeled using random effects.[6] Graphs portray age, time period, and cohort differences. We describe the associations of other predictors with work values by assessing predicted probabilities of holding particular work values at illustrative levels of each explanatory variable, while holding the others constant at average values.

Results

Figure 1 shows how overall commitment to work as a central life activity varies with age, period, and cohort. Solid lines represent trends by age, period, and cohort in the estimated probability that one would continue to work in the event that s/he were to become wealthy. Grey areas represent confidence bands around those trends, while the dotted line shows the estimated probability that an average person would continue to work.[7]

In the upper panel of Figure 1, we see that aging effects are dominant—after adjusting for period and cohort differences—in shaping whether people would continue to work if they were to become wealthy. At average values of other predictors, an estimated 80 percent of younger workers say that they would continue to work; the "continue" percentage declines monotonically (to about 55 percent) until age 65, after which it increases somewhat. The upswing in the latter age groups likely reflects selection into the labor force beyond the conventional age of retirement.[8]

The prominence of work as a central life interest also varies across periods (middle panel of Figure 1), though differences among periods are much smaller than those among age groups; holding other predictors constant at average values, period-specific proportions of people who would continue to work vary between about 0.67 and 0.72. Somewhat higher proportions of Americans regarded work as a central life interest between 1976 and 1990; this then dipped a bit in 1991–1995, before beginning to increase gently until 2011–2016.

Cohort effects on work as a central life interest are statistically detectable, but substantively minor, as shown by the small cohort variations seen in the lower panel of Figure 1. Aside from a slightly lower propensity to continue working among people born between 1955 and 1969, the estimated cohort differences display little pattern. Our results for the seven indicators of importance placed on specific work facets also reflect an absence of pronounced cohort differences. This relative lack of cohort effects casts doubt on speculations about the distinctiveness of work values held by the Millennial generation, or its predecessors.

Age, generation, and time period differences in types of work values

Turning to the valuation placed on specific aspects of work, the differences that arise most consistently have to do with changes over *time periods*. These are statistically significant and substantively meaningful for six of the seven ratings of the importance of specific aspects of work that we examined (all except flexible hours), as shown in Figure 2.[9]

FIGURE 1
Work as a Central Life Interest: Age, Period, and Cohort Differences

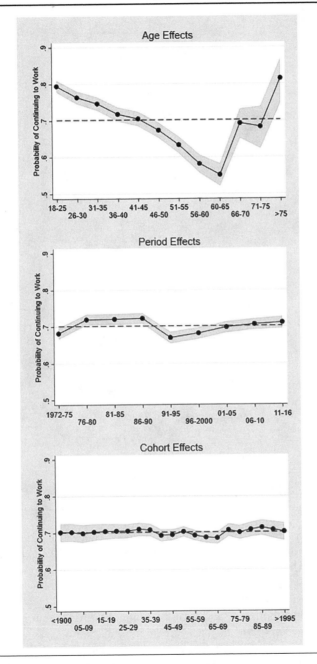

FIGURE 2
Period Differences in Work Values

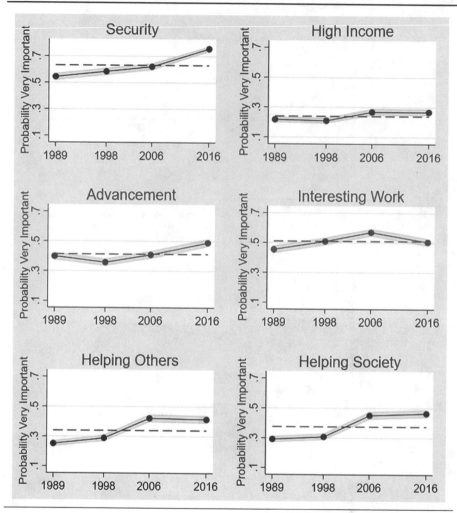

In general, people seem to demand more of their jobs in recent periods, assigning more importance to most work facets than in previous periods. In particular, we find that, in recent periods, people assign greater priority to jobs that have security, high income, and opportunities for advancement—especially after 2006 (for security) and 1998 (for income and promotion chances). These results are consistent with both H3 and a problematic rewards situational explanation asserting that workers tend to place greater emphasis on work values that they find most difficult to realize. Opportunities for advancement with one's employer and to obtain high incomes have generally declined in recent decades, leading Americans to see their work increasingly in market-oriented, instrumental terms (see Kalleberg 2009; Kalleberg and Marsden 2013). It also seems eminently plausible that the large rise in the importance assigned to job security in 2016 (by which time the adjusted probability of a "very important" rating of security exceeded 0.7) reflects painful memories throughout the society of the Great Recession that began in December 2007, together with the heightened insecurity and increasingly precarious work characteristic of the United States and other rich democracies in this period (e.g., Kalleberg 2018).

Other notable period-related differences include a general rise in the importance assigned to the three intrinsic work values (interesting jobs, and work that helps others and society). The ratings of these are notably higher in 2006 and 2016 by comparison with 1989 and 1998. The rise in the importance of having interesting work from the late 1990s to the mid-2000s may reflect the greater availability of such jobs (which would be consistent with a reinforcement explanation), as corporate restructuring led to reductions in middle management and gave workers in many organizations more opportunities to participate in decision-making, thereby increasing opportunities to obtain challenging work that utilized their skills (Kalleberg 2009). The greater importance placed on helping others and society—additional sources of intrinsic meaning from work—also increased markedly until 2006, after which it levelled off or grew more slowly. The economic crisis of 2007–09 thus appears to have led people to place more priority on extrinsic aspects of work.

Age differences in work values are displayed in Figure 3. These are generally somewhat smaller than the period differences shown in Figure 2, though some notable variations across age groups are evident.

The importance people place on jobs offering high income is greatest between the ages of 26 and 45, in line with H2. Family responsibilities are most pressing at those ages. Valuation of opportunities for advancement declines more or less steadily with age until the midlife years, after which it levels off. Younger people (aged 18–25) place the most emphasis on interesting work, perhaps reflecting the idealism of those with less experience in the labor market, though age-related variations here are modest. Work that helps others or society is somewhat less valued by the oldest age groups.

By contrast, differences among cohorts or generations are very small, unpatterned, and usually not statistically significant. For this reason, we do not display them in a separate figure. In particular, Millennials do not appear to differ from members of other generations in their work values, even the importance of flexible schedules. Thus, we find no support for H1.

Structural mechanisms

People from more advantaged social origins (i.e., whose parents have more education) are more likely to assign high importance to interesting work and less apt to emphasize security, high income, good promotion opportunities, or jobs that help society and others, supporting H4 (see Table 1). A person whose parents have eight years of education, and who is average on other predictors, has a predicted probability of 0.66 of rating security as "very important," for example; this falls to 0.58 for an otherwise-similar person with college-educated (16 years)

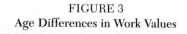

FIGURE 3
Age Differences in Work Values

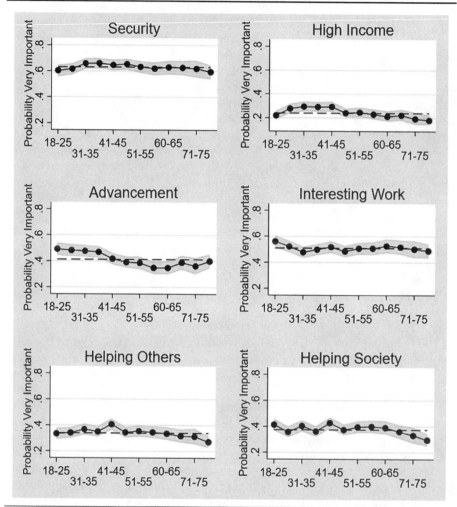

parents. Those with more highly educated parents are also less likely to regard contributing to society as a high priority; we speculate that those who experience disadvantaged conditions are more inclined to try to help others avoid them.

Those who have more resources in the labor market are more likely to value intrinsic rewards as opposed to extrinsic factors such as security and advancement (which are valued more by less advantaged members of the labor force)—providing a great deal of empirical support for H5 (see Table 1). Respondents with more education more often place high importance on interesting work and less on having secure, high paying jobs with greater promotion opportunities. More educated people are also more apt to say they would continue working if

TABLE 1

Adjusted Predicted Probabilities of Holding Work Values, at Selected Illustrative Values of Respondent Characteristics

	"Very Important" Rating of . . .							
Explanatory Variable	Continue Working	Secure Job	High Income	Advancement	Interesting Job	Help Others	Help Society	Flexible Hours
Sex								
Male	**0.72**	**0.60**	0.25	0.41	0.50	**0.30**	**0.35**	**0.14**
Female	**0.68**	**0.65**	0.24	0.41	0.52	**0.37**	**0.39**	**0.16**
Race								
Black	0.69	**0.70**	**0.40**	**0.55**	0.51	**0.41**	**0.44**	**0.20**
Nonblack	0.70	**0.62**	**0.22**	**0.39**	0.51	**0.33**	**0.36**	**0.14**
Education								
8 years	**0.65**	**0.74**	**0.36**	**0.47**	**0.46**	0.36	0.36	**0.20**
12 years	**0.69**	**0.66**	**0.27**	**0.43**	**0.50**	0.34	0.37	**0.16**
16 years	**0.73**	**0.57**	**0.19**	**0.38**	**0.54**	0.33	0.38	**0.13**
Marital Status								
Married	**0.69**	**0.61**	**0.21**	0.40	**0.48**	0.33	0.37	0.16
Unmarried	**0.72**	**0.65**	**0.26**	0.42	**0.53**	0.35	0.38	0.14
# Children at home								
0	**0.69**	0.64	0.24	0.42	**0.52**	0.35	0.38	0.15
2	**0.72**	0.62	0.24	0.39	**0.48**	0.32	0.37	0.15
SEI of occupation								
20	0.70	**0.66**	**0.28**	**0.44**	**0.47**	0.33	0.37	0.14
45	0.70	**0.63**	**0.24**	**0.41**	**0.51**	0.34	0.37	0.15
70	0.71	**0.60**	**0.21**	**0.38**	**0.55**	0.35	0.38	0.16
Parental Education[a]								
8 years	0.70	**0.66**	**0.26**	**0.45**	**0.47**	0.32	**0.37**	0.15
12 years	0.70	**0.62**	**0.21**	**0.42**	**0.49**	0.30	**0.34**	0.15
16 years	0.71	**0.58**	**0.17**	**0.38**	**0.51**	0.28	**0.31**	0.14
(N)[b]	(21,950)	(5,219)	(5,193)	(5,198)	(5,205)	(5,199)	(5,198)	(5,177)

Note: Entries give the predicted probability of holding a work value among people in the indicated group, holding all other predictors (including age, period and cohort) constant at average values. **Bold** entries correspond to statistically significant ($p<0.05$) differences.
[a]Estimates for parental education are based on a separate model that excludes observations made in 2006.
[b]For parental education, N is smaller by roughly 1,500.

they were to become financially independent, perhaps reflecting a greater intrinsic appeal of their work activities or a greater opportunity cost of exiting the labor force. By and large, higher occupational status is associated with work values in the same way that higher education is, though those with higher SEI scores are no more likely than those with lower ones to regard work as a central life interest.

Black respondents are more likely than nonblack ones to place greater importance on most of the specific values, including security, high income, advancement, helping both others and society, and flexible schedules, though not having interesting jobs. Blacks do not differ significantly from nonblacks in whether they would continue working if they no longer needed to earn an income, though.

Turning to gender differences, we find that men are more apt to see work as a central feature of their lives, but for the most part less likely to regard the seven specific facets of jobs as highly as women do. Women assign significantly greater importance than men to having secure jobs, jobs in which they can help both others and society, and flexible working hours.

Married people are significantly less apt than the unmarried to see work as a continuing life activity, and to regard security, high income, and interesting work as having high importance. We conjecture that having a spouse is an alternative source of fulfillment that the unmarried lack. We also found that having children at home raises the prospect that one regards working as a central life interest, while reducing emphasis on having interesting work.

Conclusion

We examined how three distinct processes—generational shifts, aging, and changes over time periods—result in temporal differences in work values in the United States. Our analyses of data from the GSS and the ISSP showed that the most widespread differences in work values have to do with variations in the *time periods* during which people live. In particular, in recent periods Americans tend to place greater importance on jobs that provide security, high income, and greater opportunities for advancement; this is consistent with the view that these job rewards have become more difficult to attain in recent years, and, thus, more problematic for workers.

We found significant overall age differences in the centrality of work within peoples' lives, a steady decline until the conventional age of retirement (65). Our results also indicate that people in their prime working ages place greater importance on income and security, while younger people are most apt to value interesting work.

On the other hand, we found few if any meaningful differences in work values among people in different cohorts or generations. This finding suggests that much speculation about the distinctiveness of values for particular generations lacks a strong empirical grounding, at least for the United States. The work values of young people may well be different from those of older ones, but such age differences do not appear to be attributable mainly to either youth or cohort membership. To the extent that we are seeing "global generations" (Edmunds and Turner 2005) that have similar patterns of work values (and other attitudes and ideologies) in different countries, then, these similarities are likely due more to parallel developments during those time periods (such as technological innovations that shape the structure of work in similar ways among countries, or that promote diffusion across countries) than to specific generational characteristics.

We also found evidence that those from more advantaged social origins and with more labor market resources were more apt to assign greater importance to interesting work and less to extrinsic rewards such as high income, security, and opportunities for advancement. These findings too are consistent with a "problematic rewards" explanation.

The centrality of period differences in work values underscores the profound impacts of work structures and the availability of various types of job rewards—coupled with cultural narratives about the role of work within societies at particular times—on peoples' attitudes toward work. This highlights the importance of understanding differences in work values in terms of the larger environments in which people live. In turn, this points to the need to examine how work values vary across countries that have different labor market and social welfare protection institutions, economic conditions, and cultural values. The articles in this issue of *The ANNALS* illustrate some of these cross-country differences.

Notes

1. Differing research designs allow one to distinguish different temporal components of change. In a cross-sectional study at a single point in time, historical period does not vary, and age is equal to time of survey minus year of birth—so differences in work values by age could reflect aging, generational differences, or some mixture of the two. With repeated cross-sectional data like those we study here, separate associations of work values with age, birth cohort, and historical time period can be estimated, subject to particular assumptions. An accelerated longitudinal design or prospective cohort panel (Yang and Land 2013) follows several distinct birth cohorts—repeatedly observing individual subjects in them—and thereby traces within-cohort change for real as distinct from "synthetic" cohorts, together with age- and period-related differences.

2. Of course, experiences outside and inside the work context can operate together to shape work values. Work values formed prior to labor force entry, for example, predispose people toward selecting jobs that have particular characteristics (Johnson 2005).

3. See Marsden and Smith (2012) for an overview of the GSS's basic study design and content, and Smith et al. (2017) or http://www.gss.norc.org/ for many more details. See http://www.issp.org for information about the ISSP; the 1998, 2006, and 2016 U.S. data about work orientations were collected one year later than those for most other ISSP member countries.

4. We use the average of separate reports about the mother and the father to represent educational origins if both are available, and otherwise a report about a single parent. Because the 2006 GSS did not ask the respondents who answered the ISSP work orientations questions to also answer questions about parental education, we are unable to simultaneously estimate differences by parental education and the effect of being observed in 2006. For all predictors other than parental education, findings presented here are based on analyses that include the cases from 2006. Findings for parental education are from identical analyses that omit the 2006 observations; in the latter, findings for predictors other than parental education are substantively similar to those displayed.

5. See Hout, Smith, and Marsden (2016) on the construction of these scores; higher scores indicate higher standing. For those who are currently unemployed or retired, the SEI measure refers to the respondent's most recent occupation.

6. We use listwise deletion as a missing value treatment. We obtain similar findings using the intrinsic estimator described by Yang and Land (2013). Estimates were obtained via the xtmelogit routine implemented in Stata (Rabe-Hesketh and Skrondal 2012). Because estimating generalized linear mixed models with crossed random effects makes very intensive demands on computation time, we present estimates based on a Laplace approximation.

7. The temporal trends displayed in our figures are adjusted for other temporal components (e.g., cohort and period in the case of age) as well as the other explanatory variables listed in Table 1.

8. Only labor force participants are asked the "central life interest" question. Hence those who have already stopped working (or looking for work) because they have sufficient wealth or other assured income sources are not among those questioned.

9. Temporal variations in the rating of flexible hours are minor and unpatterned, so we do not display the corresponding graphs in Figures 2 and 3.

References

Bernstein, Paul. 1997. *American work values: Their origin and development*. Albany, NY: State University of New York Press.

Costanza, David P., Jessica M. Badger, Rebecca L. Fraser, Jamie B. Severt, and Paul A. Gade. 2012. Generational differences in work-related attitudes: A meta-analysis. *Journal of Business Psychology* 27:375–94.

Edmunds, June and Bryan S. Turner. 2005. Global generations: Social change in the twentieth century. *The British Journal of Sociology* 56:559–77.

Goldthorpe, John H., David Lockwood, Frank Bechhofer, and Jennifer Platt. 1968. *The affluent worker: Industrial attitudes and behavior*. Cambridge: Cambridge University Press.

Gruenberg, Barry. 1980. The happy worker: An analysis of educational and occupational differences in determinants of job satisfaction. *American Journal of Sociology* 86:247–71.

Hout, Michael, Tom W. Smith, and Peter V. Marsden. 2016. Prestige and socioeconomic scores for the 2010 Census codes. GSS Methodological Report 124. Chicago, IL: NORC.

Howe, Neil, and William Strauss. 1991. *Generations: The history of America's future, 1584 to 2069*. New York, NY: Harper Collins.

Jenkins, Ryan. 2018. This is why millennials care so much about work-life balance. Available from https://www.inc.com/ryan-jenkins/this-is-what-millennials-value-most-in-a-job-why.html (accessed May 17, 2018).

Johnson, Monica Kirkpatrick. 2001. Job values in the young adult transition: Stability and change with age. *Social Psychology Quarterly* 64:297–317.

Johnson, Monica Kirkpatrick. 2005. Family roles and work values: Processes of selection and change. *Journal of Marriage and the Family* 67:352–69.

Kalleberg, Arne L. 1977. Work values and job rewards: A theory of job satisfaction. *American Sociological Review* 42 (1): 124–43.

Kalleberg, Arne L. 2009. Precarious work, insecure workers: employment relations in transition. *American Sociological Review* 74:1–22.

Kalleberg, Arne L. 2018. *Precarious lives: Job insecurity and well-being in rich democracies*. Cambridge: Polity Press.

Kalleberg, Arne L., and Karyn A. Loscocco. 1983. Aging, values, and rewards: Explaining age differences in job satisfaction. *American Sociological Review* 48:78–90.

Kalleberg, Arne L., and Peter V. Marsden. 2013. Changing work values in the United States, 1973–2006. *Social Science Research* 42:255–70.

Kohn, Melvin L. 1969. *Class and conformity: A study in values*. Homewood, IL: Dorsey.

Lorence, Jon. 1987. Age differences in work involvement: Analyses of three explanations. *Work and Occupations* 14:533–57.

Mannheim, Karl. 1927/1952. The problem of generations. In *Essays in the sociology of knowledge*, ed. and trans. Paul Kecskemeti, 276–322. London: Routledge and Kegan Paul.

Marsden, Peter V., and Tom W. Smith. 2012. Appendix: The General Social Survey Project. In *Social trends in American life: Findings from the General Social Survey since 1972*, ed. Peter V. Marsden, 369–78. Princeton, NJ: Princeton University Press.

Maslow, Abraham. 1954. *Motivation and personality*. New York, NY: Harper and Row.

Martin, Jack K., and Steven A. Tuch. 1993. Black-white differences in the value of job rewards revisited. *Social Science Quarterly* 74:884–901.

Pfau, Bruce N. 7 April 2016. What do millennials really want at work? The same things the rest of us do. *Harvard Business Review*.

Quiggin, John. 7 March 2018. Millennial means nothing. *New York Times*, A27.

Rabe-Hesketh, Sophia, and Anders Skrondal. 2012. *Multilevel and longitudinal modeling using stata*. 3rd ed. College Station, TX: Stata Press.

Salancik, Gerald R., and Jeffrey Pfeffer. 1977. An examination of need satisfaction models of job attitudes. *Administrative Science Quarterly* 22:427–56.

Smith, Tom W., Michael Davern, Jeremy Freese, and Michael Hout. 2017. *General Social Surveys, 1972–2016: Cumulative Codebook*. Chicago, IL: NORC.

Twenge, Jean M. 2006. *Generation Me: Why today's young Americans are more confident, assertive, entitled – and more miserable than ever before*. New York, NY: Free Press.

Yang, Yang, and Kenneth C. Land. 2013. *Age-period-cohort analysis: New models, methods and empirical applications*. Boca Raton, FL: CRC Press.

Extrinsic and Intrinsic Work Values: Findings on Equivalence in Different Cultural Contexts

MAURICE GESTHUIZEN,
DANIEL KOVAREK,
and
CAROLIN RAPP

Academic literature emphasizes the importance of work values to job satisfaction and commitment. There is agreement that work values are multidimensional—most often identified as having extrinsic and intrinsic elements. However, little work has gone into assessing the measurement invariance of work values in different contexts. In this contribution, we ask, Do we find similar patterns of extrinsic and intrinsic work values across different cultural contexts? As such, we investigate the validity of *work values* when they are applied in cross-national analyses by identifying sets of items that can be translated into scales of extrinsic and intrinsic work values that carry a similar meaning in those cultural contexts. We thus want to know which items that make up *work values* are best understood in diverse contexts and are most suitable for cross-cultural analysis. We tackle this issue by relying on the European Values Study 2008, as well as the CUPESSE data from 2016. The results reveal that there is a trade-off between the number of items researchers use to study work values and the number of countries analyzed if we aim for a more equivalent analysis of work values across Europe.

Keywords: work values; scalogram analysis; cross-cultural research; measurement equivalence

The contributions of this volume of *The ANNALS* underscore the general importance of analyzing work values in broad context. Work values define the general importance of work in one's life as well as one's adherence to existing norms. Further, they are guidelines for employers in selecting adequate employees. Throughout the literature, as well as in this

Maurice Gesthuizen is an assistant professor in the Department of Sociology at Radboud University (Nijmegen, the Netherlands). His major research interests include educational inequality, economic vulnerability, social capital, and their interrelations. He has published widely on these subjects in international scientific journals.

Correspondence: m.gesthuizen@maw.ru.nl

DOI: 10.1177/0002716219829016

volume, work values have been analyzed from different angles, in particular their multiple causes—at the individual or contextual level—as well as their potential consequences for one's life satisfaction, economic self-sufficiency, or nonelectoral political participation (Cemalcilar, Secinti, and Sumer 2018; Elizur 1984; Gesthuizen and Verbakel 2011; Lechner et al. 2018; Visser, Gesthuizen, and Kraaykamp 2019; Yankelovich 1985). Another large part of the literature engages with the question of how work values change between generations and over decades (Jin and Rounds 2012; Krahn and Galambos 2013; Lechner et al. 2017; Meriac, Woehr, and Banister 2010; Twenge et al. 2010).

Yet there is little previous academic work on the basic question of what we understand work values to be (Elizur et al. 1991; Halman and Müller 2006; Kaasa 2011; Leuty and Hansen 2011; Vecerník 2003) and whether the measurement of work values is accurate and comparable across cultural contexts. Equivalence is an important issue in cross-cultural research. If we, for example, analyze the most important determinants of work values, we assume that these concepts—or better, the scales we use—are understood the same way in different contexts: each measured item has the same meaning across countries. The meaning of certain concepts may differ as they depend on the cultural, economic, and political setting within a country (Gesthuizen and Verbakel 2014). Does the importance of a secure job have the same emphasis in a country with a strong welfare state compared to a country with very low social security? Do inhabitants of those countries interpret *security* in a similar fashion and think of the same features related to this concept? Likewise, preferring a secure job over not experiencing too much pressure may, for instance, decisively differ among countries: in one nation, the bulk of the population might prefer security; whereas in the other nation, work pressure occupies the minds of most.

Accordingly, it is the aim of this contribution to empirically test the comparability of measurements of dimensions of work values, as well as to assess the extent to which there is conceptual invariance among a wide-range of countries. We base our analysis on two datasets, the European Values Study and the Cultural Pathways to Economic Self-Sufficiency and Entrepreneurship (CUPESSE) 2016 survey. By means of scalogram analysis,[1] we test whether there are similar patterns for selected items of intrinsic and extrinsic work values across countries.

Daniel Kovarek is a PhD candidate in the Department of Political Science at Central European University. His research interests include voting behavior, public opinion, and party politics.

Carolin Rapp is an assistant professor in the Department of Political Science at the University of Copenhagen. Her research lies in the intersection among political sociology, political psychology, and social policy research. Her research has appeared in, for example, the Journal of Politics, Journal of Ethnic and Migration Studies, *and* Social Science Research.

NOTE: The research leading to these results received funding from the European Union Seventh Framework Programme under grant agreement no. 613257 – CUPESSE (Cultural Pathways to Economic Self-Sufficiency and Entrepreneurship).

Dimensions of Work Values

Schwartz (1992, 1994, 20) posits that values encompass five dimensions: "a value is a (1) belief (2) pertaining to desirable end states or modes of conduct, that (3) transcends specific situations, (4) guides selection or evaluation of behavior, people, and events, and (5) is ordered by importance relative to other values to form a system of value priorities." Work values define the general motivation to work and what kind of work we are looking for. The research on work values is thereby spread over multiple disciplines such as sociology, psychology, economics, and political science (Cemalcilar, Secinti, and Sumer 2018), which leads to a large variety of understandings and variances in the analysis of work values. The literature largely agrees that work values contain different dimensions and subconcepts. The most common distinction thereby is between intrinsic and extrinsic work values (Gesthuizen and Verbakel 2014; Kaasa 2011; Kalleberg 1977; Ros, Schwartz, and Surkiss 1999).

Preferences for work may differ between individuals: some may prefer a job that offers economic benefits, whereas others may look for self-fulfillment in a job. The first refers to extrinsic work values, which cover tangible things such as income, working hours, pension schemes, or insurances. In that sense, these values are external to the individual as they are not connected to the way one works or to the content of one's work (Kaasa 2011). Hallman and Müller (2006, 119) even go as far as saying that the main purpose of extrinsic values is to reduce the general unpleasant character of work by providing favorable circumstances. In other words, even if someone does not like the content of her work, she might still appreciate it if it provides a decent pay or other amenities. However, following Ester, Braun, and Vinken (2006, 90), extrinsic work values "are no longer sufficient to do the job" of fostering economic development in Europe, as they are outdated. To be compatible with the changes on the European labor market, workers have to augment or even change their traditional mindset and enhance intrinsic work values.

Intrinsic work values are the mirror image of extrinsic values: they describe the desired content of one's work and not the general circumstances of it. According to Arendt (2013, 140), intrinsic values evolve around personal development and self-fulfillment in work. They stress the importance that an individual places on the "opportunities for further development of personal skills and an interest in the work promoted by the activity" (Tarnai et al. 1995, 140). Someone high on these values may, for example, prefer a job where he has the freedom to decide what he does, even though it means having less security (an extrinsic value). Thus, the focus lies more on the personally defined goals of work, instead of individual wealth or security (Yankelovich 1985). Intrinsic work values apply to the accelerated European labor market. Individuals are supposed to take responsibility in their jobs, be creative, and strive for self-fulfillment instead of working in a typical nine-to-five manner (Ester, Braun, and Vinken 2006). In that sense, the increased importance of intrinsic work values is in line with the pronounced individualization in European societies (Halman, Sieben, and van Zundert 2011).

Even though the literature agrees on these two dimensions of work values, we cannot be certain if these two are present or, better said, understood in the same way in every country. The institutional structure in a country, the religious background, or the current labor market may have a great impact on how the items that are supposed to measure a certain dimension of work values are interpreted (Gesthuizen and Verbakel 2014). Moreover, in surveys and studies, a large number of items measuring both extrinsic and intrinsic work values are usually used (e.g., at least five items per dimension), which raises the question of what pattern these items show in different cultural contexts. Can we be sure that the structure of these items and how they are understood are equivalent across countries? Or that they sum up to the same scale? Our aim is to assess the general patterns of work values' measures, that is, their cross-national comparability and scalability. More precisely, what would be the best way to assess extrinsic and intrinsic work values in cross-cultural research? Do we need a huge battery of items, or may some specific items suffice? These are our guiding questions in this contribution. In what follows, we test for measurement equivalence of extrinsic and intrinsic work values in different European countries, based on scalogram analysis.

Data and Methods

To test for measurement equivalence of the scales resulting from the most commonly used extrinsic and intrinsic work values items, we rely on European Value Study (EVS) data from 2008 (EVS 2011). The dataset comprises nineteen items on work values. Yet we focus in our analysis on the ten most often used, relating to the extrinsic-intrinsic distinction (see e.g., Ester, Braun, and Vinken 2006; Gesthuizen and Verbakel 2014; Halman and Müller 2006). The EVS 2008/2010 question is, *"Here are some aspects of a job that people say are important. Please look at them and tell me which ones you personally think are important in a job:* (1) good pay, (2) not too much pressure, (3) good job security, (4) good hours, (5) generous holidays, (6) opportunity to use initiative, (7) a job in which you feel you can achieve something, (8) a responsible job, (9) a job that is interesting, (10) a job that meets one's abilities." The first five items refer to extrinsic work values, whereas the latter five signify intrinsic work values. The potential answers then are whether a respondent mentioned the respective item (=1) or not (=0). The EVS asked for these items in forty-seven countries, which we take into account in our analyses. Our sample comprises 67,214 respondents. A list of these countries is included in Figures A3 through A12 in the online appendix.

As the EVS data already are 10 years old, we rely on the CUPESSE data (Tosun et al. 2018) to test the robustness of our findings. This dataset comprises ten items asking about work values and was conducted in eleven European countries in 2016; findings obtained from this additional dataset are listed in the online appendix (Tables A1–A4).[2] The aim of the CUPESSE project was to capture the intergenerational transmission of work values, among other values. The focus was thereby on young adults between 18 and 35. There are 19,996 respondents in the dataset.

FIGURE 1
Item Difficulties of Extrinsic and Intrinsic Work Values, EVS

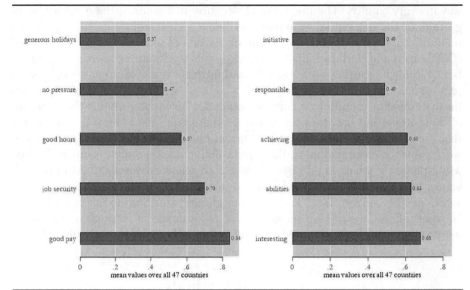

Figure 1 summarizes the mean values for each of the ten EVS items, grouped by work value dimension. Starting with the extrinsic dimension, it is clear that the importance that individuals attach to the specific extrinsic work values differs: a well-paying job is on average mentioned by 84 percent of all respondents, followed respectively by "job security" (70 percent), "good hours" (57 percent), "not too much pressure" (47 percent), and "generous holidays" (37 percent). There is a clear rank order in item difficulties, "having a well-paid job" being the least difficult item (i.e., most popular: highest average) and "generous holidays" the most difficult (i.e., least popular: lowest average). In the CUPESSE data, we also find such a rank order in item difficulties (see online appendix Figure A1).

Within the intrinsic dimension, a rank order of item difficulties also appears: 68 percent find "having an interesting job" important, followed by "a job that meets one's abilities," "a job in which you feel you can achieve something," "a responsible job," and "a job that offers the opportunity to use initiative" (respectively, 63, 61, 49, and 49 percent). On average, the same applies for the CUPESSE data.

Method

We use scalogram (Mokken) analysis (Mokken 1971; Sijtsma and Meijer 2016; Sijtsma and Molenaar 2002) to test whether and to what extent the items underlying each work value dimension have a similar structure/pattern, as well as sufficient scalability, if we compare the countries in our datasets. Scalogram analysis is based on item-response theory. It assumes that the answer that a respondent gives to an item (important vs. not important)—which is part of a certain latent construct, here extrinsic and intrinsic work values—not only depends on his true (unmeasured) attitude regarding this construct, but also on the difficulty of this particular item that is developed to measure it. For instance, an individual can, in reality, attach an above-average importance to extrinsic work values; but given that "generous holidays" is a difficult item, not many respondents consider this item as particularly important for extrinsic work values (see, e.g., Figure 1), so this individual will most likely score "generous holidays" as not important (0). Thus, the more difficult the item, the stronger, in theory, it expresses the latent construct to be measured. Given a respondent's true position on the latent continuum of "finding extrinsic work values important" (continuum ranging from left = less difficult items to right = more difficult items), she finds the manifest items of extrinsic work values important (observed score 1) that are positioned at her left of the continuum, whereas the items positioned at the right are evaluated as not important (observed score 0). In scalogram analysis, the score a respondent gets on the scale of, in this example, extrinsic work values then simply is a summation of the scores "important" (1). The higher this scale score, the more someone values extrinsic work characteristics.[3]

The H-parameters (*Loevinger's parameters of homogeneity*) indicate the strength of the scale as a whole and the deviation from the assumed pattern if all combinations of items are included in one formula. H-parameters >.30 and <.40 indicate a weak scale, H-parameters >.40 and <.50 indicate moderate scales, whereas H-parameters >.50 indicate strong scales. Moreover, scalogram analysis provides additional tests—the first and second criterion of monotonicity, also called monotone homogeneity and double monotonicity—which are important, if not crucial, for assessments of cross-national equivalence, and are based on so called rest score methods (see van der Ark 2012). A test of the first criterion of monotonicity implies that, in our example, those who in reality value extrinsic job characteristics more than intrinsic also have a higher probability of answering "important" to "having a secure job" or, for that matter, whatever item measuring extrinsic work values. The second criterion of monotonicity implies that the item response functions of two or more items do not intersect. If they do not intersect, for every respondent on every position on the latent continuum (thus varying in how they value extrinsic job characteristics), the rank order of item difficulties is uniform: everyone rank orders the items in the same way. This uniformity, both across countries (similar rank orders in item difficulties) and within countries across respondents, is vital for our assessment of equivalence and invariance. If we find similar patterns across and within nations, the underlying structure of the scales is similar, and we can safely assume that the items are understood similarly and the scale scores can be compared across groups.

If we find, for a combination of items, similar rank orders of item difficulties for a set of countries, sufficiently high H-parameters, and no violations of the first and second criteria of monotonicity, we conclude that for this set of countries, the measurement of the dimension of work values is equivalent. Excluding items could result in fewer deviations and thus a larger pool of countries that can be compared on the construct, yet at the cost of substantial aspects of the meaning of the concept. For instance, if "having a secure job" needs to be excluded to achieve comparability of *extrinsic work values* across nations, the concept of extrinsic work values does not contain this aspect anymore. Because "job security" is part of the theoretical concept, excluding "job security" diminishes the internal validity of the theoretical concept, and it becomes more "narrow."

Results

We present our results in several steps. First, we present for both dimensions of work values the rank order of item difficulties for each country separately and compare them to the rank order that is found when calculated for all countries at the same time (the overall pattern). Deleting items from the set means that we achieve a larger pool of countries for which the dimension of work values is comparable. We therefore also determine the order of deleting items from the set so that with each single deletion, we retain as many countries as possible that match with the overall pattern (Table 1). Second, detailed analyses show the scalability (H-parameters) and violations of the first and second criteria of monotonicity for each item in each county, in every step of deleting an item from the analysis (Tables 2–3). Finally, for the combination of items within a work value dimension that generates the highest number of nations with equivalent scales, we present for each country average scores on the scales of extrinsic and intrinsic work values. These scales are standardized z-scores, so that the overall average is zero, and the average country scores depict whether and to what extent they are above or below average (Figure 2). These findings show the rank order among countries in valuing extrinsic and intrinsic work characteristics, based on measures that can be compared cross-nationally.

Starting with the extrinsic dimension of work values, the light gray areas in Table 1 show that out of the forty-seven countries, twenty-two have a pattern of rank order in item difficulties that matches the overall pattern: good pay showing the highest rate of agreement, after which the order of importance, respectively, is job security, good hours, no pressure, and generous holiday (see also Figure 1). The dark gray areas depict the deviations from the general pattern, meaning a different rank order in item difficulties. For Azerbaijan, for instance, we see that "experiencing not too much pressure" causes a large deviation from the overall pattern: in this country it is the least difficult, most important work value, instead of the second most difficult according to the general pattern. The column for no pressure also shows that this item causes deviations in many nations. Deleting this item would make most countries switch from deviating to not deviating from the overall pattern (thirteen to be precise; see Tables 2–3). After "no pressure" is deleted, eliminating "job security" from the analyses would result in the highest gain in terms of countries following the overall pattern (nine in total). Deleting "good hours," in a final step, would add the last three countries to the pool of countries having a similar rank order in item difficulty.

(text continues on p. 77)

TABLE 1

Item Difficulties of Extrinsic and Intrinsic Work Values, EVS

| | Extrinsic Work Values | | | | | Intrinsic Work Values | | | | | |
	Good Pay	Job Security[b]	Good Hours[c]	No Pressure[a]	Generous Holidays	Interesting[c]	Abilities[b]	Achieving	Responsible[a]	Initiative	N
Albania	.96	.76	.68	.62	.59	.52	.71	.58	.35	.45	1,534
Azerbaijan	.72	.58	.53	.79	.36	.54	.79	.56	.65	.45	1,379
Austria	.67	.71	.45	.30	.26	.69	.59	.56	.47	.45	1,470
Armenia	.96	.83	.79	.76	.46	.88	.81	.73	.65	.67	1,400
Belgium	.60	.31	.30	.15	.16	.43	.37	.36	.31	.33	1,502
Bosnia Herzegovina	.93	.69	.69	.59	.55	.68	.63	.58	.31	.33	1,512
Bulgaria	.98	.87	.73	.56	.46	.79	.84	.77	.44	.41	1,259
Belarus	.93	.55	.62	.31	.48	.72	.54	.52	.30	.39	1,459
Croatia	.85	.68	.55	.50	.35	.64	.57	.55	.35	.35	1,380
Cyprus	.93	.80	.83	.63	.34	.79	.79	.68	.65	.50	966
Northern Cyprus	.96	.96	.90	.85	.39	.53	.91	.84	.80	.72	458
Czech Republic	.84	.61	.45	.46	.36	.65	.54	.47	.39	.40	1,715
Denmark	.54	.45	.31	.17	.17	.62	.39	.56	.48	.50	1,487
Estonia	.94	.71	.74	.47	.31	.82	.71	.60	.35	.50	1,456
Finland	.59	.69	.54	.31	.19	.78	.54	.61	.48	.33	1,134
France	.57	.28	.20	.05	.10	.59	.36	.45	.48	.33	1,495
Georgia	.98	.90	.60	.40	.35	.82	.64	.75	.57	.57	1,353
Germany	.74	.80	.28	.20	.12	.63	.56	.51	.43	.41	2,061
Greece	.94	.54	.53	.47	.19	.65	.59	.46	.55	.33	1,483
Hungary	.86	.81	.46	.19	.16	.44	.46	.43	.38	.17	1,511
Iceland	.80	.48	.46	.21	.09	.71	.54	.69	.30	.56	807
Ireland	.89	.77	.67	.45	.51	.75	.64	.66	.59	.53	776
Italy	.76	.74	.53	.51	.22	.67	.68	.68	.43	.52	1,454
Latvia	.89	.63	.55	.32	.36	.70	.56	.51	.34	.34	1,408
Lithuania	.96	.72	.63	.49	.43	.82	.70	.54	.42	.46	1,496

(continued)

TABLE 1 (CONTINUED)

	Extrinsic Work Values					Intrinsic Work Values					
	Good Pay	Job Security[b]	Good Hours[c]	No Pressure[a]	Generous Holidays	Interesting[c]	Abilities[b]	Achieving	Responsible[a]	Initiative	N
Luxembourg	.82	.69	.63	.52	.36	.85	.81	.79	.76	.73	1,507
Malta	.91	.84	.74	.64	.34	.79	.75	.60	.53	.60	1,363
Moldova	.98	.93	.88	.72	.79	.94	.93	.92	.82	.86	1,402
Montenegro	.94	.67	.69	.57	.51	.68	.64	.55	.48	.36	1,516
Netherlands	.74	.46	.60	.49	.47	.71	.81	.63	.52	.78	1,474
Norway	.58	.60	.27	.20	.11	.58	.30	.63	.38	.42	1,088
Poland	.93	.78	.54	.70	.41	.76	.63	.66	.53	.48	1,421
Portugal	.89	.89	.68	.57	.59	.79	.73	.74	.62	.59	1,490
Romania	.95	.84	.74	.47	.50	.69	.78	.70	.55	.59	1,224
Russian Federation	.94	.71	.48	.36	.51	.70	.57	.52	.36	.59	1,394
Serbia	.91	.83	.61	.59	.41	.71	.68	.69	.53	.46	1,512
Slovak Republic	.92	.69	.52	.38	.40	.67	.58	.55	.47	.44	1,324
Slovenia	.76	.73	.29	.54	.33	.79	.59	.74	.53	.57	1,299
Spain	.77	.52	.45	.33	.17	.28	.24	.25	.15	.13	1,492
Sweden	.60	.53	.46	.32	.17	.60	.32	.61	.49	.63	1,187
Switzerland	.56	.55	.24	.19	.10	.66	.46	.52	.50	.46	1,253
Turkey	.98	.97	.90	.84	.55	.58	.90	.85	.83	.78	2,273
Ukraine	.93	.61	.56	.31	.57	.71	.57	.48	.32	.38	1,429
Macedonia	.96	.86	.78	.76	.57	.77	.79	.79	.77	.68	1,188
Great Britain	.74	.66	.52	.24	.30	.69	.43	.66	.39	.45	1,535
Northern Ireland	.90	.74	.69	.41	.52	.71	.55	.57	.46	.46	422
Kosovo	.96	.86	.75	.79	.68	.72	.79	.78	.68	.66	1,601
Overall	*.84*	*.70*	*.57*	*.46*	*.37*	*.68*	*.62*	*.61*	*.49*	*.49*	64,349

NOTE: Light gray: pattern equivalent to the grand total; dight gray: deviation from pattern.
a. First item excluded from pattern evaluation.
b. Second item excluded from pattern evaluation.
c. Third item excluded from pattern evaluation.

68

TABLE 2A
Cross-National Equivalence of Extrinsic Work Values, Scalogram Analysis, EVS

	Good Pay	Job Security	Good Hours	No Pressure	Generous Holidays		Violations	
	Hi	Hi	Hi	Hi	Hi	H	Mon 1	Mon 2
Albania	.44	.36	.38	.35	.36	.36	No	No
Azerbaijan	.20	.33	.31	.33	.19	.27	No	No
Austria	.53	.52	.60	.57	.63	.57	No	No
Armenia	.31	.47	.39	.43	.54	.44	No	No
Belgium	.35	.24	.29	.26	.38	.30	No	Yes
Bosnia Herzegovina	.43	.48	.51	.44	.47	.47	No	No
Bulgaria	.45	.52	.55	.44	.49	.49	No	No
Belarus	.49	.30	.36	.44	.39	.37	No	No
Croatia	.43	.35	.45	.41	.54	.44	No	No
Cyprus	.46	.35	.44	.48	.56	.45	No	No
Northern Cyprus	.46	.39	.51	.50	.37	.46	No	No
Czech Republic	.55	.41	.43	.43	.49	.45	No	No
Denmark	.29	.26	.34	.34	.42	.32	No	No
Estonia	.56	.49	.48	.58	.60	.54	No	No
Finland	.28	.32	.35	.40	.56	.37	No	No
France	.24	.27	.29	.45	.46	.32	No	No
Georgia	.54	.65	.71	.65	.64	.66	No	No
Germany	.32	.22	.41	.38	.50	.37	No	No
Greece	.60	.28	.39	.35	.58	.38	No	Yes
Hungary	.39	.35	.50	.50	.51	.46	No	No
Iceland	.39	.35	.50	.50	.51	.46	No	No
Ireland	.53	.47	.58	.54	.61	.55	No	No
Italy	.39	.48	.52	.47	.67	.49	No	Yes
Latvia	.48	.46	.50	.60	.55	.52	No	No

	Good Pay	Job Security	Good Hours	Generous Holidays		Violations	
	Hi	Hi	Hi	Hi	H	Mon 1	Mon 2
Albania	.43	.32	.39	.40	.38	No	No
Azerbaijan	.21	.28	.29	.17	.24	No	No
Austria	.50	.49	.60	.71	.57	No	No
Armenia	.30	.45	.45	.55	.46	No	No
Belgium	.36	.25	.28	.44	.32	No	No
Bosnia Herzegovina	.49	.46	.52	.54	.50	No	No
Bulgaria	.52	.54	.58	.60	.57	No	No
Belarus	.49	.26	.33	.37	.33	No	No
Croatia	.46	.34	.48	.58	.46	No	No
Cyprus	.46	.37	.41	.52	.43	No	No
Northern Cyprus	.43	.35	.44	.38	.40	No	No
Czech Republic	.58	.40	.45	.53	.48	No	No
Denmark	.29	.24	.31	.48	.31	No	No
Estonia	.54	.43	.45	.64	.50	No	No
Finland	.29	.31	.31	.60	.35	No	No
France	.23	.24	.27	.45	.28	No	No
Georgia	.44	.62	.71	.72	.67	No	No
Germany	.31	.23	.42	.53	.36	No	No
Greece	.65	.32	.41	.54	.42	No	Yes
Hungary	.37	.32	.46	.61	.42	No	No
Iceland	.37	.32	.46	.61	.42	No	No
Ireland	.58	.45	.56	.66	.56	No	No
Italy	.41	.46	.57	.72	.52	No	No
Latvia	.46	.40	.44	.57	.46	No	No

(continued)

TABLE 2B (CONTINUED)

	Good Pay	Job Security	Good Hours	No Pressure	Generous Holidays		Violations		Good Pay	Job Security	Good Hours	Generous Holidays		Violations	
	Hi	Hi	Hi	Hi	Hi	H	Mon 1	Mon 2	Hi	Hi	Hi	Hi	H	Mon 1	Mon 2
Lithuania	.54	.39	.38	.44	.45	.42	No	No	.55	.32	.36	.48	.40	No	No
Luxembourg	.42	.44	.43	.43	.54	.45	No	No	.44	.40	.45	.60	.46	No	No
Malta	.56	.50	.60	.58	.65	.58	No	No	.54	.48	.58	.75	.58	No	No
Moldova	.35	.41	.43	.46	.37	.41	No	No	.35	.40	.35	.34	.36	No	No
Montenegro	.56	.41	.44	.42	.43	.44	No	No	.55	.38	.44	.49	.45	No	No
Netherlands	.41	.41	.45	.38	.43	.42	No	Yes	.45	.41	.44	.47	.44	No	No
Norway	.24	.19	.41	.35	.48	.32	No	No	.23	.17	.43	.51	.30	No	No
Poland	.45	.40	.43	.38	.48	.43	No	No	.48	.39	.47	.52	.47	No	No
Portugal	.48	.51	.61	.55	.60	.56	No	Yes	.49	.47	.62	.67	.57	No	No
Romania	.56	.48	.48	.52	.49	.50	No	No	.54	.46	.44	.50	.47	No	No
Russian Federation	.66	.48	.41	.47	.44	.46	No	No	.67	.49	.38	.44	.45	No	No
Serbia	.59	.49	.55	.52	.61	.55	No	No	.58	.45	.61	.66	.58	No	No
Slovak Republic	.57	.44	.57	.57	.54	.54	No	No	.54	.40	.53	.58	.51	No	No
Slovenia	.43	.48	.49	.54	.52	.49	No	No	.42	.45	.45	.50	.46	No	No
Spain	.31	.22	.33	.35	.48	.33	No	Yes	.31	.19	.33	.49	.31	No	Yes
Sweden	.32	.32	.41	.42	.56	.39	No	No	.33	.28	.39	.61	.37	No	Yes
Switzerland	.34	.23	.31	.30	.44	.31	No	Yes	.33	.25	.32	.45	.32	No	No
Turkey	.21	.49	.62	.63	.68	.58	No	No	.18	.44	.58	.69	.51	No	No
Ukraine	.62	.47	.47	.60	.54	.52	No	No	.62	.44	.42	.53	.47	No	No
Macedonia	.33	.55	.51	.52	.55	.52	No	Yes	.31	.51	.52	.58	.51	No	No
Great Britain	.44	.37	.49	.48	.57	.52	No	No	.44	.35	.45	.66	.46	No	No
Northern Ireland	.64	.40	.52	.60	.59	.54	No	No	.61	.36	.46	.61	.50	No	No
Kosovo	.47	.43	.43	.41	.36	.41	No	No	.43	.42	.46	.35	.41	No	Yes

NOTE: Hi: Item H (criterion: at least .30); H: Scale H (criterion: at least .30); Mon 1: violation of the first criterion of monotonicity based on rest score method; Mon 2: violation of the second criterion of monotonicity based on rest score method; Unk: violation of the second criterion of monotonicity based on rest score method is unknown, since at least three items are needed for this test; light gray: pattern equivalent to the grand total, based on rank order in item difficulties; dark gray: Does not meet (minimum) criterion (violations and Scale H).

TABLE 2B
Cross-National Equivalence of Extrinsic Work Values, Scalogram Analysis, EVS

	Good Pay	Good Hours	Generous Holidays			Violations		Good Pay	Generous Holidays			Violations[a]
	Hi	Hi	Hi	Hi	H	Mon 1	Mon 2	Hi	Hi	Hi	H	Mon 1
Albania	.38	.46	.46	.45	.45	No	No	.38	.38	.38	.38	No
Azerbaijan	.11	.27	.20	.20	.20	No	No	-.02	-.02	-.02	-.02	No
Austria	.57	.62	.72	.64	.64	No	No	.72	.72	.72	.72	No
Armenia	.31	.49	.53	.48	.48	No	No	.41	.41	.41	.41	No
Belgium	.40	.39	.50	.43	.43	No	No	.55	.55	.55	.55	No
Bosnia Herzegovina	.56	.56	.59	.57	.57	No	No	.63	.63	.63	.63	No
Bulgaria	.57	.60	.61	.60	.60	No	No	.62	.62	.62	.62	No
Belarus	.59	.42	.45	.46	.46	No	No	.72	.72	.72	.72	No
Croatia	.60	.58	.66	.61	.61	No	No	.78	.78	.78	.78	No
Cyprus	.49	.49	.62	.53	.53	No	No	.72	.72	.72	.72	No
Northern Cyprus	.44	.43	.51	.46	.46	No	No	.58	.58	.58	.58	No
Czech Republic	.67	.53	.58	.58	.58	No	No	.78	.78	.78	.78	No
Denmark	.38	.38	.49	.41	.41	No	No	.52	.52	.52	.52	No
Estonia	.50	.61	.73	.63	.63	No	No	.72	.72	.72	.72	No
Finland	.30	.32	.64	.38	.38	No	No	.64	.64	.64	.64	No
France	.27	.33	.48	.35	.35	No	No	.45	.45	.45	.45	No
Georgia	.56	.72	.72	.71	.71	No	No	.54	.54	.54	.54	No
Germany	.46	.46	.59	.50	.50	No	No	.71	.71	.71	.71	No
Greece	.66	.69	.71	.69	.69	No	No	.69	.69	.69	.69	No
Hungary	.48	.53	.66	.56	.56	No	No	.72	.72	.72	.72	No
Iceland	.48	.53	.66	.56	.56	No	No	.72	.72	.72	.72	No
Ireland	.65	.68	.72	.69	.69	No	No	.74	.74	.74	.74	No
Italy	.54	.57	.70	.60	.60	No	No	.70	.70	.70	.70	No
Latvia	.55	.55	.59	.56	.56	No	No	.64	.64	.64	.64	No

(continued)

TABLE 2B (CONTINUED)

| | Good Pay | Good Hours | Generous Holidays | | Violations | | Good Pay | Generous Holidays | | Violations[a] |
	Hi	Hi	Hi	H	Mon 1	Mon 2	Hi	Hi	H	Mon 1
Lithuania	.57	.49	.53	.52	No	No	.79	.79	.79	No
Luxembourg	.48	.52	.65	.55	No	No	.65	.65	.65	No
Malta	.67	.67	.79	.71	No	No	.88	.88	.88	No
Moldova	.45	.28	.32	.32	No	No	.60	.60	.60	No
Montenegro	.57	.55	.58	.56	No	No	.65	.65	.65	No
Netherlands	.44	.45	.54	.48	No	No	.56	.56	.56	No
Norway	.48	.49	.56	.50	No	No	.56	.56	.56	No
Poland	.57	.53	.54	.54	No	No	.64	.64	.64	No
Portugal	.63	.64	.68	.65	No	No	.70	.70	.70	No
Romania	.61	.47	.48	.50	No	No	.65	.65	.65	No
Russian Federation	.68	.37	.39	.42	No	No	.75	.75	.75	No
Serbia	.74	.68	.72	.71	No	No	.84	.84	.84	No
Slovak Republic	.72	.64	.65	.65	No	No	.77	.77	.77	No
Slovenia	.62	.38	.46	.47	No	Yes	.73	.73	.73	No
Spain	.42	.48	.68	.52	No	No	.72	.72	.72	No
Sweden	.46	.46	.69	.51	No	No	.73	.73	.73	No
Switzerland	.47	.37	.49	.44	No	No	.70	.70	.70	No
Turkey	.19	.60	.68	.55	No	No	.26	.26	.26	No
Ukraine	.61	.50	.52	.52	No	No	.67	.67	.67	No
Macedonia	.41	.49	.57	.51	No	No	.64	.64	.64	No
Great Britain	.56	.57	.69	.61	No	No	.73	.73	.73	No
Northern Ireland	.72	.63	.70	.68	No	No	.87	.87	.87	No
Kosovo	.47	.39	.38	.40	No	No	.42	.42	.42	No

NOTE: Hi: Item H (criterion: at least .30); H: Scale H (criterion: at least .30); Mon 1: violation of the first criterion of monotonicity based on rest score method; Mon 2: violation of the second criterion of monotonicity based on rest score method; Unk: violation of the second criterion of monotonicity based on rest score method is unknown, since at least three items are needed for this test; light gray: pattern equivalent to the grand total, based on rank order in item difficulties; dark gray: Does not meet (minimum) criterion (violations and Scale H).

a. Violation of the second criterion of monotonicity based on rest score method is unknown, since at least three items are needed for this test.

TABLE 3A
Cross-National Equivalence of Intrinsic Work Values, Scalogram Analysis, EVS

	Interesting	Abilities	Achieving	Responsible	Initiative		Violations		Interesting	Abilities	Achieving	Initiative		Violations	
	Hi	Hi	Hi	Hi	Hi	H	Mon 1	Mon 2	Hi	Hi	Hi	Hi	H	Mon 1	Mon 2
Albania	.36	.36	.43	.43	.41	.40	No	Yes	.32	.34	.42	.43	.38	No	Yes
Azerbaijan	.33	.42	.38	.38	.16	.33	No	Yes	.29	.40	.36	.16	.29	No	Yes
Austria	.60	.52	.53	.51	.54	.54	No	No	.60	.54	.52	.58	.56	No	No
Armenia	.65	.52	.55	.47	.53	.54	No	No	.66	.56	.55	.59	.59	No	No
Belgium	.24	.29	.26	.25	.33	.28	Yes	Yes	.25	.31	.28	.34	.29	No	No
Bosnia Herzegovina	.48	.49	.47	.53	.58	.51	No	No	.44	.50	.45	.62	.50	No	No
Bulgaria	.56	.53	.59	.58	.59	.57	No	No	.52	.52	.57	.66	.57	No	No
Belarus	.57	.47	.49	.55	.54	.52	No	No	.57	.44	.48	.54	.50	No	No
Croatia	.45	.44	.46	.51	.55	.48	No	No	.41	.42	.44	.60	.46	No	No
Cyprus	.54	.40	.51	.51	.64	.52	No	Yes	.53	.41	.54	.64	.53	No	No
Northern Cyprus	.49	.61	.58	.51	.42	.51	No	No	.48	.62	.58	.42	.51	No	No
Czech Republic	.54	.58	.56	.56	.54	.56	No	No	.51	.57	.57	.57	.56	No	No
Denmark	.30	.26	.28	.28	.31	.29	No	No	.28	.29	.28	.31	.29	No	No
Estonia	.52	.45	.50	.55	.52	.51	No	No	.50	.42	.48	.53	.48	No	No
Finland	.50	.40	.42	.43	.46	.44	No	No	.50	.40	.42	.47	.44	No	No
France	.32	.37	.29	.29	.44	.34	No	No	.38	.38	.34	.42	.38	No	No
Georgia	.62	.63	.64	.63	.61	.63	No	No	.56	.65	.60	.68	.63	No	No
Germany	.39	.40	.38	.38	.44	.40	No	No	.38	.41	.39	.47	.41	No	No
Greece	.48	.41	.42	.46	.58	.46	Yes	Yes	.47	.42	.43	.58	.47	Yes	Yes
Hungary	.25	.29	.31	.32	.54	.32	No	No	.24	.29	.32	.56	.32	No	No
Iceland	.28	.36	.37	.48	.41	.38	No	No	.26	.36	.31	.38	.33	No	No
Ireland	.50	.53	.53	.54	.60	.54	No	No	.50	.53	.52	.62	.54	No	No
Italy	.47	.45	.44	.58	.51	.49	No	No	.44	.41	.41	.49	.44	No	No
Latvia	.47	.41	.49	.53	.59	.50	No	No	.45	.38	.48	.62	.47	No	Yes

(continued)

TABLE 3A (CONTINUED)

	Interesting	Abilities	Achieving	Responsible	Initiative		Violations		Interesting	Abilities	Achieving	Initiative		Violations	
	Hi	Hi	Hi	Hi	Hi	H	Mon 1	Mon 2	Hi	Hi	Hi	Hi	H	Mon 1	Mon 2
Lithuania	.47	.39	.51	.49	.46	.47	Yes	No	.42	.39	.49	.48	.45	No	No
Luxembourg	.47	.46	.44	.40	.50	.45	No	No	.50	.50	.45	.52	.49	No	No
Malta	.68	.66	.63	.60	.64	.64	No	No	.68	.67	.66	.68	.67	No	No
Moldova	.57	.52	.53	.55	.54	.54	No	No	.54	.52	.50	.57	.53	No	No
Montenegro	.50	.50	.51	.50	.62	.52	No	Yes	.47	.51	.53	.65	.54	No	No
Netherlands	.54	.61	.55	.61	.57	.57	No	No	.51	.59	.55	.55	.55	No	No
Norway	.34	.31	.31	.36	.36	.34	No	No	.31	.33	.29	.35	.32	No	No
Poland	.50	.47	.47	.48	.54	.50	No	No	.50	.48	.48	.58	.51	No	No
Portugal	.61	.65	.65	.68	.72	.66	No	No	.59	.63	.64	.74	.65	No	No
Romania	.49	.51	.52	.51	.50	.51	No	No	.47	.51	.51	.53	.50	No	No
Russian Federation	.53	.45	.51	.46	.51	.49	No	Yes	.52	.45	.52	.55	.51	No	Yes
Serbia	.48	.49	.49	.53	.58	.51	No	No	.44	.48	.46	.64	.50	No	No
Slovak Republic	.61	.55	.54	.59	.64	.58	No	No	.57	.54	.54	.68	.58	No	No
Slovenia	.57	.57	.57	.56	.56	.57	No	No	.54	.58	.55	.59	.57	No	No
Spain	.35	.32	.33	.33	.39	.34	No	No	.35	.33	.32	.42	.35	No	No
Sweden	.30	.39	.29	.41	.38	.35	No	Yes	.28	.39	.28	.31	.31	No	No
Switzerland	.35	.25	.31	.30	.35	.31	No	Yes	.35	.27	.32	.32	.31	No	No
Turkey	.78	.70	.71	.65	.64	.69	No	No	.77	.73	.74	.66	.72	No	No
Ukraine	.51	.50	.53	.54	.55	.53	No	No	.49	.49	.53	.56	.52	No	No
Macedonia	.46	.51	.53	.40	.59	.50	No	Yes	.51	.56	.57	.63	.57	No	Yes
Great Britain	.44	.42	.45	.43	.47	.44	No	Yes	.43	.44	.47	.48	.45	No	No
Northern Ireland	.52	.45	.51	.48	.57	.51	No	Yes	.54	.47	.51	.59	.53	No	No
Kosovo	.44	.40	.33	.46	.31	.39	No	Yes	.40	.38	.26	.31	.34	No	Yes

NOTE: Hi: Item H (criterion: at least .30); H: Scale H (criterion: at least .30); Mon 1: violation of the first criterion of monotonicity based on rest score method; Mon 2: violation of the second criterion of monotonicity based on rest score method; Unk: Violation of the second criterion of monotonicity based on rest score method is unknown, since at least three items are needed for this test; light gray: pattern equivalent to the grand total, based on rank order in item difficulties; dark gray: Does not meet (minimum) criterion (violations and Scale H).

TABLE 3B
Cross-National Equivalence of Intrinsic Work Values, Scalogram Analysis, EVS

	Interesting	Achieving	Initiative		Violations		Achieving	Initiative		Violations[a]
	Hi	Hi	Hi	H	Mon 1	Mon 2	Hi	Hi	H	Mon 1
Albania	.34	.44	.44	.40	No	No	.56	.56	.56	No
Azerbaijan	.25	.31	.15	.24	No	Yes	.21	.21	.21	No
Austria	.61	.54	.60	.58	No	No	.55	.55	.55	No
Armenia	.68	.58	.62	.62	No	No	.56	.56	.56	No
Belgium	.27	.26	.30	.28	No	No	.29	.29	.29	No
Bosnia Herzegovina	.46	.45	.58	.49	No	No	.56	.56	.56	No
Bulgaria	.55	.57	.69	.60	No	No	.71	.71	.71	No
Belarus	.61	.56	.58	.58	No	No	.55	.55	.55	No
Croatia	.48	.47	.60	.51	No	No	.58	.58	.58	No
Cyprus	.61	.62	.70	.64	No	No	.69	.69	.69	No
Northern Cyprus	.45	.53	.40	.45	No	No	.47	.47	.47	No
Czech Republic	.52	.54	.56	.54	No	No	.58	.58	.58	No
Denmark	.28	.28	.33	.30	No	No	.33	.33	.33	No
Estonia	.54	.55	.56	.55	No	No	.57	.57	.57	No
Finland	.51	.44	.53	.49	No	No	.47	.47	.47	No
France	.39	.32	.43	.38	No	No	.36	.36	.36	No
Georgia	.52	.59	.69	.60	No	No	.74	.74	.74	No
Germany	.39	.40	.46	.42	No	No	.46	.46	.46	No
Greece	.50	.49	.58	.53	No	No	.56	.56	.56	No
Hungary	.30	.33	.54	.37	No	No	.58	.58	.58	No
Iceland	.23	.28	.40	.30	No	No	.46	.46	.46	No
Ireland	.49	.55	.63	.56	No	No	.67	.67	.67	No
Italy	.44	.45	.50	.46	No	No	.52	.52	.52	No
Latvia	.56	.58	.67	.60	No	No	.67	.67	.67	No

(continued)

TABLE 3B (CONTINUED)

	Interesting	Achieving	Initiative		Violations		Achieving	Initiative		Violations[a]
	Hi	Hi	Hi	H	Mon 1	Mon 2	Hi	Hi	H	Mon 1
Lithuania	.53	.50	.51	.51	No	No	.49	.49	.49	No
Luxembourg	.50	.46	.50	.48	No	No	.47	.47	.47	No
Malta	.74	.65	.65	.67	No	No	.61	.61	.61	No
Moldova	.55	.53	.55	.54	No	No	.53	.53	.53	No
Montenegro	.52	.53	.67	.57	No	No	.66	.66	.66	No
Netherlands	.49	.50	.55	.51	No	No	.58	.58	.58	No
Norway	.29	.26	.38	.31	No	No	.36	.36	.36	No
Poland	.48	.53	.63	.54	No	No	.65	.65	.65	No
Portugal	.61	.66	.73	.67	No	No	.77	.77	.77	No
Romania	.47	.50	.53	.50	No	No	.57	.57	.57	No
Russian Federation	.58	.56	.60	.58	No	No	.58	.58	.58	No
Serbia	.48	.49	.61	.52	No	No	.61	.61	.61	No
Slovak Republic	.59	.59	.69	.62	No	No	.68	.68	.68	No
Slovenia	.50	.52	.65	.55	No	No	.66	.66	.66	No
Spain	.36	.33	.43	.37	No	No	.39	.39	.39	No
Sweden	.25	.25	.30	.26	No	No	.29	.29	.29	No
Switzerland	.37	.36	.36	.36	No	No	.35	.35	.35	No
Turkey	.75	.74	.66	.72	No	No	.65	.65	.65	No
Ukraine	.55	.55	.56	.56	No	No	.56	.56	.56	No
Macedonia	.52	.59	.60	.57	No	No	.69	.69	.69	No
Great Britain	.41	.43	.55	.46	No	No	.57	.57	.57	No
Northern Ireland	.58	.57	.64	.60	No	No	.62	.62	.62	No
Kosovo	.33	.28	.29	.30	No	No	.23	.23	.23	No

NOTE: Hi: Item H (criterion: at least .30); H: Scale H (criterion: at least .30); Mon 1: violation of the first criterion of monotonicity based on rest score method; Mon 2: violation of the second criterion of monotonicity based on rest score method; Unk: Violation of monotonicity based on rest score method is unknown, since at least three items are needed for this test; light gray: pattern equivalent to the grand total, based on rank order in item difficulties; dark gray: Does not meet (minimum) criterion (violations and Scale H).

a. Violation of the second criterion of monotonicity based on rest score method is unknown, since at least three items are needed for this test

FIGURE 2

Differences in Extrinsic and Intrinsic Work Values across Countries (EVS), Based on Most Equivalent Scales

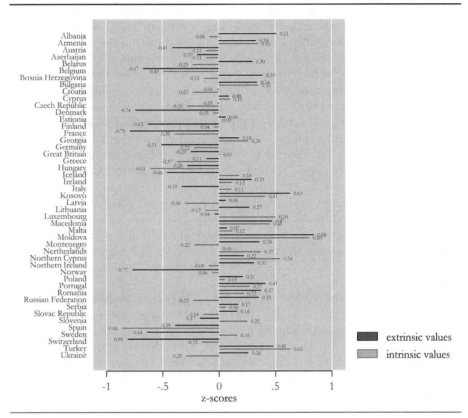

For the intrinsic dimension of work values, we see straightaway that fewer countries, nine in total, have a pattern equivalent to the overall rank order of item difficulties. We also see more dark gray areas compared to the extrinsic dimension, depicting numerous deviations from the general pattern. Removing "a responsible job" first from the analyses adds the most countries to the pool of "nondeviators." A job that meets one's abilities is the second item generating the highest wins, and finally having an interesting job. For the intrinsic dimension of work values, the Netherlands and Sweden can never achieve a rank order in item difficulties similar to the overall pattern, as in these countries "using initiative" is held to be more important (less difficult) than "the ability to achieve something," which in the overall pattern initiative is the most difficult intrinsic work value.

Tables 2 and 3 show the scalability parameters (Hi and H) and violations of the first and second criterion of monotonicity (Mon1 and Mon2) for each step in the process of deleting items from the scale. Again, light gray areas in Tables 2 and 3 depict the countries that have a rank order in item difficulties similar to the overall pattern. Dark gray cells show where violations are; that is, Hi- or H-parameters below .30 and significant violations of the first or second criterion of monotonic-ity. The results reveal that if a researcher wishes to study the construct of extrinsic work values with as many items as possible in a cross-national comparison, it would be premature to state that he or she could do so for twenty-two countries. Tables 2 and 3 show that for five (Greece, Italy, Portugal, Spain, and Switzerland) out of the twenty-two countries with a rank order similar to the overall pattern, the second criterion of monotonicity is violated, meaning that respondents *within* those countries differ in their rank order of item difficulties. Consequently, we may state that the fewer items we use, the more countries are similar to the over-all pattern and the fewer violations regarding scalability and monotonicity.

Detecting the countries similar to the overall pattern and without any viola-tion, seventeen countries can be safely compared when using all extrinsic work value items (see Table 2A); twenty-nine if the scale is based on "good pay," "job security," "good hours," and "generous holidays" (see Table 2A); forty-three if "good pay," "good hours," and "generous holidays" are used to calculated sum-mated cumulative scales (see Table 2B); and forty-five if "good pay" and "gener-ous holidays" are used to calculate scale scores (see Table 2B). Azerbaijan and Turkey remain incomparable due to insufficient scalability; that is, for those nations, the two remaining items cannot be used for cumulative scaling, even though the rank order of item difficulties is similar to the overall pattern (see Table 2B).

For the dimension of intrinsic work values, eight countries can be safely com-pared if all five items are to be used (see Table 3A). Cross-national comparisons are possible for seventeen countries if "a responsible job" is not included in the scale (see Table 3A), for thirty-four nation if "a job that meet one's abilities" is excluded subsequently (see Table 3B), and for forty-two nations if the scale is solely based on "the possibility to achieve something" and "the possibility to use initiative" (see Table 3B). For the dimension of intrinsic work values, problems remain for Azerbaijan, Belgium, the Netherlands, Sweden, and Kosovo, due to insufficient scalability, deviating rank orders, or both.

In the end, equivalence analyses are used to find answers to comparative research questions on differences among countries and to explain them. Even though we did not formulate such theoretically guided research questions, we end this result section by presenting average scores of countries on the extrinsic and intrinsic dimension of work values. Figure 2 summarizes these averages. Both scales are based on two items, so they achieve as high a level of comparabil-ity as possible. Furthermore, the scale scores have been calculated for all forty-seven countries together and standardized using z-scores, meaning that the average across all countries is zero, and each score depicts to what extent its rate of valuing extrinsic and intrinsic work characteristics is below or above average. Note that even though they are in Figure 2, for Azerbaijan, Belgium, the Netherlands, Sweden, and Kosovo, the scale is not equivalent for the intrinsic dimension; while for the extrinsic dimension, strictly speaking, Azerbaijan and Turkey cannot be included in the comparison.

On average, the importance attached to extrinsic work characteristics is high-est in Eastern European countries such as Albania, Bosnia Herzegovina, Bulgaria, and Moldova; and lowest in Scandinavian countries such as Norway and Sweden, but also in Switzerland. Intrinsic work values are on average rated highest in Moldova, Luxembourg, and Northern Cyprus; while inhabitants of Belgium, Hungary, and Spain appreciate intrinsic work characteristics well below the European average. Figure 2 also shows that both dimensions of work values are positively correlated: on average, higher averages of extrinsic work values go hand-in-hand with higher averages of intrinsic work values, implying that the importance of work, irrespective of which characteristic it is about, varies between countries. Yet the correlations are most often weak to moderate (see Table A5 in the online appendix), underscoring that even though related, both dimensions of work values can be distinguished empirically.

We conduct the same tests of scale equivalence for the CUPESSE data, and those results are displayed in the online appendix. The results support our findings from the EVS: the more countries we want to compare, the fewer items we should use, at the cost of the "richness" of the theoretical construct. Here also, internal validity is traded for external validity.

Discussion and Conclusion

The leading question of this contribution was whether people in different cultural contexts (i.e., different countries) have similar or different things in mind when they think about extrinsic or intrinsic work values. Prior research has underscored cohort differences, showing that different age groups emphasize different values (Lechner et al. 2017; Meriac, Woehr, and Banister 2010; Twenge et al. 2010), and previous work has also tried to assess the measurement equivalence of these values across countries (Leuty and Hansen 2011; Vecerník 2003).

In contrast to these prior studies, though, our work assesses the general scalability of the most commonly used work value measures. Testing the scalability of items is important because it allows the researcher to take empirical realities into account when comparing respondents across cultures with respect to the same concept. Trade-offs between internal validity (if a measurement of values is valid for a given country) and external validity (if a measurement that is valid for one country can be applied in another country) are unavoidable, but a transparent process of narrowing the list of items used for measurement (or countries to which those items are applied) contributes to a well-justified case selection in cross-national comparative studies, as long as one can argue that the most important items are included.

Our findings add to the general discussion of how many items are needed to accurately measure a given construct and how much added value comes from including a battery of items for a given measurement. Some argue that single-item measures offer more advantages than multi-item measures (Gardner et al. 2016). Single-item measures circumvent the issue of measurement invariance across cultural contexts. However, they might not suffice to capture the many dimensions of certain constructs. For this particular research on work values, we have seen that the extrinsic and intrinsic dimensions consist of multiple items that capture the different aspects of each dimension. Each dimension is indeed made up of multiple facets, but using more and more items to measure a particular aspect of work values can result in less comparability across countries. Researchers are thus faced with the trade-off between the "richness" of the scale and the number of countries to which that scale can be justifiably applied in comparative analyses. The more countries we want to compare, the fewer items we should use.

Another takeaway of our analysis is the apparent difference of the cross-national comparability of work values on the two dimensions: the number of items that one is able to safely compare (in the European context, at least) differs substantially. Whereas for extrinsic values, twenty-two countries are comparable if all items are used based on the results of our scalogram analysis, the corresponding number of countries drops to only eight when we look at intrinsic values. In a similar fashion, the analysis on the intrinsic dimension also yielded a higher number of incomparable countries.

These findings resonate with prior research that points out the challenges of capturing intrinsic work values. Some of the literature emphasizes the varied and possibly overlapping measures of intrinsic work values, the context- and interaction-dependent dynamic of intrinsic orientations, as well as the growing prevalence of "intrinsic life satisfaction" outside the workplace, embedded into an emerging hedonistic value pattern in postindustrial and modern countries (Sortheix, Chow, and Salmela–Aro 2015). These make cross-cultural comparisons of intrinsic motivations more difficult and also more costly (in terms of the trade off of particular subdimensions [items] to gain more comparability).

Our finding that both dimensions of work values are positively correlated (Table A5 in the online appendix) tallies with results of previous research (Gesthuizen and Verbakel 2011) that emphasizes that these dimensions are not inversely related (as was argued earlier in Ester, Braun, and Vinken 2006; Yankelovich 1985). Following the logic of Hauff and Kirchner (2015), extrinsic values cannot be substituted for intrinsic ones (or vice versa): people formulate additional work-life demands and attach higher importance to work value sets without neglecting previously dominant dimensions. Hence, this contribution reiterates the message that work values are not only systematically interrelated, but have distinguishable dimensions, one of which can be enhanced without compromising the other. As generations or times change, people might attach higher importance to novel work-related expectations while leaving more traditional, income- or security-related dimensions intact as well.

Our results also illustrate how Eastern European respondents value the extrinsic dimension more than individuals from other EVS countries. In this sense, our analyses support previous studies (Ester, Braun, and Vinken 2006; Hauff and Kirchner 2015; Kaasa 2011; Parboteeah, Cullen and Paik 2013) that argued for extrinsic values being more important in less-developed countries. In general, the predominance of income and security-related work values concerns the significantly lower share of "postmodern demanders" among employees in postcommunist Eastern European countries, as well as the overall positive relationship between modernization or individualization and the importance attached to intrinsic work values. Similarly, the negative relationship between postindustrialization and extrinsic work values is perceived as a manifestation of shifting from materialist to postmaterialist values. Apart from cross-cultural comparisons, future research should focus on cases clearly violating the second criterion of monotonicity, identifying and explaining within-nation variability, that is, specific value patterns among respondent subgroups of a given country.

In sum, this article emphasizes the trade-off that researchers need to make between (1) covering the most possible subdimensions of a latent construct and (2) equivalencies that are desirable in cross-cultural research. Future research on work values could concentrate on the comparable cases, where all aspects of a given dimension (extrinsic or intrinsic) can be included in the analyses, preserving the wealth of the construct. Or, depending on the research question, one with a multilevel design could seek the inclusion of the most possible (i.e., comparable) countries and opt for getting rid of a particular number of items, sacrificing the full meaning of the concept measured and risking the omission of substantial aspects of the meaning. We recommend that other researchers compare the results they get by employing scales consisting of a varying number of items (if not using the full one), as well as with a complete pool of countries, *with* the set of safely comparable ones, as ways of performing robustness checks. Nonetheless, the question remains: How many items are enough to measure the complex nature of extrinsic and intrinsic work values, to rightfully reject or confirm hypotheses, as well as to come to valid overall conclusions within cross-national studies? Our findings suggest that researchers should focus on the most important items for each scale to truly capture work values in cross-cultural research.

Notes

1. Scalogram analysis, also known as Mokken scale analysis or Guttman scaling, is designed for analyzing nominal or ordinal items (finding a job characteristic important versus not important). Items indicating a latent theoretical construct (extrinsic work values, for instance) have substantially different averages. Since the items we analyze have these characteristics, scalogram analysis is preferred over other methods such as multigroup explanatory factor analysis, which usually relies on interval items that have approximately similar averages. See also note 3.

2. The question wording mirrors the one from the EVS, whereby the items slightly differ: (1) secure job, (2) high income, (3) job leaving enough time for leisure activities, (4) job allowing to balance work with other commitments, (5) job allowing to help others, (6) job allowing to learn new things, (7) job allowing me to develop my creativity, (8) job allowing me to meet and interact with people, (9) job giving me a feeling of self-worth, and (10) job allowing me to work independently. The first four items represent extrinsic values, whereas the latter six are intrinsic values. The answer categories were originally on a 4-point Likert scale from *strongly disagree* to *strongly agree*, but we recoded them into binary responses for the analyses, strongly agree being coded (1) and strongly disagree until agree being coded (0).

3. The assumptions of scalogram analysis differ from those of scaling methods based on classical test theory—multi-group explanatory factor analysis (MG-EFA) for instance—which assume that averages on

the manifest items belonging to a dimension are more or less similar, after which scale scores are based on the average scores on the underlying ordinal/interval items. Obviously, the items we use are dichotomous and differ substantially in their averages. This also implies that equivalence tests performed with methods relying on classical test theory (configural, metric, and scalar invariance tested with MGCFA) are likely to generate invalid results. This likely pertains to both the equivalence results, and to the dimensional structure found if tests would be performed to assess (invariance in) multidimensionality. The characteristics of our EVS items are simply not fit for these methods.

References

Arendt, Hannah. 2013. *The human condition*. Chicago, IL: University of Chicago Press.

Cemalcilar, Zeynep, Ekin Secinti, and Nebi Sumer. 2018. Intergenerational transmission of work values: A meta-analytic review. *Journal of Youth and Adolescence* 47 (8): 1559–79.

Elizur, Dov. 1984. Facets of work values: A structural analysis of work outcomes. *Journal of Applied Psychology* 69 (3): 379–89.

Elizur, Dov, Ingwer Borg, Raymond Hunt, and Istvan Magyari Beck. 1991. The structure of work values: A cross cultural comparison. *Journal of Organizational Behavior* 12 (1): 21–38.

Ester, Peter, Michael Braun, and Henk Vinken. 2006. Eroding work values? In *Globalization, value change and generations. A cross-national and intergenerational perspective*, eds. Peter Ester, Michael Braun, and Peter Mohler, 89–113. Leiden: Brill.

European Values Study. 2011. European Values Study 2008: Integrated dataset (EVS 2008): GESIS Data Archive, Cologne. Available from dbk.gesis.org (accessed 29 September 2018).

Gardner, Donald G., L. L. Cummings, Randall B. Dunham, and Jon L. Pierce. 2016. Single-item versus multiple-item measurement scales: An empirical comparison. *Educational and Psychological Measurement* 58 (6): 898–915.

Gesthuizen, Maurice, and Ellen Verbakel. 2011. Job preferences in Europe. *European Societies* 13 (5): 663–86.

Gesthuizen, Maurice, and Ellen Verbakel. 2014. Work values in Europe: Modernization, globalization, institutionalization and their moderating impact on the occupational class effect. In *Value contrasts and consensus in present-day Europe: Painting Europe's moral landscapes*, eds. Wilhelmus A. Arts and Loek Halman, 329–53. Boston, MA: Brill.

Halman, Loek, and Hans Müller. 2006. Contemporary work values in Africa and Europe: Comparing orientations to work in African and European societies. *International Journal of Comparative Sociology* 47 (2): 117–43.

Halman, Loek, Inge Sieben, and Marga van Zundert. 2011. *Atlas of European values. Trends and traditions at the turn of the century*. Leiden: Brill.

Hauff, Sven, and Stefan Kirchner. 2015. Identifying work value patterns: cross-national comparison and historical dynamics. *International Journal of Manpower* 36 (2): 151–68.

Jin, Jing, and James Rounds. 2012. Stability and change in work values: A meta-analysis of longitudinal studies. *Journal of Vocational Behavior* 80 (2): 326–39.

Kaasa, Anneli. 2011. Work values in European countries: Empirical evidence and explanations. *Review of International Comparative Management / Revista de Management Comparat International* 12 (5): 852–62.

Kalleberg, Arne L. 1977. Work values and job rewards: A theory of job satisfaction. *American Sociological Review* 42 (1): 124–43.

Krahn, Harvey J., and Nancy L. Galambos. 2013. Work values and beliefs of "Generation X" and "Generation Y." *Journal of Youth Studies* 17 (1): 92–112.

Lechner, Clemens M., Florencia M. Sortheix, Richard Göllner, and Katariina Salmela-Aro. 2017. The development of work values during the transition to adulthood: A two-country study. *Journal of Vocational Behavior* 99:52–65.

Lechner, Clemens M., Florencia M. Sortheix, Martin Obschonka, and Katariina Salmela-Aro. 2018. What drives future business leaders? How work values and gender shape young adults' entrepreneurial and leadership aspirations. *Journal of Vocational Behavior* 107:57–70.

Leuty, Melanie E., and Jo-Ida C. Hansen. 2011. Evidence of construct validity for work values. *Journal of Vocational Behavior* 79 (2): 379–90.

Meriac, John P., David J. Woehr, and Christina Banister. 2010. Generational differences in work ethic: An examination of measurement equivalence across three cohorts. *Journal of Business and Psychology* 25 (2): 315–24.

Mokken, R. J. 1971. *A theory and procedure of scale analysis: With applications in political research.* Methods and Models in the Social Sciences 1. Boston, MA: De Gruyter Mouton.

Ros, Maria, Shalom H. Schwartz, and Shoshana Surkiss. 1999. Basic individual values, work values, and the meaning of work. *Applied Psychology* 48 (1): 49–71.

Schwartz, Shalom H. 1992. Universals in the content and structure of values: Theoretical advances and empirical tests in 20 countries. *Advances in Experimental Social Psychology* 25 (1): 1–65.

Schwartz, Shalom H. 1994. Are there universal aspects in the structure and contents of human values? *Journal of Social Issues* 50 (4): 19–45.

Sijtsma, Klaas, and Rob R. Meijer. 2016. A method for investigating the intersection of item response functions in Mokken's nonparametric IRT model. *Applied Psychological Measurement* 16 (2): 149–57.

Sijtsma, Klaas, and Ivo W. Molenaar. 2002. *Introduction to nonparametric item response theory.* Measurement Methods for the Social Sciences vol. 5. Thousand Oaks, CA: Sage Publications.

Sortheix, Florencia M., Angela Chow, and Katariina Salmela-Aro. 2015. Work values and the transition to work life: A longitudinal study. *Journal of Vocational Behavior* 89:162–71.

Tarnai, Christian, Holger Grimm, Dirk John, and Rainer Watermann. 1995. Work values in European comparison: School education and work orientation in nine countries. *Tertium Comparationis: Journal für Internationale Bildungsforschung* 1 (2): 139–63.

Tosun, Jale, Jos. L. Arco-Tirado, Maurizio Caserta, Zeynep Cemalcilar, Markus Freitag, Felix H.risch, Carsten Jensen, Bernhard Kittel, Levente Littvay, and Martin Lukeš, et al. 2018. Perceived economic self-sufficiency: A country- and generation-comparative approach. *European Political Science.* doi:10.1057/s41304-018-0186-3.

Twenge, Jean M., Stacy M. Campbell, Brian J. Hoffman, and Charles E. Lance. 2010. Generational differences in work values: Leisure and extrinsic values increasing, social and intrinsic values decreasing. *Journal of Management* 36 (5): 1117–42.

van der Ark, L. Andries. 2012. New developments in Mokken scale analysis in R. *Journal of Statistical Software* 48 (5): 1–27.

Vecerník, Jirí. 2003. Skating on thin ice: A comparison of work values and job satisfaction in CEE and EU countries. *International Journal of Comparative Sociology* 44 (5): 444–71.

Visser, Mark, Maurice Gesthuizen, and Gerbert Kraaykamp. 2019. Work attitudes and political participation: A cross-national analysis. *The ANNALS of the American Academy of Political and Social Science* (this volume).

Yankelovich, Harvey. 1985. *The world at work: An international report on jobs, productivity, and human values.* New York, NY: Octagon Books.

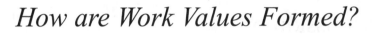

How are Work Values Formed?

Inter-generational Transmission of Work Values in Czech Republic, Spain, and Turkey: Parent-Child Similarity and the Moderating Role of Parenting Behaviors

By
NEBI SÜMER,
DANIELA PAUKNEROVÁ,
MIHAELA VANCEA,
and
ELIF MANUOĞLU

Although public debates emphasize a weakening of work values and ethics over the last few decades, little attention has been paid to the transmission of work values between parents and children. It is still unclear what kind of parental behavior is critical and if culture influences the intergenerational transmission of work values. Based on socialization and value transmission theories, we explore the question by comparing three countries with different cultural characteristics: Czech Republic, Spain, and Turkey. We used data from the CUPESSE project collected from young adults aged 18 to 35 and their parents. Turkish young adults and parents reported higher levels of moral- and gender-based work values than their Spanish and Czech counterparts. Parent-child similarity in work values was the highest among the Turkish families and the lowest among the Czech families. Overall, we find that stronger moral and redistributive work values and weaker gender role–based work values are associated with high levels of parental warmth and autonomy granting and low levels of perceived psychological control. Results suggested that family climate, rather than specific paternal and maternal parenting behaviors, have more substantial effect on the value transmission. We discuss implications that consider the role of cultural orientation and gender roles.

Keywords: value transmission; work values; parenting behaviors

Social scientists generally regard the family as a primary socialization agent among whom values, attitudes, ideologies, and norms are passed on from one generation to the next in all cultures (Kulik 2002; Trommsdorff 2016). Work values and ethics are fundamental agents guiding job-related beliefs, attitudes, and behaviors and managing motivation and commitment in organizational settings (Consiglio et al. 2017; Kooij et al. 2011). Intergenerational transmission of work values is particularly important in a context of contemporary job relations and insecure labor market conditions,

Correspondence: nebisumer@sabanciuniv.edu

DOI: 10.1177/0002716219830953

as well as of increasing youth unemployment (De Vos, Buyens, and Schalk 2005; Jin and Rounds 2012).

Considering the recent changes in work environments and the intergenerational differences in work values, ethic, and attitudes, we analyze the degree of work value similarity between parents and young adults. We then explore the moderating role of three fundamental types of parenting behaviors (i.e., emotional warmth, autonomy granting, and psychological control) in parent-child work value similarity since the degree of parenting quality reflected *via* particular parenting styles and behaviors is argued to be associated with parent-child similarity in work values (Cemalcilar, Secinti, and Sümer 2018). Finally, we aim to examine if parent-child work value similarity and the potential moderating effect of parenting behaviors vary across cultures, by comparing three countries with different cultural characteristics: Czech Republic, Spain, and Turkey. According to Hofstede, Hofstede, and Minkov's (2010) model of dimensional cultural classification, Czech Republic could be classified as individualistic, Spain as moderately collectivist, and Turkey as collectivist. We use this classification as the general framework to better understand potential cultural differences in parent-child work value similarity and the moderating role of parenting behaviors in these three cultures. In sum, we seek to answer two global questions in this study: Are work values transmitted similarly in all cultural contexts? Does the quality of parenting behaviors moderate the transmission of work values within the family?

There is no commonly agreed-upon conceptualization or operational definition of *work values*. As discussed in several articles in this volume (e.g., Gesthuizen, Kovarek, and Rapp) work values, as an umbrella term, are studied in multiple disciplines with different conceptualizations and classifications, referring to diverse domains from job importance to work attitudes, and/or ethics. In this article, we focus on three specific aspects of work values: work ethics (or moral work

---

Nebi Sümer is a professor of psychology in the Faculty of Arts and Social Sciences at Sabancı University, Turkey. His research interests are parenting behaviors, attachment dynamics across the lifespan, road user behaviors, and the effects of unemployment and job insecurity.

Daniela Pauknerová is an associate professor and head of the Department of Managerial Psychology and Sociology in the Faculty of Business Administration at University of Economics, Prague. Her research interests include social, work, and organizational psychology; leadership; and cross-cultural psychology.

Mihaela Vancea is a researcher and lecturer in Political and Social Sciences at the Universitat Pompeu Fabra. Her research interests include subjects such as international migration and immigrant rights; network society; energy transition; and the relationship between education, employment, and health.

Elif Manuoglu is a PhD student in the Department of Psychology at Middle East Technical University, Turkey. Her research interests include the effects of social media use on well-being, intrinsic and extrinsic motivation, and parenting behaviors.

NOTE: This study was supported by the project, Cultural Pathways to Economic Self-Sufficiency and Entrepreneurship (CUPESSE; Seventh Framework Program; Grant Agreement No. 61325).

values), redistributive work values, and gender roles–based work values. Considering that work ethics refers to "moral embeddedness" or "centrality" of work in one's life, our conceptualization of work values captures mainly the moral dimension in the work ethics, and thus, we give it the name *moral work values*.

Parent-Child Value Similarity and Intergenerational Transmission Processes

Past work has consistently shown that parents transmit their values to their offspring, but how this transmission occurs and what specific values or parenting behaviors are associated with the transmission have not been fully explored (Cemalcilar, Secinti, and Sümer 2018). Socialization theory emphasizes the significance of early childhood experiences and parenting quality in the family context (Ranieri and Barni 2012) and social learning via modeling (Döring et al. 2017) for the maintenance and transmission of culture specific knowledge, beliefs, values, and attitudes across generations (Schönpflug 2001). However, both the value priorities and the way families transmit their values to next generations continuously change with rapidly changing socioeconomic and cultural contexts (Grusec and Davidov 2007; Schwartz 2014; Trommsdorff 2009a, 2016).

The transmission of values between parents and children consists of a series of complex, selective, and bidirectional processes that may take place through various pathways or transmission belts (Kraaykamp, Cemalcilar, and Tosun, this volume; Kohn 1983; Schönpflug 2001) and may be directly influenced by the family climate (Roest, Dubas, and Gerris 2009). Family socialization is not only a direct transmission process through which children learn behavioral patterns and attitudes from their parents, but also an indirect one, by parents' choice of outside socialization settings or groups (Kulik 2002).

Some scholars acknowledge that intergenerational value transmission is stronger between same-sex relationships than between opposite-sex relationships (e.g., Acock and Bengtson 1978; Kandler, Gottschling and Spinath 2016). Accordingly, more parent-to-child value transmissions would take place within same-sex compared to cross-sex dyads (Boehnke, Ittel, and Baier 2002; Roest, Dubas, and Gerris 2010). Other studies found no effect of gender (Boehnke 2001; Whitbeck and Gecas 1988) or only same-sex similarities for father-son relations (Kulik 2002). Various studies (Acock and Bengtson 1978; Roest, Dubas, and Gerris 2010) also showed that intergenerational transmission does not occur only in same-sex parent-child pairs, but also in opposite-sex pairs. The lack of consistency in the literature suggests that there may be moderators of this effect and that the content or salience of the value or attitude under investigation may also play a role (Cemalcilar, Secinti, and Sümer 2018; Roest, Dubas, and Gerris 2010).

The gender role model of socialization theory assumes that transmission processes may be gendered. Both children's developmental stage (Pinquart and Silbereisen 2004) and values (Schwartz and Rubel 2005) influence the transmission belt between parents and children. Accordingly, the transmission of values from parents to children may vary in time as well as within and across cultures that have more or less traditional gender roles (Schwartz 2014).

Past researchers have explored parent-child similarity in various value-specific domains, such as career choice (Bryant, Zvonkovic, and Reynolds 2006), prosocial education (Döring et al. 2017), general cultural values (Hofstede 2001), familism values (Padilla et al. 2016), and multicultural values (Friedlmeier and Trommsdorff 2011). Brannen (2006) found two specific cultural patterns of intergenerational transmission of values: solidaristic patterns are predominate in families that share the culture of giving across generations, while a family mutuality pattern is maintained through a culture of work among men and a culture of care among women.

In a context of a welfare state and aging population, work values' transmission processes between parents and children acquire a particular significance, as they may predict different work-related outcomes, such as career choice (Bryant, Zvonkovic, and Reynolds 2006), self-employment (Laspita et al. 2012), work ethics (Lee, Padilla, and McHale 2016), or cultural attitudes toward gender roles in the family and labor market (Kulik 2002; Roest, Dubas, and Gerris 2010; Farré and Vella 2013; Andersson and Hammarstedt 2011). Moreover, culture-specific value priorities shape the meaning and implication of work in a given culture (Schwartz 1999).

Cultural differences in traditionalism and cultural value orientations, such as collectivism, individualism, or power distance, lead to selective value transmission (Phalet and Schönpflug 2001). Consistent with this line of research, past studies have documented that based on a collectivistic achievement orientation, Turkish immigrant adolescents in Western Europe tend to combine family loyalty with achievement orientation (Phalet and Schönpflug 2001). Similarly, Schönpflug (2001) compared Turkish immigrant adolescents and their German counterparts and found that Turkish family styles with more traditional characteristics act as a transmission belt between Turkish parents and children. Therefore, considering that Turkish culture has been identified as more traditional and collectivist with relatively higher levels of power distance and masculinity compared to Spanish and Czech cultures (Hofstede, Hofstede, and Minkov 2010), we expect stronger parent-child similarity in work values within Turkish families than their Spanish and Czech counterparts.

The moderating role of parenting behaviors

Parenting behaviors have been found to moderate intergenerational value transmission. Past studies conducted in various contexts have consistently shown that compared to authoritarian and neglectful parenting styles, authoritative parenting style defined by high emotional warmth and control of children is associated with an optimal social and emotional development in childhood and adolescence, as well as psychological well-being (Steinberg et al. 1991; Smetana 2017). Supportive parenting behavior together with autonomy granting and low psychological control is linked with higher social initiatives (Barber et al. 2005), which is critical for self-sufficiency and entrepreneurship. A longitudinal study showed that if the earlier relationship was emotionally close between parent and child, value transmission was stronger in the children (Min, Silverstein, and Lendon 2012).

Studies have documented emotional warmth, psychological control, and autonomy granting as the core dimensions of parenting behaviors (Soenens and Vansteenkiste 2010). Parental warmth and autonomy granting, which are characterized by positive emotions, support, and responsiveness, are the universally positive parenting behaviors leading to optimal development in all cultures. Psychological control, however, is the fundamental characteristic of authoritarian parenting that includes intrusive parenting, guilt induction, and love withdrawal that hinder children's ability to become independent and develop a healthy sense of self and personal identity (Barber and Harmon 2002). Psychological control is associated with internalizing and externalizing problems, especially in Western individualistic cultures (Smetana 2017).

Parenting behaviors that provide warmth, support, and autonomy are generally associated with psychological adjustment (Khaleque 2013) and other positive outcomes such as high self-esteem and academic achievement and low risky health behaviors for adolescents across cultures (Supple et al. 2006). Parents granting autonomy to their children encourage their independent expression and support democratic family decision-making. Psychologically controlling parents, however, do not usually promote their children's autonomy. Interestingly enough, parents who are low in psychological control do not necessarily grant autonomy to their children (Kunz and Grych 2013). Therefore, psychological control and autonomy granting appears to be distinct parenting constructs rather than opposite ends of the parental control continuum (Silk et al. 2003).

Previous studies have shown that in cultures where interdependence is emphasized, higher parental control over children, such as stressing obedience, is commonly observed compared to cultures that emphasize independence (Chao 1994; Smetana 2017), implying a cultural variation in the use of psychological control. Consistently, cultural differences in psychological control are much larger than cultural differences in emotional warmth (Trommsdorff 2009b). Considering the potential cultural adaptivity of psychological control, Kagitcibasi (2007) asserted that different aspects of psychological control might function differently in varying cultural settings. As she stated, "higher levels of parental control are seen in sociocultural contexts where independence of the child is not a goal of parenting" (p. 175). In sum, past work has demonstrated that certain parenting behaviors can promote value transmission but others hinder it, suggesting the potential for a moderating effect of parenting in value transmission. However, the pattern of moderation, especially with respect to parental psychological control, is expected to differ between collectivistic and individualistic cultures. Thus, we expect that the effect of psychological control on intergenerational value transmission will be stronger among young adults from Czech Republic compared to those from Spain and Turkey who have an interdependent family structure.

Cultural variation in work values

Social and cultural norms, expectations, and gender roles in a given culture, which are acquired by children from their earliest years onward, are rooted much deeper in the human mind than are workplace or organizational cultures (Hofstede 2011). The degrees of individualism and collectivism in a society have been extensively used as the most descriptive characteristics of cultures. *Collectivism* refers to the extent to which people in a society are integrated into groups, whereas *individualism* reflects the degree to which members of the cultures have relatively loose ties. In collectivistic cultures, from birth onward individuals are integrated into strong, cohesive in-groups, often extended families. Hofstede, Hofstede, and Minkov's (2010) eminent classification as well as Hofstede's recent work (2011) identify Turkey as a collectivistic culture with relatively high levels of power distance, masculinity, and uncertainty avoidance in comparison with Czech Republic and Spain.

According to Supple et al. (2009), basic values such as participating in family decision-making and those values having long-term consequences for adulthood, such as the freedom to choose one's education and career, vary across national cultures and are less common in young individuals coming from traditional or collectivistic cultures, where family dependency may be stronger. Confirming this expectation, in her study of Turkish parents and children in Germany, Schönpflug (2001) showed that collectivistic values were much more easily transmitted across generations than individualistic ones, even after controlling for gender and educational status of parents and their children. However, a recent meta-analysis (Cemalcilar, Secinti, and Sümer 2018) suggested that past literature is largely scarce in examining parent-child work value similarity in varying cultural contexts, yet they showed that there were no significant differences in parent-child value similarity in the limited number of samples from individualistic and collectivistic cultures. Hence, in this study, using data from three distinct cultural contexts, Turkey, Spain, and Czech Republic, we analyze the role of parenting behaviors and different cultural contexts in the intergenerational transmission of work values.

Current study

In this study, based on the socialization and cultural arguments, we aim to explore (1) the degree of work value similarity between parents and children (young adults) as an indicator of intergenerational transmission, (2) cross-country differences on the main domains of work values (moral, gender-based, and redistributive), and (3) the moderating effect of parenting behavior (warmth, autonomy granting, and psychological control) in parent-child work value similarity.

Considering the influence of parental emotional warmth on value transmission, we expect young adults perceiving higher levels of positive parenting to depict higher work value similarity with their parents in the three countries. However, the moderating role of psychological control may vary between individualistic and collectivist cultural contexts. In the current study, we use samples from Czech Republic, Spain, and Turkey, representing cultural contexts with decreasing levels of individualism (and increasing levels of collectivism) according to Hofstede, Hofstede, and Minkov's (2010) model of dimensional cultural classification.

Specifically, we expect parental psychological control to have a stronger negative effect in Czech Republic (individualistic context) than in both Spain and Turkey (collectivist contexts). Finally, considering potential effects of gender roles on the transmission of work values, we expect that fathers' values would have a stronger effect on the transmission process in Turkey, where gender division of labor is common, than in both Czech Republic and Spain.

In sum, we specifically seek to answer four questions: (1) What is the degree of parent-child similarity in three domains of work values (moral, redistributive, gender-based) across cultures with varying levels of individualism/collectivism? (2) Does the strength of parent-child similarity in work values vary between father-child and mother-child dyads? (3) Are there any cultural (country) differences on the mean levels of work values? and (4) Do parenting behaviors moderate the effect of parents' work values in the transmission process?

Methods

Participants

The current study is based on the Cultural Pathways to Economic Self-Sufficiency and Entrepreneurship (CUPESSE) survey data[1] from three countries: Czech Republic, Spain, and Turkey. A total of 6,056 young individuals, representing the three selected countries, participated in this study (see Table 1). About half of the participants were female in each country. Young participants were requested to give the contact address of their parents for further data gathering.

Measures

Work values were assessed for both young adults and their parents through a seven-item questionnaire (see Table 2). We assessed three types (domains) of work values, namely, moral work value (MWV), redistributive work value (RWV), and gender role–based work value (GWV). Items were rated on a 4-point Likert scale (1 = *strongly disagree* to 4 = *strongly agree*). Due to the design of the study, each respondent's mother or father participated in the research.

A series of exploratory factor analyses on the items of works values across parents and youth samples in each country suggested that the first five items of work values (see Table 2), representing the moral and ethical aspects of work values, clustered into a single factor in all subsamples with the acceptable reliability values. Therefore, we calculated the mean of the five items and named this as MWV in further analyses. Reliability coefficients (Cronbach's alpha) for the five-item MWV factor across the samples ranged from .48 (Turkish youths and Spanish mothers) to .59 (Turkish fathers).

The remaining two items, "Everyone should have the right to a minimum income even if they are not working" and "A man's job is to earn money; a woman's job is to look after the home and family," were used as single-item measures. Considering

TABLE 1
Sample Characteristics

	Czech Republic		Spain		Turkey	
	N	Mean Age (SD)	N	Mean Age (SD)	N	Mean Age (SD)
Youth[a]	1,214	27.3 (5.03)	1,826	27.6 (5.0)	3,016	25.8 (5.3)
Mother	503	52.36 (6.86)	742	55.06 (6.53)	411	50.18 (7.93)
Father	199	56.12 (7.62)	412	55.51 (6.84)	119	55.52 (7.01)

a. Within the youth sample, 57.1 percent in Czech Republic, 51.1 percent in Spain, and 50.4 percent in Turkey are females.

TABLE 2
Items of the Three Types of Work Values

Moral work values (MWV)	To fully develop your talents, you need to have a job.
	It's humiliating to receive money without having to work.
	If welfare benefits are too high there is no incentive to find work.
	Work is a duty towards society.
	Work should always come first even if it means less spare time.
Redistributive work value (RWV)	Everyone should have the right to a minimum income even if they are not working.
Gender role–based work value (GWV)	A man's/husband's job is to earn money; a woman's/wife's job is to look after the home and family.

their corresponding contents, we labeled these items as RWV and GWV, respectively. These three dimensions of work values were used in the analyses.

Parenting behaviors were assessed from youth samples using only an eight-item measure, consisting of three subscales representing emotional warmth (three items), psychological control (two items), and autonomy granting (three items) (see Table 3). Participants responded to the items for their mothers and fathers separately using a yes/no scale (yes = 1; no = 2). Responses were then recoded into a dummy variable (yes = 1), and three separate subscales (emotional warmth, psychological control, and autonomy granting), for maternal and paternal parenting behaviors, were created based on the mean value of the items in each parenting dimension.

Results

Degree of parent-child similarity in work values across cultures

To answer the first research question, we calculated via dyadic correlations across the three dimensions of work values separately in the three countries.[2] As

TABLE 3
Items of the Parenting Behaviors Dimensions

Emotional warmth	I felt that warmth and tenderness existed between me and my mother/father
	I felt that my mother/father was proud when I succeeded in something I did
	If things went badly for me my mother/father tried to comfort and encourage me
Psychological control	My mother/father always tried to change how I felt or thought about things
	My mother/father blamed me for other family members' problems
Autonomy granting	My mother/father emphasized that every family member should have some say in family decisions
	My mother/father encouraged me to be independent
	My mother/father allowed me to choose my own direction in life

NOTE: Respondents rated the same items separately for their mothers and fathers.

TABLE 4
Correlations of Youth-Parent Work Values

	Mother's Work Values	Father's Work Values
Czech Republic		
Youth's MWV	.18***	.16*
Youth's RWV	.11**	.01
Youth's GWV	.16***	.14*
Spain		
Youth's MWV	.13***	.22***
Youth's RWV	.26***	.22***
Youth's GWV	.09**	.09*
Turkey		
Youth's MWV	.34***	.40***
Youth's RWV	.29***	.17*
Youth's GWV	.32***	.23**

NOTE: Due to the design of the study, either the mother or father of each respondent participated in the research. Hence, correlations between mother-youth and father-youth self-reported work values are independent from each other. In other words, they are from dyads from different families.
$*p < .05.$ $**p < .01.$ $***p < .001.$

presented in Table 4, all the dyadic correlations were significant except for the RWV in the father-child dyad in Czech Republic. There was a weak to moderate level parent-child value similarity in all countries with correlations varying between .09 and .40. A relatively higher level of similarity was found in MWV in father-child dyad. Parent-child similarity in the three work value dimensions was significantly higher in Turkey than in Czech Republic and Spain.

Variability between father-child and mother-child dyads

We compared two significant correlation coefficients for mother-child and father-child on the same value dimension to answer the second research question (see Table 4). Results indicated that none of the dyadic correlations differed significantly, suggesting a similar transmission pattern of work values to children from both parents.

Given that young adults and parents responded separately, with no common method variance problem, the significant correlations showed that work values were significantly similar between parents and children in all three countries. However, parent-child similarity was the highest in Turkey and the lowest in Czech Republic, with Spain in between. As expected, parent-child similarity, especially in MWV, was the highest in Turkey, suggesting that family members share the same work value system and have strong family cohesion. There were no significant differences between mother-child and father-child in the ratings of work values in the three countries, suggesting that value transmission within the family is indeed based on family climate rather than on parents' gender.

Cultural differences on the mean levels of parents' and youths' work values

As presented in online appendix Table A1, the mean levels of three value dimensions were significantly different. For instance, in a scale varying from one to four, young adults from Turkey reported higher mean levels of MWV than the other two countries. The largest cross-cultural differences were observed in GWV. Turkish young adults and their parents endorsed the traditional GWV, suggesting that "breadwinning" is a man's job while "caregiving" and "domestic work" are a woman's duty. The next highest rating of GWV value was from Czech respondents, followed finally by the Spanish respondents' rating.

Comparison of the mean scores of work values among the three countries yielded significant differences in both young adults' and parents' reports. As presented in online appendix Table A1, Turkish young participants reported the highest level of MWV as well as of RWV and GWV, in comparison to Czech and Spanish young respondents. Czech youths reported significantly higher levels of MWV and GWV and a lower level of RWV than those from Spain. The pattern of values observed among parents was similar to that of young adults, with the exception of Czech fathers' MWV. There was no significant difference between fathers' MWV in Czech Republic and Spain.

Examination of effects size of differences among countries using partial Eta squares indicated the largest GWV differences in mothers, fathers, and young adults (.42, .41, and .28, respectively). Although the lowest effect size of difference across countries was observed on fathers' MWV (.09), all differences among countries were large in magnitude, basically stemming from Turkish participants' higher ratings. The differences between Czech Republic and Spain were small to moderate in magnitude.

Comparison of the three value dimensions within each country showed the highest rating of MWV (as the most important one) in Czech Republic, in comparison with the ratings of GWV and RWV, among both young respondents and their parents. Spanish young respondents and their parents rated RWV higher than MWV and GWV. Turkish young respondents and their mothers rated the RWV higher than the other work values, while Turkish fathers rated MWV as the highest. Young adults and their parents in all countries rated the GWV as the least important work value.

In sum, moral and redistributive work values were rated above the mean value in all three countries, with the highest ratings in Turkey. Spain and Czech Republic were similar in MWV ratings with small differences. Spanish participants reported the highest rating in RWV and the lowest in GWV.

Do parenting behaviors moderate the transmission of work values?

As expected, overall, young adults perceived higher levels of emotional warmth (M_{mother} = 1.91, SD = 0.23; M_{father} = 1.83, SD = 0.30) and autonomy granting (M_{mother} = 1.76, SD = 0.30; M_{father} = 1.73, SD = 0.32), and lower levels of psychological control (M_{mother} = 1.27, SD = 0.33; M_{father} = 1.26, SD = 0.33).

To analyze if parenting behaviors moderate the similarity (transmission) between parents' and young adults' work values, we first examined the correlations between work values (reported by both parents and young adults) and the three types of parenting behaviors reported by young adults, and then we tested the moderation hypotheses using moderated regression analyses.

Some of the correlations between young adults' work values and perceived parenting behaviors were significant and generally in the expected direction (see Table 5). For instance, psychological control was significantly and positively correlated with GWV, particularly in Spain. Mothers' warmth was positively associated with RWV in Turkey. Autonomy granting was positively correlated with MWV in both Spain and Turkey.

The correlations between work values and parenting behaviors reported by young participants were relatively weak, though mostly significant. One noteworthy moderate correlation was noted between perceived psychological control from both mothers and fathers and the GWV in all countries. Especially in Spain and Czech Republic, if families had high psychological control, young adults tended to be more gendered-biased and traditional in their work attitudes. Maternal psychological control in Czech Republic and paternal psychological control in Turkey were weakly but significantly correlated with RWV.

Correlations between young respondents' reports of parenting behaviors and parents' reports of work values yielded a relatively different pattern with a few significant correlations (see online appendix Table A2). Significant negative correlations between emotional warmth from both mothers and fathers and their GWV, especially in the Czech Republic, suggested that when parents tend to be

TABLE 5
Correlations between Youth's Work Values and Their Ratings
of Mother's and Father's Parenting Behaviors

	MWV	RWV	GWV
Czech Republic (N = 1,106)[a]			
Mother's emotional warmth	−.01	−.00	.02
Mother's psychological control	.07°	.07°	.10°
Mother's autonomy granting	.05	.03	.01
Father's emotional warmth	−.02	−.00	.01
Father's psychological control	.09°	.04	.14°°°
Father's autonomy granting	.06	.03	−.03
Spain (N = 1,745)			
Mother's emotional warmth	.03	.02	−.05°
Mother's psychological control	.18°°	.02	.31°°
Mother's autonomy granting	.07°	.01	.08°
Father's emotional warmth	.03	−.01	−.00
Father's psychological control	.19°°	.02	.26°°
Father's autonomy granting	.07°	−.01	.05°
Turkey (N = 2,859)			
Mother's emotional warmth	.03	.17	.01
Mother's psychological control	−.05°	.02	.09°°°
Mother's autonomy granting	.06°	.03	−.00
Father's emotional warmth	.05°	.03	.00
Father's psychological control	−.04°	.04°	11°°
Father's autonomy granting	.07°°	.01	−.02

a. Sample sizes decreased due to missing values in items measuring parental behaviors.
°p < .05. °°p < .01. °°°p < .001.

very traditional and believe in a gender division of work, they are perceived as less warm and highly controlling by their children.

Finally, hierarchical regression analyses were conducted to see whether parental work values and parenting behaviors predicted young adults' work values and importantly whether parenting behaviors moderated the link between parents' and young adults' value similarity. Analyses were conducted separately for the three types of work values and for mothers and fathers across the three countries (separately). All predictor variables were centered. To predict young adults' work values in the first step, we entered the gender to control for its effect; in the second step, we entered parent's self-reported work values and youth's ratings of their parents' parenting behaviors. Finally, we entered the interaction terms that were created by multiplying parental behaviors and parents' specific work values in the last step (see online appendix Tables A3, A4, and A5).

The findings showed that gender contributed significantly to the model only in Spain and accounted for 1 percent of the variation in young respondents in the

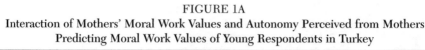

FIGURE 1A

Interaction of Mothers' Moral Work Values and Autonomy Perceived from Mothers
Predicting Moral Work Values of Young Respondents in Turkey

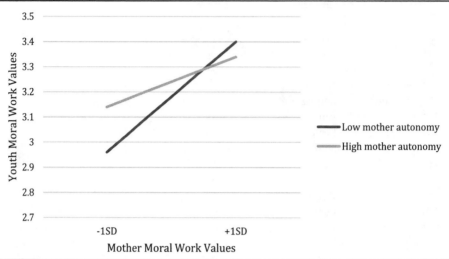

first step. Overall, regressions revealed significant effects of both maternal and
paternal work values and parenting behaviors in predicting young adults' work
values in the second step. Perceived psychological control predicted youth's
GWV, especially in Czech Republic and Spain. Perceived autonomy granting
from fathers predicted youth's GWV negatively and the RWV positively in
Turkey, suggesting that paternal autonomy granting as a positive parenting
behavior enhances less gender-biased and more redistributive work values.

There were four statistically significant interactions in the last step in these
analyses, indicating the moderating effect of parenting behaviors on parent-child
work values similarity. All interactions reflected a similar pattern, suggesting that
when emotional warmth and autonomy granting were high and psychological
control was low in the family, and parents held more positive work values, such
as high moral and redistributive work values, young adults reported higher levels
of MWV and RWV and lower levels of GWV.

In Turkey, as mothers exhibited higher levels of MWV, young respondents had
higher ratings of these values. However, when mothers showed lower levels of
MWV and were perceived as granting low autonomy, young respondents reported
lower levels of MWV as well (see Figure 1a). Almost the same pattern was seen
regarding maternal warmth in Spain: when mothers reported lower levels of
RWV and were perceived as cold (low warmth) by their children, young respondents reported lower levels of RWV (see Figure 1b).

In Turkey, when fathers' warmth was high regardless of fathers' rating of
GWV, young respondents reported higher levels of GWV. However, when
fathers' warmth was lower, fathers' rating of GWV did make a difference.
Accordingly, young respondents reported lower levels of GWV when fathers'

FIGURE 1B

Interaction of Mothers' Redistributive Work Value and Warmth perceived from Mothers
Predicting Redistributive Work Value of Young Respondents in Spain

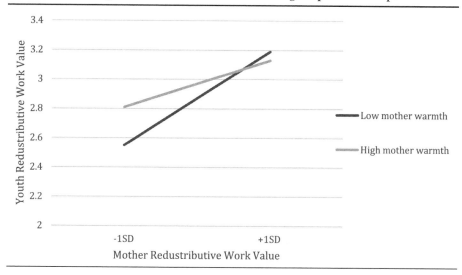

FIGURE 1C

Interaction of Fathers' Gender Role–Based Work Value and Warmth Perceived from
Fathers Predicting Young Respondents' Gender Role–Based Work Value in Turkey

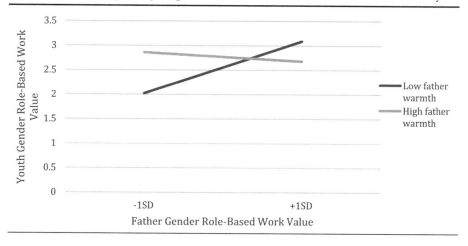

levels of GWV and warmth were lower (see Figure 1c). Another significant inter-action in Turkey (see Figure 1d) showed that when mothers exhibited lower levels of RWV and high psychological control, young respondents reported lower levels of RWV.

In sum, these moderated effects suggest that autonomy granting and warmth positively influence the intergenerational transmission of MWV and RWV, while

FIGURE 1D
Interaction of Mothers' Redistributive Work Value and Psychological Control Perceived from Mothers Predicting Redistributive Work Value of Young Respondents in Turkey

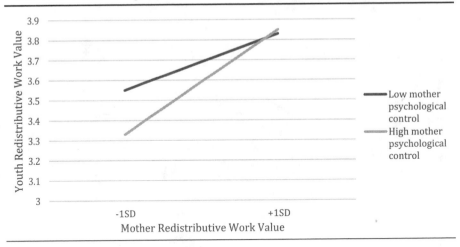

psychological control has a negative influence on this transmission. The moderating impact of parental behavior on the intergenerational transmission of GWV is nevertheless less clear.

Conclusion

This study examined parent-child similarity in work values and cultural differences in the intergenerational transmission of these values by focusing on respondents (parents and young adults) from Turkey, Czech Republic, and Spain. We found no significant differences in work value ratings between mother-child and father-child pairs in the three countries, suggesting that value transmission within the family is based more on the whole family climate rather than on specific mother/father behavior. Higher levels of parental warmth were related to higher work values similarity between parents and young adults in all three countries, suggesting a pancultural effect. If families exhibited high psychological control, young people tended to be more gender-biased and traditional in their work attitudes, especially in Spain and Czech Republic. Positive family climate seems to create optimal conditions for the transmission of positive work values. Parental psychological control had a stronger effect in Czech Republic compared to both Spain and Turkey, supporting Kagitcibasi's (2007) conceptual explanations that parental control may not be associated with negative outcomes in the collectivistic/relational cultures with strong family ties.

In line with previous studies demonstrating no significant effect of gender on parent-to-child value transmission (Boehnke 2001; Whitbeck and Gecas 1988), our results suggested similar transmission patterns of work values to young adults from both fathers and mothers. However, we could not explore if transmission patterns differ across father-son, father-daughter, mother-son, and mother-daughter dyads. For instance, Roest, Dubas, and Gerris (2010) found bidirectional father-son transmission, but not a mother-daughter transmission of a moral work value (i.e., work as duty). Future research should explore parent-to-child work value transmissions within same-sex compared to cross-sex dyads.

Although there was a weak to moderate level of parent-child work value similarity in all countries, Turkey came first, followed closely by Spain and finally Czech Republic. Particularly in terms of moral and gender-based work values, parent-child similarity was higher in Turkey than in the other two countries, suggesting a strong work value system and family cohesion as well as the predominance of traditional gender roles in Turkey. Phalet and Schönpflug (2001) argue that because collectivism enables family cohesion and cooperation across generations, values are most readily and strongly transmitted in collectivistic cultures. Our finding supports this claim and shows that work value transmission is stronger in collectivistic cultures (Turkey and Spain) than individualistic ones (Czech Republic). These findings are also supported by previous studies conducted on the Turkish population (Kagitcibasi 2007) that described the Turkish family structure as emotionally interdependent with high family cohesion and goal-oriented parental control and authority. Therefore, high parental control may not have the same negative effect in the Turkish cultural context as in individualistic cultures with independent family structures.

Respondents from Turkey and Czech Republic reported more gendered work values than those from Spain. These results, although in line with previous studies that found predominant cultural attitudes toward gender roles in the family and labor market (Kulik 2002; Roest, Dubas, and Gerris 2010; Farré and Vella 2013; Andersson and Hammarstedt 2011), are somehow surprising in the case of Czech Republic, a rather individualistic country. Czech Republic has experienced a transition from a communist regime, based on a full-employment labor force model, to a more democratic but also unstable regime in terms of young adults' employment. Moreover, a family policy system based on an old Bismarckian family policy approach was implemented in Czech Republic that has encouraged a rather traditional family model based on a clear gender division. Therefore, although Czech Republic is more individualistic than Turkey, traditional gender roles seem to prevail.

When we examined the moderating effect of parenting behavior on the intergenerational transmission of work values, the interactions reflected almost a similar pattern among the three countries. Of four significant interactions, three of them were in the case of mother-child dyad. Specifically, when mothers' warmth and autonomy granting were high and psychological control was low, and mothers exhibited high levels of moral and redistributive work values, young adults exhibited high levels of these work values and low levels of gender role–based work values. However, the pattern in Turkey seemed to change when fathers' warmth was low. In this case, young individuals did not adopt their fathers' values if their fathers also showed low gender-based work values. These findings suggest that mothers' and fathers' warmth may not have the same influence in terms of work value transmission within the family. Therefore, future studies should explore if maternal and paternal parenting behaviors have differential effects on work value transmission among sons and daughters, separately.

There are significant differences in the mean ratings of values between the countries, with Turkey having the highest ratings on the majority of values. However, it is important to note that because the sample sizes were large, especially for young adults, even very small differences across the three countries could have emerged as significant. Therefore, the effect sizes need to be taken into consideration in interpreting these findings. Significant differences between countries with relatively large effects were in the ratings of GWV. As expected, Turkish participants, especially parents, endorsed traditional gender roles at work much more than their counterparts in the other two countries. Moreover, parenting behaviors were measured with a few items in a dummy coded format that lowered the reliability of certain dimensions, range restriction, and reduced variances, which could have attenuated the effect sizes. Findings should be interpreted with caution considering these limitations.

Although we could not find a clear cultural pattern in the transmission of work values between parents and young adults across the three countries, the study brings in new empirical evidence in favor of the moderating effect of parenting behaviors, while showing a still pervasive gender-biased transmission of work values in some countries. These findings suggest the importance of family and employment policies that promote positive and egalitarian work values and attitudes, especially to combat the intergenerational transmission of traditional gender roles that put women at a disadvantage in many countries. Emotional warmth and autonomy granting seem to be universally positive parenting behaviors that create an optimal climate for the intergenerational transmission of moral and redistributive work values. Overall, our findings suggest that, regardless of cultural differences, when the family climate at home is positive and parents endorse ethical (moral) and redistributive work values, with less emphasis on the traditional gender roles at work, youth are more likely to adopt their parents' work values.

Notes

1. For more details on the samples and design of the CUPESSE dataset, see Tosun et al. (2018).

2. Since each respondent's mother or father participated in the study, analyses containing self-reported work values of parents are independent from each other. In other words, they are from dyads from different families.

References

Acock, Alan C., and Vern L. Bengtson.1978. On the relative influence of mothers and fathers: A covariance analysis of political and religious socialization. *Journal of Marriage and the Family* 4 (3): 519–30.

Andersson, Lina, and Mats Hammarstedt. 2011. Transmission of self-employment across immigrant generations: The importance of ethnic background and gender. *Review of Economics of the Household* 9 (4): 555–77.

Barber, Brian K., and Elizabeth L. Harmon. 2002. Violating the self: Parental psychological control of children and adolescents. In *Intrusive parenting: How psychological control affects children and adolescents*, ed. Brian K. Barber, 15–52. Washington, DC: American Psychological Association.

Barber, Brian K., Heidi E. Stolz, Joseph A. Olsen, W. Andrew Collins, and Margaret Burchinal. 2005. Parental support, psychological control, and behavioral control: Assessing relevance across time, culture, and method. *Monographs of the Society for Research in Child Development* 70 (4): 1–147.

Boehnke, Klaus. 2001. Parent-offspring value transmission in a societal context. *Journal of Cross-Cultural Psychology* 32:241–55.

Boehnke, Klaus, Angela Ittel, and Dirk Baier. 2002. Value transmission and "Zeitgeist": An under-researched relationship. *Sociale Wetenschappen* 45:28–43.

Brannen, Julia. 2006. Cultures of intergenerational transmission in four-generation families. *Sociological Review* 54 (1): 133–54.

Bryant, Brenda K., Anisa M. Zvonkovic, and Paula Reynolds. 2006. Parenting in relation to child and adolescent vocational development. *Journal of Vocational Behavior* 69 (1): 149–75.

Cemalcilar, Zeynep, Ekin Secinti, and Nebi Sümer. 2018. Parent-child work value similarity: A meta-analytic review. *Journal of Youth and Adolescence* 47:1559–79.

Chao, Ruth K. 1994. Beyond parental control and authoritarian parenting style: Understanding Chinese parenting through the cultural notion of training. *Child Development* 65:1111–19.

Consiglio, Chiarra, Roberto Cenciotti, Laura Borgogni, Guido Alessandri, and Shalom H. Schwartz. 2017. The WVal: A new measure of work values. *Journal of Career Assessment* 25:405–22.

De Vos, Ans, Dirk Buyens, and René Schalk. 2005. Making sense of a new employment relationship: Psychological contract-related information seeking and the role of work values and locus of control. *International Journal of Selection and Assessment* 13:41–52.

Döring, Anna K., Elena Makarova, Walter Herzog, and Anat Bardi. 2017. Parent–child value similarity in families with young children: The predictive power of prosocial educational goals. *British Journal of Psychology* 108 (4): 737–56.

Farré, Lídia, and Francis Vella. 2013. The intergenerational transmission of gender role attitudes and its implications for female labor force participation. *Economica* 80 (318): 219–47.

Friedlmeier, Mihaela, and Gisela Trommsdorff. 2011. Are mother–child similarities in value orientations related to mothers' parenting? A comparative study of American and Romanian mothers and their adolescent children. *European Journal of Developmental Psychology* 8 (6): 661–80.

Gesthuizen, Maurice, Daniel Kovarek, and Carolin Rapp. 2019. Extrinsic and intrinsic work values: Findings on equivalence in different cultural contexts. *The ANNALS of the American Academy of Political and Social Science* (this volume).

Grusec, Joan E., and Maayan Davidov. 2007. Socialization in the family: The roles of parents. In *Handbook of socialization theory and research*, eds. Joan E. Grusec and Paul D. Hastings, 284–308. New York, NY: Guilford.

Hofstede, Geert. 2001. *Culture's consequences: Comparing values, behaviors, institutions, and organizations across nations*, 2nd ed. Thousand Oaks, CA: Sage Publications.

Hofstede, Geert. 2011. Dimensionalizing cultures: The Hofstede model in context. *Online Readings in Psychology and Culture* 2 (1).

Hofstede, Geert, Gert Jan Hofstede, and Michael Minkov. 2010. *Cultures and organizations: Software of the mind*. New York, NY: McGraw-Hill.

Jin, Jing, and James Rounds. 2012. Stability and change in work values: A meta-analysis of longitudinal studies. *Journal of Vocational Behavior* 80 (2): 326–39.

Kagitcibasi, Cigdem. 2007. *Family, self, and human development across cultures: Theory and applications*. Revised 2nd ed. Hillsdale, NJ: Lawrence Erlbaum.

Kandler, Christian, Juliana Gottschling, and Frank M. Spinath. 2016. Genetic and environmental parent-child transmission of value orientations: An extended twin family study. *Child Development* 87 (1): 270–84.

Khaleque, Abdul. 2013. Perceived parental warmth, and children's psychological adjustment, and personality dispositions: A meta-analysis. *Journal of Child and Family Studies* 22 (2): 297–306.

Kohn, Melvin L.1983. On the transmission of values in the family: A preliminary formulation. In *Research in sociology of education and socialization. A research annual. Personal change over the life course*, ed. Alan C. Kerckhoff, 3–12. Greenwich, CT: JAI Press.

Kooij, Dorien T. A. M., Annet H. de Lange, Paul G. W. Jansen, Ruth Kanfer, and Josje S. E. Dikkers. 2011. Age and work related motives: Results of a meta-analysis. *Journal of Organizational Behavior* 32:197–225.

Kraaykamp, Gerbert, Zeynep Cemalcilar, and Jale Tosun. 2019. Transmission of work attitudes and values: Comparisons, consequences, and implications. *The ANNALS of the American Academy of Political and Social Science* (this volume).

Kulik, Liat. 2002. Like-sex versus opposite-sex effects in transmission of gender role ideology from parents to adolescents in Israel. *Journal of Youth and Adolescence* 31:451–57.

Kunz, Hauser Jennifer, and John H. Grych. 2013. Parental psychological control and autonomy granting: Distinctions and associations with child and family functioning. *Parenting* 13 (2): 77–94.

Laspita, Stavroula, Nicola Breugst, Stephen Heblich, and Holger Patzelt. 2012. Intergenerational transmission of entrepreneurial intentions. *Journal of Business Venturing* 27 (4): 414–35.

Lee, Bora, Jenny Padilla, and Susan M. McHale. 2016. Transmission of work ethic in African-American families and its links with adolescent adjustment. *Journal of Youth & Adolescence* 45 (11): 2278–91.

Min, Joohong, Merril Silverstein, and Jessica P. Lendon. 2012. Intergenerational transmission of value over the family life course. *Advances in Life Course Research* 17 (3): 112–20.

Padilla, Jenny, Susan M. McHale, Michael J. Rovine, Kimberly A. Updegraff, and Adriana J. Umaña-Taylor. 2016. Parent-youth differences in family values from adolescence into young adulthood: Developmental course and links with parent-youth conflict. *Journal of Youth and Adolescence* 45 (12): 2417–30.

Phalet, Karen, and Ute Schönpflug. 2001. Intergenerational transmission of collectivism and achievement values in two acculturation contexts: The case of Turkish families in Germany and Turkish and Moroccan families in the Netherlands. *Journal of Cross-Cultural Psychology* 32 (2): 186–201.

Pinquart, Martin, and Rainer K. Silbereisen. 2004. Transmission of values from adolescents to their parents: The role of value content and authoritative parenting. *Adolescence* 39 (153): 83–100.

Ranieri, Sonia, and Daniela Barni. 2012. Family and other social contexts in the intergenerational transmission of values. *Family Science* 3 (1): 1–3.

Roest, Annette M. C., Judith Semon Dubas, and Jan R. M Gerris. 2009. Value transmissions between fathers, mothers, and adolescent and emerging adult children: The role of the family climate. *Journal of Family Psychology* 23 (2): 146–55.

Roest, Annette M. C., Judith Semon Dubas, and Jan R. M. Gerris. 2010. Value transmissions between parents and children: Gender and developmental phase as transmission belts. *Journal of Adolescence* 33 (1): 21–31.

Schönpflug, Ute. 2001. Intergenerational transmission of values: The role of transmission belts. *Journal of Cross-Cultural Psychology* 32 (2): 174–85.

Schwartz, Shalom H. 1999. A theory of cultural values and some implication for work. *Applied Psychology: An International Review* 48 (1): 23–47.

Schwartz, Shalom H. 2014. National culture as value orientations: Consequences of value differences and cultural distance. In *Handbook of the economics of art and culture*, vol. 2, eds. Victor A. Ginsburgh and David Throsby, 547–86. Amsterdam: Elsevier.

Schwartz, Shalom H., and Tammy Rubel. 2005. Sex differences in value priorities: Cross-cultural and multimethod studies. *Journal of Personality and Social Psychology* 89 (6): 1010–28.

Silk, Jennifer S., Amanda S. Morris, Tomoe Kanaya, and Laurence Steinberg. 2003. Psychological control and autonomy granting: Opposite ends of a continuum or distinct constructs? *Journal of Research on Adolescence* 13 (1): 113–28.

Soenens, B., and M. Vansteenkiste. 2010. A theoretical upgrade of the concept of parental psychological control: Proposing new insights on the basis of self-determination theory. *Developmental Review* 30 (1): 74–99.

Smetana, Judith G. 2017. Current research on parenting styles, dimensions, and beliefs. *Current Opinion in Psychology* 15:19–25.

Steinberg, Laurence, Nina S. Mounts, Susie D. Lamborn, and Sanford M. Dornbusch. 1991. Authoritative parenting and adolescent adjustment across varied ecological niches. *Journal of Research on Adolescence* 1 (1): 19–36.

Supple, Andrew J., Sharon R. Ghazarian, James M. Frabutt, Scott W. Plunkett, and Tovah Sands. 2006. Contextual influences on Latino adolescent ethnic identity and academic outcomes. *Child Development* 77 (5): 1427–33.

Supple, Andrew J., Sharon R. Ghazarian, Gary W. Peterson, and Kevin R. Bush. 2009. Assessing the cross-cultural validity of a parental autonomy granting measure: Comparing adolescents in the United States, China, Mexico, and India. *Journal of Cross-Cultural Psychology* 40 (5): 816–33.

Tosun, Jale, José Arco-Tirado, Maurizio Caserta, Zeynep Cemalcilar, Markus Freitag, Felix Hörisch, Carsten Jensen, Bernhard Kittel, Levebte Littvay, Martin Lukes, et al. 2018. Perceived economic self-sufficiency: A country- and generation-comparative approach. *European Political Science*. Advance online publication. doi.org/10.1057/s41304-018-0186-3.

Trommsdorff, Gisela. 2009a. Intergenerational relations and cultural transmission. In *Cultural transmission: Psychological, developmental, social, and methodological aspects*, ed. Ute Schönpflug, 126–60. Cambridge, MA: Cambridge University Press.

Trommsdorff, Gisela. 2009b. A social change and a human development perspective on the value of children. In *Perspectives on human development, family and culture*, eds. Sevda Bekman and Ayhan Aksu-Koç, 86–107. Cambridge, MA: Cambridge University Press.

Trommsdorff, Gisela. 2016. Intergenerational relations in cultural context and in socio-economic change. In *Youth in education: The necessity of valuing ethnocultural diversity*, eds. Christiane Timmerman, Noel Clycq, Marie Mc Andrew, Alhassane Balde, Luc Braeckmans, and Sara Mels, 11–26. London: Routledge.

Whitbeck, Les B., and Viktor Gecas. 1988. Value attributions and value transmission between parents and children. *Journal of Marriage and the Family* 50 (3): 829–40.

The Transmission of Work Centrality within the Family in a Cross-Regional Perspective

By
BERNHARD KITTEL,
FABIAN KALLEITNER,
and
PANOS TSAKLOGLOU

Young adults' work values evolve as they are socialized into education and work. We study a core concept of work values, *work centrality*, and distinguish between an extrinsic dimension, that is, the relative importance of work; and an intrinsic dimension, that is, nonfinancial employment commitment. Using data collected by the CUPESSE project on two generations of families in nine European countries, we explore the congruence of work values between parents and adolescents and the effect of the regional-level social and economic context on young adults' work values. We find, first, that parental influence is the most robust determinant of extrinsic and intrinsic work centrality in adolescents. Second, the relative importance of work to young women varies across regions, but the variation is explained in part by female labor force participation rates in those regions. Third, differing patterns of extrinsic and intrinsic work centrality across European regions are explained, in part, by gender, education, and subjective financial satisfaction.

Keywords: work values; intergenerational transmission; employment commitment; labor force participation; regions; Europe; multilevel analysis

Work values are important to labor market participation. They are concrete conceptions of the multidimensional concept of the meaning of work (Nord et al. 1988; Dekas and Baker 2014; Ros, Schwartz, and Surkiss 1999). We focus on one core work value, *work centrality*, defined as the subjective belief that work is important in one's life (Walsh and Gordon

Bernhard Kittel is a professor of economic sociology at the University of Vienna. His main research interests are justice attitudes and group decision-making and youth labor markets. Recent publications have appeared in the Journal of Public Economics, Political Research Quarterly, *the* Journal of Youth Studies, *and* Sociological Inquiry.

Correspondence: bernhard.kittel@univie.ac.at

DOI: 10.1177/0002716219827515

ANNALS, *AAPSS*, 682, March 2019

2008; Rosso, Dekas, and Wrzesniewski 2010; Ros, Schwartz, and Surkiss 1999) and further differentiate this concept into two components according to the important distinction between extrinsic and intrinsic motivations (Harpaz and Fu 1997).

We aim to shed light on three related questions: First, how important is the transmission of work centrality within the family? Second, in what way does work centrality vary across Europe? Third, which contextual factors influence work centrality? Following established measures (Rosso, Dekas, and Wrzesniewski 2010), we operationalize the extrinsic component as the relative importance of work compared to leisure (Relative Importance of Work or RIW) and the intrinsic component as the intention to work in the absence of financial necessity (Nonfinancial Employment Commitment or NEC). While both dimensions measure the general importance of work, they highlight different aspects of the meaning of work in the life of an individual. RIW emphasizes the social role of work, including the need to work to make a living, while NEC focuses on the subjective value of work, and we expect these dimensions of work centrality to be affected by sociodemographic and contextual factors in different ways.

We study three sets of determinants of work centrality: individual factors such as the characteristics of the present job and the family situation, socialization effects due to transmission within the family, and the social role of respondents in the wider society (Gallie, Felstead, and Green 2012; Kalleberg 1977; Kalleberg and Marsden 2013). Although there is much evidence suggesting the relevance of socialization effects (Roberts and Bengtson 1999; Johnson 2002), the relationship is far from perfect. We address this gap by studying the factors affecting the deviation of youth work values from their parents' values after taking transmission effects into account for both aspects of work centrality.

We combine the three levels in a single model and argue that while individual work values are rooted in familial socialization, the socioeconomic and cultural contexts play an important role as well. In contrast to previous studies (Turunen and Nätti 2017; Esser 2009; Parboteeah and Cullen 2003), we conceptualize the context not at the level of countries but at the regional level, which is arguably more immediately relevant in socioeconomic and cultural

Fabian Kalleitner is a PhD candidate in the Department of Economic Sociology at the University of Vienna. His current research focuses on fiscal sociology and biased perceptions, status attainment processes, and web survey methodology.

Panos Tsakloglou is a professor at the Athens University of Economics and Business. His research focuses on inequality, poverty, social exclusion, and the redistributive role of public policies and has been published in the Quarterly Journal of Economics, *the* Economic Journal, *the* Journal of Development Economics, *and the* Journal of European Social Policy.

NOTE: This research was funded under the EU Seventh Framework Programme collaborative research project CUPESSE (Cultural Pathways to Economic Self-Sufficiency and Entrepreneurship; grant agreement number 613257). We are grateful for very helpful comments from anonymous reviewers. We also want to thank the participants of the workshop "Work Attitudes and Values in Post-Crisis Europe" in Heidelberg 2018, especially Anne-Marie Parth, for their comments and suggestions.

terms. Whereas country-level averages constitute a baseline, within-country variations in economic prosperity, labor market conditions, and cultural values are large in European countries, most notably along the center-periphery and the urban-rural cleavages (Lipset and Rokkan 1967; Hooghe and Marks 2018). Living conditions in urban metropoles and rural peripheries are more similar across countries than within countries. Furthermore, social institutions such as the family culture follow different political cleavages than current national borders (Alesina et al. 2015; Duranton, Rodríguez-Pose, and Sandall 2009). Also, a welfare or employment regime perspective has been shown to be only of limited use in a work value context (Steiber 2013). Thus, a focus on country-level comparisons may conceal more than illuminate. As a second research question, then, we ask what socioeconomic and cultural factors in the region condition individual deviations in the transmission of work values within the family in addition to individual factors.

We study these questions with data from the Cultural Pathways to Economic Self-Sufficiency and Entrepreneurship (CUPESSE) project, which is unique in providing data that systematically trace the transmission of work values from parents to their children across different European countries (Tosun et al. 2018). We analyze these questions for NEC and RIW separately. By merging the CUPESSE data with regional (NUTS-2) social and economic indicators from EUROSTAT and controlling for country effects, we integrate contextual variation into the analysis.[1]

Dimensions of Work Centrality

Research on work values has a long tradition in sociology (Weber 1904/2005; Durkheim 1893/2014). Most researchers define work values in terms of outcomes people desire and seek through work (Brief 1998; Cherrington 1980; Nord et al. 1988). Despite several critiques and extensions (Gallie 2007; Halaby 2003) and the introduction of newer classifications (Wrzesniewski et al. 1997), the two-factor model of intrinsic and extrinsic values has remained dominant in research classifications (Kalleberg and Marsden 2013; Mortimer et al. 1996; Johnson, Sage, and Mortimer 2012).

Work centrality is often supposed to transcend the distinction between intrinsic and extrinsic work values (Rosso, Dekas, and Wrzesniewski 2010; Ros, Schwartz, and Surkiss 1999). As stated above, a high level of work centrality means that one sees work as an important aspect of life itself. Work centrality influences decisions about work, especially during economic hardship, when greater efforts are necessary (Johnson, Sage, and Mortimer 2012). It also enhances job search efforts, vocational aspirations, the school-to-work transition, job search intensity, job selection, and job satisfaction (Kanfer, Wanberg, and Kantrowitz 2001; Hitlin 2006; Jin and Rounds 2012; Bal and Kooij 2011; Kalleberg 1977).

Although RIW and NEC have both been used in combined scales of work centrality (England and Harpaz 1983; Harpaz and Fu 1997), we argue that these

FIGURE 1
Relative Importance of Work (RIW)

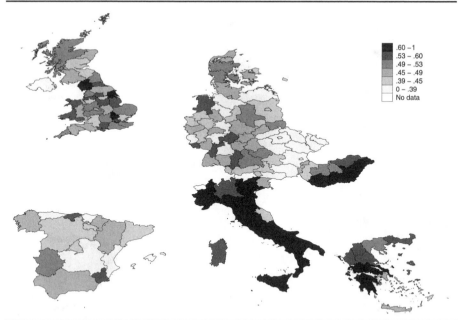

NOTE: RIW: Work should come first, even at the expense of leisure. $N = 15,949$.

two indicators measure conceptually distinct dimensions of the value assigned to work. First, we conceptualize the RIW as the subjective relevance of work in life by contrasting feelings about work to feelings about leisure from a utilitarian perspective. Our measure of RIW is based on parts of Furnham's (1990) operationalization of Weber's (1904/2005) concept of work ethic. He interpreted work centrality as "leisure avoidance." This approach results in the item, "Work should always come first even if it means less spare time," which is then rated on a 4-point Likert scale ranging from *strongly disagree* to *strongly agree*.[2] We dichotomize this scale by categorizing the first two answers as "low work centrality" (53 percent of respondents) and the second two as "high work centrality" (47 percent of respondents).

Figure 1 depicts the distribution of RIW aggregated at the NUTS-2 level in the countries studied. We observe very high levels of RIW in Italy, in particular the southern part; Hungary; and the southeastern part of England. High levels are found in the British Midlands, in the southern part of Germany as well as Lower Saxony, and in large parts of Greece. On the other side of the scale are Spain, Austria, the Czech Republic, the eastern and northern parts of Germany, and parts of the United Kingdom. Denmark, parts of Hungary, and some areas in the United Kingdom and Germany are in the middle range of the scale.

Second, we focus on the value of work beyond the need for income. Morse and Weiss (1955) told participants to imagine that they inherited enough money

FIGURE 2
Nonfinancial Employment Commitment (NEC)

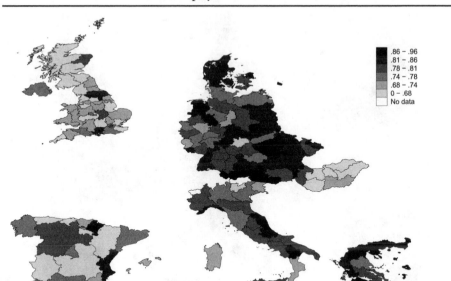

NOTE: NEC: Would continue working without financial necessity. $N = 13,658$.

to live comfortably for the rest of their lives and asked whether they intended to continue working. An astonishing 80 percent of the respondents answered yes. This idea of NEC is closely related to Weber's concept of a religious belief in work as a way toward salvation (Rosso, Dekas, and Wrzesniewski 2010). Hence, the item on employment commitment in the case of unexpected wealth refers to the importance of work as an end in itself, thereby highlighting the intrinsic value of work (Steiber 2013). Our question wording focuses on the general orientation toward work and not on the current job situation: "If you were to get enough money to live as comfortably as you would like for the rest of your life, would you continue to work or would you stop working?" Respondents could answer "Continue work" or "Stop working." More than measuring a single aspect of the work ethos, NEC should be interpreted as a way to operationalize individual work ethos in a single question. Although multi-item indicators are more frequently used in international comparisons, the measure has remained popular (Gallie, this volume; Steiber 2013; Turunen and Nätti 2017; van der Wel and Halvorsen 2015).

Figure 2 shows the share of respondents in a NUTS-2 region who believe that they would continue work even if they would not need the income from work. Most notably, Austria, Germany, and Greece score highest and Hungary scores lowest on the NEC measure. Thus, respondents in the first set of countries give work a low status in comparison to leisure but cannot imagine ceasing work even if they would not need to work. Quite the reverse order is observed in Hungary, parts of the United Kingdom, and the northeastern part of Italy: respondents tend to rate work very highly in comparison to spare time, but the share of those who would stop working if they had the opportunity is very high. In the other countries, the scores of the two variables are more aligned.

As the covariation of RIW and NEC is small (Gamma = 0.2; see Table A2 in the online appendix), our argument that the two dimensions of work centrality actually capture very different aspects of the concept is empirically supported. A principal component analysis of work centrality measures (regardless of using a one- or a three-item operationalization) and NEC results in a two-factor model (online appendix Table A3), which further supports our decision to investigate the multidimensionality of work centrality and analyze RIW and NEC separately.

We thus observe substantial variation not only in the average scores on RIW and NEC across European regions but also in the relative scores of the two variables, yielding different regional profiles of congruent and incongruent work centrality measures.

Determinants of Work Centrality

The main idea of our argument is that individual work values are embedded in a social context. We distinguish two levels of context, that is, the family as a proximate and direct source of work values and the broader socioeconomic and cultural conditions as a distant framework of opportunities and limitations motivating or restraining the development of individual work values. We first discuss the two levels of contextual conditions and then present the individual-level factors constituting the model to which the contextual conditions are added and compared.

Transmission of work centrality within the family

The family context has often been highlighted as a prime influence in shaping the value structures of children, especially work values (Kalleberg and Marsden 2013; Roberts and Bengtson 1999). Both socialization theory (Bush and Simmons 1981; Long and Hadden 1985) and social attainment theory (Blau and Duncan 1967; Mortimer 1974) suggest that work orientations are socially transmitted from parents to children through social interactions and observation. Socialization is the prime mechanism of the initial development of values and patterns of behavior (Grusec and Kuczynski 1997). Additionally, the social psychology of work stresses the connection between social origins and adult job values (Johnson 2002; Kohn and Schooler 1969). Parents are the prime agents of socialization and value development in early childhood and adolescence (Whiston and Keller 2004). We measure the intergenerational transmission of work values using value congruency between parents and children. In line with the strong empirical evidence and expectations of socialization and social attainment theory, we anticipate (H1) strong value congruency between parents and their children in both measures of work centrality.

The regional socioeconomic and cultural context

Workers may seek jobs that conform to their values, although such jobs may not be available given job market conditions (Kalleberg 1977). First, according to need-based theories (Kalleberg and Marsden 2013; Maslow 1954), RIW should be higher when jobs are scarce in a labor market. Second, consistent with a reinforcement and accentuation model, workers should emphasize the values they can obtain in their actual job (Johnson, Sage, and Mortimer 2012; Rosenberg 1979). In this case, the level of unemployment in the relevant labor market should have a positive impact on RIW but a negative one on NEC, because having a job becomes more important but the probability of having an adequate job decreases. Furthermore, people who are out of work for long periods might grow accustomed to their situation. At the regional level, this is argued to weaken the social norm of working hard (Clark 2003). Additionally, high levels of unemployment may boost the fear of losing one's job, which has also been shown to affect NEC negatively (Steiber 2013). Consequently, we expect (H2) that higher unemployment rates (operationalized by the unemployment rate of 18- to 24-year-olds at the NUTS-2 level) will lower the chances of getting a job that people are willing to work for without the extrinsic need to do so. We also include the general level of long-term unemployment in the region, which should be better suited to capturing the social norm of being unemployed.

At the individual level, high levels of subjective job insecurity have a negative effect on the employment commitment of employees (Turunen and Nätti 2017; Steiber 2013). Hence, perceived job expectations may contribute to explaining work centrality. According to status attainment theory, the primary effect of the parents' social status is enhanced by secondary effects stemming from education and employment prospects (Sewell, Haller, and Ohlendorf 1970). To capture the social status environment and assess the effect of the socioeconomic context on work centrality, we add the percentage of employees in sectors with a low human capital intensity in the NUTS-2 region. A high share of employees in these sectors should hinder the development of strong intrinsic work centrality (NEC) as chances of reaching a human capital intense job are lower (H3) (Tabellini 2010). The lower the overall skill level in the region, the higher will be the need to work for survival (RIW) and the lower the willingness to work beyond financial necessity (NEC).

Furthermore, besides these economic factors, cultural variation should also affect work values, as Weber (1904/2005) has argued in his seminal study on the protestant ethic and capitalism. Several studies have shown that work centrality is shaped by the cultural background and by social institutions (Warr 2008; Parboteeah and Cullen 2003). However, in a comparative study, England and Whitely (1990) found more similarities than differences in work centrality across countries. This result has been replicated in other studies (Snir and Harpaz

2006), which suggests that the national level may be too broad a unit of analysis to assess the effect of culture.[3]

Roughly speaking, more peripheral and more rural areas typically score higher in maintaining traditional cultural values, which affects economic development (Tabellini 2010). Traditional values such as security, conformity, and tradition have also been associated with stronger extrinsic work values (Ros, Schwartz, and Surkiss 1999). One important marker of cultural norms with respect to the organization of the family and the society is the definition of gender-specific social roles. Recent studies have attributed variation in gender roles to histori- cally grown cultural differences at the regional level (Alesina et al. 2015; Duranton, Rodríguez-Pose, and Sandall 2009). Through a variety of channels, ranging from individual identity to the existence of childcare institutions, shared convictions about social roles are captured in the aggregated participation of women in the labor market (operationalized as the female labor force participa- tion rate in the age group 25–34 at the NUTS-2 level). We expect that (H4) regions with higher female labor force participation exhibit lower RIW and higher NEC.

Measuring these factors at the regional level (NUTS-2 level), while including country effects, is a pragmatic solution that avoids excessive averaging while maintaining a reasonable number of observations per unit of analysis. Thus, we eliminate variation that is due to cultural and institutional differences between countries that could overlap with socioeconomic variation and instead focus on variation across regions.[4]

Individual factors

Given that an extensive literature has explored the individual determinants of work values, we include a set of variables that captures these factors as a baseline model to which we compare the extensions at the family and regional levels.[5] In other words, we focus on specific sociodemographic core variables that may help to explain different patterns of RIW and NEC.

Although age seems to be an important factor for work values (Hanlon 1986; Bal and Kooij 2011), age variation in our sample of young adults is too small to capture maturing effects or closeness to retirement (Highhouse, Zickar, and Yankelevich 2010). Instead, we account for different stages in the respondent's life course and the specific roles that are attached to them (Sagie, Elizur, and Koslowsky 1996) by including several sociodemographic and socioeconomic variables.

First, given the different social roles attributed to men and women and the gender-segregated occupation structures and work roles of men and women still prevalent in European societies (Mannheim 1993), we include gender as a pre- dictor. To the extent that traditional gender roles are relevant, we should observe higher RIW among men. If the gender segregation argument holds, NEC should be higher for women than for men, because women should only work if they are intrinsically motivated.

Second, parenthood raises the importance of extrinsic work rewards, which, in turn, could influence work values. This may also be the result of self selection, as people with strong extrinsic values are more likely to marry and have children early (Johnson 2001, 2005; Mortimer, Lorence, and Kumka 1986). Therefore, the presence of children should be associated with higher RIW and lower NEC.

Third, education is a way to obtain high-quality jobs that, despite some dispute about details, can better satisfy extrinsic and intrinsic work motivations (Warr 2008; Harpaz and Fu 1997; Harpaz 2002). Thus, both RIW and NEC should be positively related to education.

Fourth, apart from a small group of highly qualified professionals, migrants tend to find jobs at the lower end of the occupational status hierarchy (Hudson 2007; Wrench, Rea, and Ouali 1999). As a consequence, they hold less rewarding jobs, and we should expect higher values on RIW but lower values on NEC.

Fifth, from a need perspective, low-income earners should focus on work due to the dominance of extrinsic benefits, resulting in higher values of RIW (Kalleberg and Marsden 2013). In turn, financial need is expected to reduce intrinsic work values, leading to a diminished interest in working beyond necessity. Need-based theories thus suggest that financial stability is negatively related to RIW and positively related to NEC.

Gallie, Felstead, and Green (2012) showed, in line with earlier results (Mortimer et al. 1996; Mortimer and Lorence 1979), that low-skill occupations decrease intrinsic job preferences. In addition, jobs demanding higher skills should be positively related to both extrinsic and intrinsic job preferences, which in turn should foster the relative importance of work in life in general. Hence, the occupational skill level, measured by the grouped ISCO-1 level (Gallie 2007), should be positively related to NEC and RIW.

Data

The empirical analysis is based on data from the CUPESSE project, an interdisciplinary project on intergenerational work value transmission funded by the European Commission under the FP7 framework (Tosun et al. 2018). In this article, we use data from nine member countries of the European Union that participated in the survey (Austria, the Czech Republic, Denmark, Germany, Great Britain, Greece, Hungary, Italy, and Spain). Data were collected in two stages. First, a probability sample of at least 1,000 young adults aged 18 to 35 was drawn from each country. Then parents were surveyed, if the young adult participants provided the means of contact. Since this approach may generate a response bias toward close parent-youth relationships that may, in turn, translate into higher similarity in values favoring a positive empirical relationship, we conducted chi-squared tests of independence comparing the share of youth respondents who provided parent data with those who did not. The tests resulted in significant differences in Denmark, Italy, and Spain for RIW and in Austria and Germany for NEC. Although significant, the small values of Cramér's V indicate very weak associations (see online appendix Tables A4 and A5). Thus, although we do not know whether parents' values differ, we know that young adults who provided parent data hold roughly the same values on work centrality as those who did not. The CUPESSE data are cross-sectional, which limits our ability to draw inferences on casual relations. But because the goal of this article is to highlight parent-child similarities in RIW and NEC and the importance of the regional context, cross-sectional data should be sufficient. We merge the data with NUTS-2 Eurostat indicators of low human capital intensive jobs defined as not being employed in technology- and knowledge-intensive sectors, the youth unemployment rate of people aged 15 to 24, and the female labor force participation rate of people aged 25 to 35 in 2015 (see online appendix Table A1 for a description of variables).

Results

We estimated two-level random-intercept models where individuals (level 1) are nested in regions (level 2). The intraclass correlation coefficient (ICC) of the null model is .106 for RIW and .078 for NEC. Hence roughly 10 percent of the variation in the data is explained by regional variation if we do not account for country variation. Similar magnitudes have also been reported in multilevel regressions of work centrality with country data at level 2 (Turunen and Nätti 2017; Stam, Verbakel, and de Graaf 2013). We included country fixed effects to account for the nested structure of the regions in national cultures, welfare regimes, and legal systems. The corresponding ICCs are .021 for RIW and .025 for NEC. The null hypothesis that the between-region variance is zero is rejected (likelihood-ratio test, $p < .01$) for both dependent variables. Thus, we can assume that regional effects have a small but significant influence and that by controlling for country-level effects we have a conservative measure for regional effects on work values. Table 1 presents the results of the random-intercept models. Column 1 refers to RIW and column 2 to NEC.

Family effects

Model 1 (RIW), on the relative importance of work compared to leisure, shows a strong congruence between youth and parent work centrality even though we control for various covariates. Hypothesis 1 (H1), that parents' work values are a strong predictor of their children's work values, is thus supported. This is also the case in model 2 (NEC), where the parent effects are even larger and, once more, the single strongest of all the predictors in our analysis. The strength of the effect is even more impressive as previous studies have suggested that, more than the parents' actual work values, the children's perception of their parents' work values influences the child's work values (Whitbeck and Gecas 1988).

Regional context effects

We expected that higher unemployment rates will lower the chances of getting jobs that people are willing to work for without the extrinsic need to do so (H2).

TABLE 1
Estimates from Two-Level Random Intercept Logit Models of RIW and NEC

Dependent Variable	(1) RIW	(2) NEC
Parent RIW	0.93°°°	
	(0.068)	
Parent NEC		1.25°°°
		(0.087)
Percentage of employees in low human capital intensive sectors, NUTS-2	−0.0087	−0.017
	(0.011)	(0.016)
Youth unemployment rate 18–24, NUTS2	−0.0047	−0.0040
	(0.014)	(0.018)
Long-term unemployment rate, NUTS2	−0.010	−0.068
	(0.035)	(0.046)
Female labor force participation rate 25–34, NUTS2	−0.028°°°	−0.027°
	(0.011)	(0.014)
Male (ref. female)	0.17°°°	−0.33°°°
	(0.067)	(0.089)
Highest level of education	−0.11°°°	0.13°°°
	(0.021)	(0.028)
Children (ref. no children)	−0.075	−0.12
	(0.088)	(0.11)
Migration background (ref. no migration background)	0.23°°	0.22
	(0.099)	(0.14)
Financial satisfaction	0.096°°	0.028
	(0.044)	(0.058)
Employment status (ref. high-skilled employed)		
Intermediate	0.068	−0.28°°
	(0.10)	(0.14)
Semi and nonskilled	0.11	−0.064
	(0.14)	(0.18)
Unemployed	0.15	−0.22
	(0.13)	(0.17)
Educ./training	−0.22°°	−0.090
	(0.097)	(0.13)
Other	−0.13	−0.50°°°
	(0.13)	(0.17)
Constant	1.81	3.17°°
	(1.17)	(1.54)
Observations	4,456	3,573
Number of groups	132	132

NOTE: Standard errors in parentheses. Country fixed effects included (not shown).
°$p < .1$. °°$p < .05$. °°°$p < .01$.

TABLE 2
Level 2 Estimates of Two-Level Random Intercept Logit Models of RIW

	(1)	(2)	(3)	(4)	(5)	(6)
Percentage of employees in low human capital intensive sectors		−0.0073 (0.012)				−0.0087 (0.011)
Youth unemployment rate			0.019°° (0.0075)			−0.0047 (0.014)
Long-term unemploy-ment rate				0.043°° (0.020)		−0.010 (0.035)
Female labor force par-ticipation rate					−0.028°°° (0.0079)	−0.028°°° (0.011)
ICC	0.019	0.019	0.015	0.017	0.010	0.010
Level 2 variance	0.063	0.064	0.051	0.058	0.034	0.033
PRV, %	—	+1.6	19.0	7.9	46.0	47.6

NOTE: PRV: Proportional reduction in variance component compared to model 1. $N = 4{,}456$; number of level 2 groups = 132. The models include all level 1 controls used in Table 1 and country dummies.
°$p < .1$. °°$p < .05$. °°°$p < .01$.

The analysis indicates that the coefficient fails to reach statistical significance in the full model. However, stepwise inclusion of the regional-level indicators shows that regions with higher unemployment rates and especially with higher long-term unemployment rates have higher levels of RIW (see Table 2). Hence, we cannot find a detrimental effect of unemployment on the social norm of work. In contrast, the results suggest that in regions with high unemployment RIW becomes more salient, which could be interpreted as an effect of the higher salience of the need for extrinsic job rewards.[6]

Contrary to our expectations, we find no statistically significant negative influence of the percentage of employment in sectors with low human capital intensity in the region on RIW or NEC (H3). While these results render the importance of occupational macro effects on work centrality unimportant, we emphasize that this result must be interpreted with caution. The cross-sectional character of our data might be insufficient to reveal the discouraging effects of low occupational opportunities over time. Furthermore, lower expectations stemming from parent-child congruency might mediate the effects of the actual occupational structure. In sum, model effects (Tables 2 and 3) indicate that regional socioeconomic variables are more relevant for RIW than for NEC, as the full model reduces residual level 2 variance for the latter only to a limited extent (13.3 percent), while it cuts the residual variance level 2 for RIW nearly in half (47.6 percent).

In regions with higher female labor force participation rates, respondents reported lower rates of RIW. This supports our hypothesis that cultural norms

TABLE 3
Level 2 Estimates of Two-Level Random Intercept Logit Models of NEC

	(1)	(2)	(3)	(4)	(5)	(6)
Percentage of employees in low human capital intensive sectors		−0.019 (0.015)				−0.017 (0.016)
Youth unemployment rate			−0.0010 (0.0093)			−0.0040 (0.018)
Long-term unemployment rate				−0.019 (0.024)		−0.068 (0.046)
Female labor force participation rate					−0.010 (0.010)	−0.027° (0.014)
ICC	0.022	0.023	0.023	0.023	0.021	0.019
Level 2 variance	0.075	0.079	0.076	0.076	0.070	0.065
PRV, %	–	+5.3	+1.3	+1.3	6.7	13.3

NOTE: PRV = proportional reduction in variance component compared to model 1. N = 3,573; number of level 2 groups = 132. The models include all level 1 controls used in Table 1 and country dummies.
°$p < .1$.

about the familial distribution of labor might discourage women to work. We calculated separate models by gender, which suggested that the estimated coefficient indeed results from a negative effect for women only for both RIW and NEC (online appendix Table A7). Thus, in regions with low rates of female labor force participation, which arguably reflect strong traditional values, the importance of work relative to leisure is more salient for women. Contrary to our expectations, this regional effect is also negative for NEC. Studying the results more closely, we find that the regional rate of female labor force participation becomes significant only when controlling for the unemployment rate in the region as well, indicating that women living in regions with a high rate of unemployment and a high female labor force participation rate respond that they are less willing to continue their job if they have no financial necessity to do so. This shows the relevance of high-quality occupations for women, as women who face the risk of unemployment may be more likely to discontinue their job careers in favor of their families, resulting in cumulating disadvantages for their career and earning possibilities.

Individual effects

Male respondents consider work more important than leisure when compared to women but are less inclined to answer that they will continue work without financial necessity to do so. Although we anticipated that people in different stages of their life course would be affected by the specific work roles attached to them, the presence of a child in the family has no effect on work values in our main model (Table 1).[7] The current employment status indicates that for individuals in education, work is less important. The employment category "other" mostly contains individuals who are working at home or on parental leave. Since this category is predominantly populated by women, the result that individuals in this category have lower rates of NEC emphasizes the importance of gender roles for work centrality.

Education decreases RIW but is positively related to NEC. There are two possible explanations for this discrepancy: On one hand, people with higher education may self-select into positions providing rewards that motivate them to continue working even if it is not financially necessary to do so. On the other hand, the higher intrinsic work values of more educated people lead them to favor work beyond its extrinsic necessity. The data do not allow for a clear interpretation.

Migration background had the expected positive effect on RIW. However, contrary to expectations, a migration background has no significant negative influence on the NEC. This observation would require further analysis with more specific data.

Financial satisfaction positively affects RIW, while we find no significant influence on NEC. This seems to contradict need theories, which emphasize a hierarchy of rewards perspectives. However, this result would be in line with an instrumental perspective that stresses the comparative utility of work to leisure.[8] Moreover, needs may not be sufficiently pressing to raise the relative importance of work. A third potential explanation may be that for some occupational groups, work is not viewed as a way of reducing financial instability. Occupational classes fail to explain shifting patterns in the full model. However, this is mainly due to a correlation between education and occupational quality because dropping the education indicator renders the effect of occupational class significantly negative for RIW and positive for NEC. Thus, work in higher positions, which in other studies has shown to better satisfy intrinsic job motivations, influences the ability of people to enjoy work beyond extrinsic necessity, but its relative effect in addition to education is difficult to measure in a cross-sectional study. Panel studies might help to better distinguish the effect of educational attainment and occupational quality.

Discussion and Conclusion

Work centrality is a core measure of the overall importance of work in life. In this article, we have considered it as multidimensional in operation: we explore an extrinsic aspect (the relative importance of work to individuals or RIW) and an intrinsic aspect (the extent to which individuals are motivated to work even if work is not a financial necessity; what we call nonfinancial employment commitment or NEC). As expected, the extrinsic and intrinsic aspects of work centrality differ substantially across European regions.

We differentiate three levels of influence on individual work values: the family as a proximate and direct source of work values; the broader regional socioeconomic context as a more distant framework of opportunities and limitations motivating or restraining the development of individual work values; and individual core characteristics such as gender, education, and current employment status and occupation skill level. We study the importance of the transmission of work centrality within the family and the contextual and individual factors that help to explain the level of individual work centrality, in addition to transmission within the family.

We find, first, that the transmission of work values from parents to their children contributes most to the explanation of young adults' work values. Both RIW and NEC exhibit strong persistence over generations. Second, the regional female labor force participation rate reduces RIW and NEC for young women. Third, we identify three individual-level factors that help to explain variation in RIW and NEC. Women reported significantly lower levels for RIW and higher levels of NEC. Education enables individuals to obtain jobs in which rewards from work are also nonmonetary, but higher education also reduces the overall importance of work compared to leisure. The opposite seems to be the case for financial satisfaction, which favors interpretations that focus on value congruency theories rather than a need perspective.

Future research might focus on the variation in the meaning of work to individuals at different stages in their life course and the relevance of gender roles. In particular, panel studies could help to further our knowledge on the correspondence between gender roles and work values in different societal contexts. Our results indicate that socioeconomic context may play a role in determining an individual's work values. Future studies could also investigate the immediate context at the level of neighborhoods, which would yield an even better measure of the relevant socioeconomic context for individuals than the NUTS-2 regions used here. A panel perspective could also help to disentangle the effects of context and the family during the important stage of entry into the labor market. Our results may underestimate the relevance of context because the economic situation should also influence parents' work values.

Individual work centrality is shaped by the transmission of values within the family in a specific socioeconomic context and is further influenced by the individual situation. Our results indicate that for most young adults in Europe, work is a central aspect of their life, although they differ in the emphasis on its expected rewards. While nonfinancial employment commitment dominates among highly educated people and in regions with low unemployment, people in the opposite condition will be much more willing to put leisure behind work. Thus, our study indicates that the social conditions into which people are socialized as well as contextual and situational factors affect their work values, leaving only limited space for discussions about wrong "work cultures" to foster work centrality.

Notes

1. NUTS refers to "nomenclature of territorial units for statistics," which is a regional classification for the EU Member States that provides a harmonized hierarchy of regions. The NUTS classification

subdivides each Member State into regions at three different levels, covering NUTS 1, 2, and 3 from larger to smaller areas. NUTS 2 are basic regions for the application of regional policies (mostly they correspond to the first legal subdivisions below the national level) (Eurostat 2018).

2. The question wording is similar to the one used in the European Value Study (EVS) 2008 V96. We also tried to combine this measure with two other indicators used in the work ethos scale of the EVS 2008 (V95, "Work is a duty to society"; V93, "Money without job is humiliating"). Due to the very low scores on the indicators of construct reliability (Cronbach's alpha = .53, ranging from .31 in Hungary to .61 in Austria), we decided to focus on the relative importance of work compared to leisure. To explore the robustness of our results, online appendix Tables A7 and A8 show regression estimates of our main findings using a continuous three-factor variable for the relative importance of work. The main conclusions of this article remain unchanged.

3. Hofstede's (1980) concept of national variation in culture has been heavily criticized for similar reasons (McSweeney 2002).

4. Country-level differences do not only account for major cultural and institutional variation, but also explain 91 percent of the regional differences in youth unemployment rates, 51 percent of the variation of the share of lower-skill jobs, and 64 percent of the variation in young female labor force participation rates. Thus, our measure of the influence of macro level effects is conservative.

5. Since the CUPESSE data are purely cross-sectional, we cannot assess causality in a strict sense, which would require panel data.

6. Although in the full model unemployment fails to reach statistical significance, we are cautious about concluding that the variable is irrelevant, because the high negative correlation between female labor force participation rate and youth unemployment rate (–.75) may cause multicollinearity. The regional effect of unemployment might also be mediated by parent-child similarity.

7. Johnson (2005) and Stam, Verbakel, and de Graaf (2014) suggest that parenthood has different effects for men and women. We tested an interaction effect, which turned out not to be statistically significant. The gender effect disappears in a three-factor model for RIW (online appendix Table A7).

8. Replacing the variable for financial stability with personal income produces the same results, which also points to the instrumental perspective.

References

Alesina, Alberto, Yann Algan, Pierre Cahuc, and Paola Giuliano. 2015. Family values and the regulation of labor. *Journal of the European Economic Association* 13 (4): 599–630.

Bal, P. Matthijs, and Dorien Kooij. 2011. The relations between work centrality, psychological contracts, and job attitudes: The influence of age. *European Journal of Work and Organizational Psychology* 20 (4): 497–523.

Blau, Peter, and Otis Dudley Duncan. 1967. *The American occupational structure.* New York, NY: John Wiley & Sons.

Brief, Arthur P. 1998. *Attitudes in and around organizations.* Foundations for Organizational Science 9. Thousand Oaks, CA: Sage Publications.

Bush, Diane Mitsch, and Roberta G. Simmons. 1981. Socialization processes over the life course. In *Social psychology: Sociological perspectives*, eds. Morris Rosenberg and Ralph H. Turner, 133–64. New York, NY: Basic Books.

Cherrington, David J. 1980. *The work ethic: Working values and values that work.* New York, NY: Amacom.

Clark, Andrew E. 2003. Unemployment as a social norm: Psychological evidence from panel data. *Journal of Labor Economics* 21 (2): 323–51.

Dekas, Kathryn H., and Wayne E. Baker. 2014. Adolescent socialization and the development of adult work orientations. In *Adolescent experiences and adult work outcomes: Connections and causes*, 5184, eds. Heinrich R. Greve and Marc-David L. Seidel. Research in the Sociology of Work, 25. Bingley, UK: Emerald Group Publishing Limited.

Duranton, Gilles, Andrés Rodríguez-Pose, and Richard Sandall. 2009. Family types and the persistence of regional disparities in Europe. *Economic Geography* 85 (1): 23–47.

Durkheim, Emile. 1893/2014. *The division of labor in society*. New York, NY: Simon and Schuster.

England, George W., and Itzhak Harpaz. 1983. Some methodological and analytic considerations in cross-national comparative research. *Journal of International Business Studies* 14 (2): 49–59.

England, George W., and William T. Whitely. 1990. Cross-national meanings of working. In *Meanings of occupational work*, eds. Arthur P. Brief and Walter R. Nord, 65–106. Lexington, MA: Lexington Books.

Esser, Ingrid. 2009. Has safety made us lazy? Employment commitment in different welfare states. In *British social attitudes: The 25th report*, 79–106. London: Sage Publications.

Eurostat. 2018. NUTS principles and characteristics. Available from https://ec.europa.eu/eurostat/en/web/nuts/background (accessed 8 January 2018).

Furnham, Adrian. 1990. A content, correlational, and factor analytic study of seven questionnaire measures of the protestant work ethic. *Human Relations* 43 (4): 383–99.

Gallie, Duncan. 2007. Production regimes and the quality of employment in Europe. *Annual Review of Sociology* 33:85–104.

Gallie, Duncan. 2019. Research on work values in a changing economic and social context. *The ANNALS of the American Academy of Political and Social Science* (this volume).

Gallie, Duncan, Alan Felstead, and Francis Green. 2012. Job preferences and the intrinsic quality of work: The changing attitudes of British employees 1992–2006. *Work, Employment and Society* 26 (5): 806–21.

Grusec, Joan E., and Leon Ed Kuczynski. 1997. *Parenting and children's internalization of values: A handbook of contemporary theory*. New York, NY: John Wiley & Sons Inc.

Halaby, Charles N. 2003. Where job values come from: Family and schooling background, cognitive ability, and gender. *American Sociological Review* 68 (2): 251–78.

Hanlon, Martin D. 1986. Age and commitment to work: A literature review and multivariate analysis. *Research on Aging* 8 (2): 289–316.

Harpaz, Itzhak. 2002. Expressing a wish to continue or stop working as related to the meaning of work. *European Journal of Work and Organizational Psychology* 11 (2): 177–98.

Harpaz, Itzhak, and Xuanning Fu. 1997. Work centrality in Germany, Israel, Japan, and the United States. *Cross-Cultural Research* 31 (3): 171–200.

Highhouse, Scott, Michael J. Zickar, and Maya Yankelevich. 2010. Would you work if you won the lottery? Tracking changes in the American work ethic. *Journal of Applied Psychology* 95 (2): 349–57.

Hitlin, Steven. 2006. Parental influences on children's values and aspirations: Bridging two theories of social class and socialization. *Sociological Perspectives* 49 (1): 25–46.

Hofstede, Geert. 1980. *Culture's consequences: International differences in work-related values*. Cross-Cultural Research and Methodology Series, 5. Beverly Hills, CA: Sage Publications.

Hooghe, Liesbet, and Gary Marks. 2018. Cleavage theory meets Europe's crises: Lipset, Rokkan, and the transnational cleavage. *Journal of European Public Policy* 25 (1): 109–35.

Hudson, Kenneth. 2007. The new labor market segmentation: Labor market dualism in the new economy. *Social Science Research* 36 (1): 286–312.

Jin, Jing, and James Rounds. 2012. Stability and change in work values: A meta-analysis of longitudinal studies. *Journal of Vocational Behavior* 80 (2): 326–39.

Johnson, Monica Kirkpatrick. 2001. Change in job values during the transition to adulthood. *Work and Occupations* 28 (3): 315–45.

Johnson, Monica Kirkpatrick. 2002. Social origins, adolescent experiences, and work value trajectories during the transition to adulthood. *Social Forces* 80 (4): 1307–40.

Johnson, Monica Kirkpatrick. 2005. Family roles and work values: Processes of selection and change. *Journal of Marriage and Family* 67 (2): 352–69.

Johnson, Monica Kirkpatrick, Rayna Amber Sage, and Jeylan T. Mortimer. 2012. Work values, early career difficulties, and the U.S. economic recession. *Social Psychology Quarterly* 75 (3): 242–67.

Kalleberg, Arne L. 1977. Work values and job rewards: A theory of job satisfaction. *American Sociological Review* 42 (1): 124–43.

Kalleberg, Arne L., and Peter V. Marsden. 2013. Changing work values in the United States, 1973–2006. *Social Science Research* 42 (2): 255–70.

Kanfer, Ruth, Connie R. Wanberg, and Tracy M. Kantrowitz. 2001. Job search and employment: A personality–motivational analysis and meta-analytic review. *Journal of Applied Psychology* 86 (5): 837–55.

Kohn, Melvin L., and Carmi Schooler. 1969. Class, occupation, and orientation. *American Sociological Review* 34 (5): 659–78.

Lipset, Seymour Martin, and Stein Rokkan. 1967. *Party systems and voter alignments: Cross-national perspectives*, vol. 7. New York, NY: Free Press.

Long, Theodore E., and Jeffrey K. Hadden. 1985. A reconception of socialization. *Sociological Theory* 3 (1): 39–49.

Mannheim, Bilha. 1993. Gender and the effects of demographics, status, and work values on work centrality. *Work and Occupations* 20 (1): 3–22.

Maslow, Abraham H. 1954. *Motivation and personality*. New York, NY: Harper & Row.

McSweeney, Brendan. 2002. Hofstede's model of national cultural differences and their consequences: A triumph of faith - a failure of analysis. *Human Relations* 55 (1): 89–118.

Morse, Nancy C., and Robert S. Weiss. 1955. The function and meaning of work and the job. *American Sociological Review* 20 (2): 191–98.

Mortimer, Jeylan T. 1974. Patterns of intergenerational occupational movements: A smallest-space analysis. *American Journal of Sociology* 79 (5): 1278–99.

Mortimer, Jeylan T., and Jon Lorence. 1979. Work experience and occupational value socialization: A longitudinal study. *American Journal of Sociology* 84 (6): 1361–85.

Mortimer, Jeylan T., Jon Lorence, and Donald S. Kumka. 1986. *Work, family, and personality: Transition to adulthood*. New York, NY: Ablex Publishing.

Mortimer, Jeylan T., Ellen Efron Pimentel, Seongryeol Ryu, Katherine Nash, and Chaimun Lee. 1996. Part-time work and occupational value formation in adolescence. *Social Forces* 74 (4): 1405–18.

Nord, Walter R., Arthur P. Brief, Jennifer M. Atieh, and Elizabeth M. Doherty. 1988. Work values and the conduct of organizational-behavior. *Research in Organizational Behavior* 10:1–42.

Parboteeah, K. Praveen, and John B. Cullen. 2003. Social institutions and work centrality: Explorations beyond national culture. *Organization Science* 14 (2): 137–48.

Roberts, Robert E. L., and Vern L. Bengtson. 1999. The social psychology of values: Effects of individual development, social change, and family transmission over the life span. In *The self and society in aging processes*, eds. Carol D. Ryff and Victor W. Marshall, 453–82. New York, NY: Springer.

Ros, Maria, Shalom H. Schwartz, and Shoshana Surkiss. 1999. Basic individual values, work values, and the meaning of work. *Applied Psychology* 48 (1): 49–71.

Rosenberg, Morris. 1979. *Conceiving the self*. New York, NY: Basic Books.

Rosso, Brent D., Kathryn H. Dekas, and Amy Wrzesniewski. 2010. On the meaning of work: A theoretical integration and review. *Research in Organizational Behavior* 30:91–127.

Sagie, Abraham, Dov Elizur, and Meni Koslowsky. 1996. Work values: A theoretical overview and a model of their effects. *Journal of Organizational Behavior* 17:503–14.

Sewell, William H., Archibald O. Haller, and George W. Ohlendorf. 1970. The educational and early occupational status attainment process: Replication and revision. *American Sociological Review* 35 (6): 1014–27.

Snir, Raphael, and Itzhak Harpaz. 2006. The workaholism phenomenon: A cross-national perspective. *Career Development International* 11 (5): 374–93.

Stam, Kirsten, Ellen Verbakel, and Paul M. de Graaf. 2013. Explaining variation in work ethic in Europe. *European Societies* 15 (2): 268–89.

Stam, Kirsten, Ellen Verbakel, and Paul M. de Graaf. 2014. Do values matter? The impact of work ethic and traditional gender role values on female labour market supply. *Social Indicators Research* 116 (2): 593–610.

Steiber, Nadia. 2013. Economic downturn and work motivation. In *Economic crisis, quality of work, and social integration*, ed. Duncan Gallie, 195–228. New York, NY: Oxford University Press.

Tabellini, Guido. 2010. Culture and institutions: Economic development in the regions of Europe. *Journal of the European Economic Association* 8 (4): 677–716.

Tosun, Jale, José L. Arco-Tirado, Maurizio Caserta, Zeynep Cemalcilar, Markus Freitag, Felix Hörisch, Carsten Jensen, Bernhard Kittel, Levente Littvay, and Martin Lukeš, et al. 2018. Perceived economic self-sufficiency: A country- and generation-comparative approach. *European Political Science*. doi:10.1057/s41304-018-0186-3.

Turunen, Teemu, and Jouko Nätti. 2017. The effects of employee and country characteristics on employment commitment in Europe. *European Societies* 19 (3): 313–35.

van der Wel, Kjetil A., and Knut Halvorsen. 2015. The bigger the worse? A comparative study of the welfare state and employment commitment. *Work, Employment and Society* 29 (1): 99–118.

Walsh, Kate, and Judith R. Gordon. 2008. Creating an individual work identity. *Human Resource Management Review* 18 (1): 46–61.

Warr, Peter. 2008. Work values: Some demographic and cultural correlates. *Journal of Occupational and Organizational Psychology* 81 (4): 751–75.

Weber, Max. 1904/2005. *Die protestantische Ethik und der Geist des Kapitalismus*. München: FinanzBuch Verlag.

Whiston, Susan C., and Briana K. Keller. 2004. The influences of the family of origin on career development: A review and analysis. *The Counseling Psychologist* 32 (4): 493–568.

Whitbeck, Les B., and Viktor Gecas. 1988. Value attributions and value transmission between parents and children. *Journal of Marriage and Family* 50 (3): 829–40.

Wrench, John, Andrea Rea, and Nouria Ouali, eds. 1999. *Migrants, ethnic minorities and the labour market: Integration and exclusion in Europe*. London: MacMillan.

Wrzesniewski, Amy, Clark McCauley, Paul Rozin, and Barry Schwartz. 1997. Jobs, careers, and callings: People's relations to their work. *Journal of Research in Personality* 31 (1): 21–33.

Gendered Intergenerational Transmission of Work Values? A Country Comparison

By
ZEYNEP CEMALCILAR,
CARSTEN JENSEN,
and
JALE TOSUN

In this study, we examine two research questions: Are the work values of young people determined by the work values of their parents? Is the transmission of work values conditioned by the young adults' gender? We use original survey data for respondents aged 18–35 and their parents in Denmark, Germany, Turkey, and the UK to explore these questions. Our findings reveal a robust pattern: in all four countries and for all four types of work values we measure, young adults' work values are strongly influenced by their parents' work values. We also find a gender effect among German respondents: work plays a more central role in the lives of young men than in the lives of young women. Gender helps to explain attitudes toward female labor force participation in all of the countries we studied, and we find no evidence that gender conditions the effect of the intergenerational transmission of work values except for in the UK, where gender does condition the effect of family attitudes on young peoples' extrinsic work values and their views on work centrality.

Keywords: defamilization; gender; parent-child dyads; transmission; work values

Values are internalized social representations or moral beliefs that people call on to rationalize their actions (Oyserman 2002). Work values, more specifically, refer to individuals' attitudes about how important work is and whether individuals pursue tangible or intangible rewards in their jobs (see Kraaykamp, Cemalcilar, and Tosun, this volume). Empirical

Zeynep Cemalcılar is an associate professor of social psychology at Koc University, Istanbul, Turkey. Her most recent research focuses on youth autonomy and self-sufficiency, subjective socioeconomic status, brief social psychological interventions, and the role of technology in social life.

Carsten Jensen is a professor in the Department of Political Science at Aarhus University. His research is focused on the causes and consequences of redistributive politics in advanced western democracies, as well as democratic representation more broadly.

Correspondence: zcemalcilar@ku.edu.tr

DOI: 10.1177/0002716218823681

research in the social sciences has shown that work values predict a variety of work-related outcomes, including vocational aspirations, career choices, decision-making processes such as to look for a job, or to get training, job selection, as well as job satisfaction (e.g., Ros, Schwartz, and Surkiss 1999). These work-related outcomes have an impact on the well-being of individuals (e.g., Blanchflower and Oswald 2011), and how individuals participate in politics (e.g., Norris 2013) and society (e.g., Rupasingha, Goetz, and Freshwater 2006). In this article, we investigate the transmission of work values within the family. Since youth represents the phase when many critical decisions are made with regard to educational and career choices (see Busemeyer and Jensen 2012), we concentrate on the work values of 18–35 year olds (Krahn and Galambos 2014).

The acquisition of (work) values takes place primarily through socialization in family, groups, and society (Cieciuch, Schwartz, and Davidov 2015). Families are ascribed a key role in the process of value acquisition. There are two pathways that explain the effect of families on the development of values. One is a genetic explanation and assumes that parents and children share similar values because of a hereditary effect (e.g., Kandler, Gottschling, and Spinath 2016). The second is an environmental explanation and assumes that parent-child value transmission is due to socialization, in which parents both provide contextual opportunities for their children, and act as major role models (e.g., Hitlin 2006). Here, we investigate the latter phenomenon, also known as "cultural" or "intergenerational" transmission (see, e.g., Schönpflug 2001; Trommsdorff 2008; Kraaykamp and Van Eijck 2010). More precisely, we are interested in the intergenerational transmission of work values and how the outcomes of this process depend on young people's gender and the cultural context in which are they are raised. Even in a region such as Europe, with otherwise striking similarities at the economic, social, and political levels, the participation of women in the labor force varies considerably (e.g., Steiber and Haas 2012), arguably giving way to cross-country variation in the work values of men and women as well as how these differences emerge.

Work-related values have been the subject of investigation in different disciplines, including, but not limited to, psychology, sociology, business, and economics. Hence, the literature suggests various conceptualizations and operationalizations of work values (see Sparrow, Chadrakumara, and Perera 2010). Research also suggests that different types of work values may influence work and well-being outcomes differently (Arslan 2001). To acknowledge such variation in the definition of work values, and also to allow for an investigation of whether

Jale Tosun is a professor at the Institute of Political Science at Heidelberg University. Her research focuses on comparative public policy, international political economy, and public administration.

NOTE: We recognize financial support by the project Cultural Pathways to Economic Self-Sufficiency and Entrepreneurship (CUPESSE; Seventh Framework Program of the European Union; Grant Agreement No. 613257). We further acknowledge helpful comments on this article by Thomas Klein, Gerbert Kraaykamp, Kyriakos Pierrakakis and Georg Wenzelburger. Dominic Afscharian and Lucas Leopold provided research assistance.

different work values may emerge differently in different contexts, in our analyses we differentiate between four types of work-related values and test our models in four different national contexts with varying cultural, social, and economic characteristics: Denmark, Germany, Turkey, and the UK. Specifically, as our dependent variables, we use (1) *work centrality*, that is, how important work is relative to family, leisure, and personal life; (2) *intrinsic work values* that relate to intangible rewards related to the process of work, such as having an interesting job, working autonomously, or having a chance for personal growth; (3) *extrinsic work values* that relate to external rewards, including status recognition, high and stable income, and opportunities for career advancements; and (4) *gender-role work values*, which captures more specifically attitudes on the labor force participation of women (see Crompton, Brockmann, and Lyonette 2005). Jointly we refer to these four types of work-related values as *work values* and test our hypotheses separately for each of them.

This article addresses two research questions: (1) Are the work values of young people determined by the work values of their parents? (2) Is the transmission of work values conditioned by the young adults' gender? We use data originating from the Cultural Pathways to Economic Self-Sufficiency and Entrepreneurship (CUPESSE) project (see Tosun et al. 2018), and to further test the generalizability of these questions, we compare and contrast our analyses across four national contexts, with varying cultural, social, and economic characteristics. Specifically, we look at Denmark, Germany, Turkey, and the UK.

Theoretical Considerations and Hypotheses

The prolific research on the intergenerational transmission of values has focused mainly on basic values (Schwartz 1999), including openness to change, self enhancement, conservation, and self-transcendence (Grusec and Davidov 2007; Roest, Dubas, and Gerris 2009; Kraaykamp, Tolsma, and Wolbers 2013). In contrast to basic human values, work values constitute domain-specific values, and refer to the expression of basic values in the work setting (Ros, Schwartz, and Surkiss 1999). Despite being a specific type of value, a recent meta-analytical review carried out by Cemalcilar, Secinti, and Sumer (2018) with thirty studies conducted in eleven countries supported a positive but medium association ($r = .20, p < .001$) between parent work values and youth work values.

Our first research question concerns the transmission of work values within family contexts by means of socialization. Parents convey their attitudes, beliefs, and values to their children directly through active education as well as indirectly through everyday routines and through the opportunities they provide to their children (Kraaykamp, Tolsma, and Wolbers 2013; Döring et al. 2017). In line with the literature on the intergenerational transmission of (work) values (e.g., Schönpflug 2001; Trommsdorff 2008; Kraaykamp and Van Eijck 2010), we expect youth's work values to be associated with the work values of their parents. However, as work values are also likely to be affected by socialization contexts other than the parents (such as peer groups), we expect a moderate association between the work values of young people and their parents (Hypothesis H1).

Our second research question concerns whether the transmission of work values is conditioned by the young adults' gender. We utilize two hypotheses to investigate this question. As the employment participation of women started to expand in many countries in the 1980s, and given that women are still confronted with practical challenges, such as childcare, when pursuing a full-time job (Steiber and Haas 2012), it is plausible to expect a difference between the work values of women vis-à-vis men (see Gallie, this volume). The social-role approach, the dominant approach to understanding gender-role beliefs, attributes the sources of these beliefs to the different social roles performed by men and women (Eagly and Wood 2013). In the ideology of separate gender roles (traditional family model), women are primarily responsible for the home, child rearing, and maintenance of good relationships. Men, in contrast, are primarily responsible for the financial support of the family. Empirical research has shown that such differences between men and women continue to exist (e.g., Lips and Lawson 2009; see Eagly and Wood 2013 for an overview). Therefore, we hypothesize that young men will have stronger work-related values than young women (Hypothesis H2).

While H1 and H2 postulate unconditional relationships between the variables, it appears reasonable to formulate an interaction hypothesis that postulates a conditional relationship among work values, intergenerational value transmission, and gender. For example, a study by Roest, Dubas, and Gerris (2009) shows that parents do not necessarily equally transmit all basic human values, but they do so selectively, caring for their own preferences as well as their respective views on gender. In this context, Boehnke, Hadjar, and Baier (2007) suggest that values of power and achievement are more likely to be passed on to sons, whereas values of care are more likely to be transmitted to the daughters in the family. Consequently, Hypothesis H3 states that the effect of intergenerational transmission on the work values of young people is conditional on their gender.

We do not expect intra-familial value transmission to be independent of the context effects (Boehnke, Hadjar, and Baier 2007). Socialization is, by definition, a process whereby individuals acquire the values, standards, and customs of the groups and the society in which they live and acquire the ability to function in an adaptive way in their social context (Grusec and Davidov 2007). To explore whether the intergenerational transmission of work values, gender, and the interaction between both plays out differently in varying country contexts, we test these three hypotheses in four national contexts (RQ1).

As the four countries differ from each other in multitudes of cultural, socioeconomic, and political characteristics, we refrain from making specific predictions regarding cultural differences in the transmission of work-related values, with one exception. Among the four types of work values that we study, it is most probable to see some effect of culture on the gender-role-based work values. Parents' beliefs about work-related gender roles are conceived to be affected by the respective norms in the four countries. Hult and Svallfors (2002), for example, report that different national production regimes correspond to different levels and patterns of employment commitment among the working population.

Likewise, Jaeger (2006, 159) stresses the importance of "frames of reference of what individuals consider to be 'normal' or 'appropriate'" for the formation of attitudes and values (see also Gallie and Alm 2000). More specifically, the gender-role beliefs that are dominant in a culture are influenced by the distribution of gender-related tasks and power distribution (Eagly and Wood 2013). In the ideology of separate gender roles (i.e., the traditional family model), women are primarily responsible for the home, child rearing, and maintenance of good relationships. Men, in contrast, are primarily responsible for the financial support of the family. Hence, in cultures with stronger traditional gender-role beliefs, the type and strength of the values that transmit within the family may depend on the gender of the parent as well as the gender of the child. Accordingly, by contrasting our models across the four cultures, we investigate whether the intergenerational transmission of value, gender, and the interaction between both plays out differently in varying country contexts. Among the four countries included in this study, Turkey ranks highest on collectivism (Hofstede, Hofstede, and Minkov 2010). Hence, we expect Turkey to differ from the three European countries, specifically on the gender-role work value.

Data and Methodology

In this section we provide details on the database used for the analysis and the operationalization of the variables.

Data description

The selection of databases is one of the most important design choices in empirical investigation and warrants enhanced attention (see, e.g., Wenzelburger, Zohlnhöfer, and Wolf 2013). Both considerations about data quality and the availability of empirical information for being able to gauge the theoretical constructs of interest are important.

This study relies on data produced by the CUPESSE two-generation survey, which is reported on extensively by Tosun et al. (2018). CUPESSE data are nationally representative and innovative because they comprise responses from both young people (18–35 years old) and their parents. Both the youth and parental questionnaires were conducted online in Denmark, Germany, and the UK, and face-to-face using paper and pencil in Turkey. We ran analyses to rule out that the variation between the data for Turkey and the other countries stems from survey mode effects. The data collection was carried out throughout spring and fall 2016. We drew a proportionally stratified sample (taking into account age, employment status, etc.) and surveyed 1,142 young people and 403 parents in Denmark; 3,279 young people and 480 parents in Germany; 3,016 young people and 537 parents in Turkey; and 3,004 young people and 499 parents in the UK. Given the cross-sectional nature of the data, we did not apply imputation techniques for missing data.

Measurement

Work-related values. Four types of work-related values function as our dependent variables. *Work-centrality* is assessed as an additive index of the following four items: "to fully develop your talents, you need to have a job"; "it's humiliating to receive money without having to work"; "work is a duty toward society"; "work should always come first even if it means less spare time." Respondents could (strongly) (dis)agree with each statement on a scale from 0 to 3. The 4-item index had a Cronbach's alpha of 0.67. In the next set of questions, the respondents were asked to determine the importance they attributed to different characteristics of a job, with response options ranging from very unimportant (=0) to very important (=3). *Extrinsic work values* are assessed by their responses to the two items about how important it is to have a secure job and/or a high income (Cronbach's alpha: 0.61). *Intrinsic work values*, on the other hand, are assessed by their responses to the two items; job allowing me to work independently and job allowing me to develop my creativity (Cronbach's alpha: 0.57). The fourth and final dependent variable, *gender-role work values*, is operationalized by the following question: "A man's job is to earn money; a woman's job is to look after the home and family." The respondents can (very) strongly agree (=3) or disagree (=0) with this statement, a high score suggesting a more traditional perspective.

Explanatory variables. We use the parents' responses to the same questions on their work values for gauging whether these values may have been transmitted from the parents to their children. We further generate a binary variable, *female*, for differentiating between the respondents' sex. We also use the variables to generate interaction terms. Table A1 in the online appendix presents the descriptive statistics.

Control variables. We control for various factors that, based on theoretical constraints, may impede the expected associations that we investigate. Most important, familial influence on youth is likely to decline across adolescence, as other socialization sources, such as peers, gain importance (Cemalcilar et al. 2018), and therefore we control for *age*. The variable *work status* differentiates between respondents being economically inactive (e.g., due to unemployment), in employment, and in education. Further, we need to control for whether the respondents still live with their parents, since this should have an impact on the intensity of the socialization process (*living with parents*). Another factor we control for is whether the young people surveyed belong to an *immigration* group. For example, Vedder, Sabatier, and Sam (2009) observed that, for the majority groups, parent-child value similarity was high, whereas for nonmainstream families, the contextual effect was stronger than within-family influence. *Financial satisfaction* is the measurement we use to include a control for the subjective perception of the economic situation, running from very dissatisfied (=0) to very satisfied (=3). We also take into account whether the respondents have *caring* responsibilities (including children of minor age) and how they characterize their relationship with their parents (*relation mother; relation father*), ranging from "very bad" (=0) to "very good" (=4). Parents transmit values also through the opportunities they provide to their children (see Kraaykamp, Tolsma, and Wolbers 2013; Döring et al. 2017). Therefore, we control for the economic condition of the respondents during their childhood (*economy childhood*).

Findings

Considering the measurement level of the dependent variables and their distributional properties, we estimate linear regression models separately for the four operationalizations of work values. Model 1 presents the analyses concerning intergenerational transmission of work values (H1) and gender main effects (H2). Model 2 adds the two-way interaction terms for gender and intergenerational value transmission (H3). By comparing the models across the four countries, we make inferences about whether value transmission differs across national contexts. We summarize the findings for the focal variables in Table 1. For a presentation of the full models, including the effects of the control, please see online appendix Tables A2–A5.

An investigation of Table 1 supports our reasoning regarding the intergenerational transmission of work-related values (H1), for all four types of work values and for all countries (see coefficients for model 1). Yet the strength of the association between parent-child work values varies for the specific value tested, and for the four countries under investigation. In general, the transmission of work-centrality and gender-role work values is stronger than the extrinsic and intrinsic work values. The effect size is greatest for respondents from the UK, where a one-unit increase in the parents' values increases the youth respondents' values by 0.5 units (model 1). The weakest effects is for intrinsic work values in Denmark (.11 units).

When inspecting model 1 and model 2 fitted for each of the four countries, our findings do not suggest a systematic gender main effect (H2) nor a systematic interaction effect of gender and parent work values (H3). Overall, females do not significantly differ from males concerning their attitudes on the importance of work. Next, we discuss the findings for specific work-values.

For *work centrality*, we obtain a positive and significant coefficient for *female* (H2) as well as the interaction term for gender and intergenerational transmission (H3) for the respondents from the UK. The results can be interpreted as follows: a one-unit increase in the parents' values for *work centrality* leads to an increase in the youth's values for *work centrality* by 0.6 units when the respondents are men. Female respondents have 0.3-unit higher values on *work centrality* if their parents indicated that they do not value *work centrality* at all. When a respondent is female, the effect of the parents' *work centrality* on the *work centrality* of the young adults decreases by 0.2 units. Put differently, in the UK, the effect of the intergenerational transmission of *work centrality* is conditioned by the effect of gender; the effect of transmission is weaker if the respondent is a

TABLE 1
Estimation Results for Youths' Work-Related Values

	Denmark		Germany		UK		Turkey	
	Model 1	Model 2	Model 1	Model 2	Model 1	Model 2	Model 1	Model 2
Work centrality								
Parents' work centrality	0.20 $(0.06)^{***}$	0.25 $(0.09)^{***}$	0.41 $(0.05)^{***}$	0.46 $(0.07)^{***}$	0.51 $(0.04)^{***}$	0.61 $(0.06)^{***}$	0.31 $(0.04)^{***}$	0.33 $(0.06)^{***}$
Female	0.01 (0.06)	0.18 (0.22)	0.10 $(0.06)^{*}$	0.28 (0.19)	−0.04 (0.05)	0.34 $(0.16)^{**}$	−0.05 (0.04)	0.02 (0.21)
Female x parents' work centrality		−0.10 (0.12)		−0.09 (0.09)		−0.20 $(0.08)^{**}$		−0.03 (0.09)
Adjusted R^2	0.037	0.036	0.186	0.186	0.270	0.279	0.104	0.102
Extrinsic work values								
Parents' extrinsic work values	0.14 $(0.06)^{**}$	0.23 $(0.09)^{**}$	0.25 $(0.05)^{***}$	0.19 $(0.08)^{**}$	0.29 $(0.05)^{***}$	0.37 $(0.06)^{***}$	0.27 $(0.04)^{***}$	0.24 $(0.06)^{***}$
Female	0.04 (0.05)	0.32 (0.24)	0.04 (0.05)	−0.18 (0.25)	0.03 (0.05)	0.42 $(0.21)^{*}$	−0.04 (0.04)	−0.21 (0.24)
Female x parents' extrinsic work values		−0.14 (0.12)		0.09 (0.10)		−0.17 $(0.09)^{*}$		0.06 (0.09)
Adjusted R^2	0.042	0.044	0.082	0.082	0.102	0.108	0.077	0.077
Intrinsic work values								
Parents' intrinsic work values	0.11 $(0.06)^{*}$	−0.02 (0.10)	0.29 $(0.05)^{***}$	0.26 $(0.07)^{***}$	0.27 $(0.05)^{***}$	0.32 $(0.07)^{***}$	0.30 $(0.04)^{***}$	0.29 $(0.06)^{***}$
Female	−0.03 (0.07)	−0.45 $(0.27)^{*}$	0.11 $(0.06)^{*}$	0.00 (0.22)	−0.07 (0.06)	0.13 (0.20)	−0.06 (0.05)	−0.12 (0.20)
Female x parents' intrinsic work values		0.20 (0.12)		0.05 (0.10)		−0.10 (0.10)		0.03 (0.08)
Adjusted R^2	0.009	0.013	0.120	0.118	0.119	0.119	0.113	0.112
Gender-role work values								
Parents' gender-role work values	0.27 $(0.05)^{***}$	0.30 $(0.09)^{***}$	0.38 $(0.05)^{***}$	0.45 $(0.07)^{***}$	0.34 $(0.04)^{***}$	0.38 $(0.06)^{***}$	0.33 $(0.05)^{***}$	0.36 $(0.07)^{***}$
Female	−0.11 $(0.06)^{*}$	−0.10 (0.06)	−0.16 $(0.09)^{*}$	−0.03 (0.13)	−0.30 $(0.07)^{***}$	−0.20 (0.12)	−0.33 $(0.10)^{***}$	−0.22 (0.22)
Female x parents' gender-role work values		−0.05 (0.11)		−0.12 (0.09)		−0.09 (0.09)		−0.06 (0.10)
Adjusted R^2	0.082	0.080	0.217	0.218	0.200	0.200	0.107	0.106

NOTE: Adjusted R^2 are for the full model. See online appendix Tables A2–A5 for the full models.
$^{*} p < 0.05.$ $^{**}p < 0.01.$ $^{***}p < 0.001.$

female (see Figure 1). When comparing the model fit statistics obtained for the four countries, we can see that the explanatory power of the model is best for the UK, as indicated by the adjusted R^2 values.

FIGURE 1

Visualization of the Interaction Effect for Work Centrality in the UK

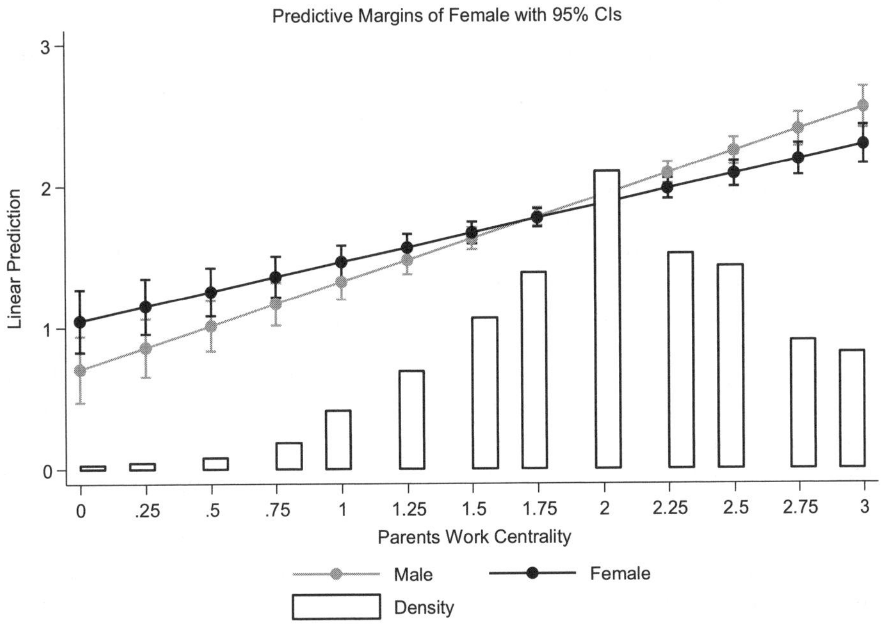

Turning to *extrinsic work values*, we obtain similar findings to the previous outcome variable. For all countries, we can observe positive and significant coefficients for the parents' *extrinsic work values*. The gender variable fails to produce coefficients at conventional levels of significance for all countries, except for in the UK. The regression results reported in Table 1 show that *female* produces a positive and significant coefficient and the interaction term between gender and the parents values' produces a negative coefficient, which is significant at the 10 percent level. The effect of the interaction effect can be interpreted as analogous to the previous one: the effect of intergenerational value transmission on *extrinsic work values* is weaker for female respondents.

The regression results for *intrinsic work values* deviate from the previous findings to the extent that the coefficient for intergenerational transmission is significant only at the 10 percent level, and even insignificant in model 2 fitted with data for Denmark. For the other countries, we continue to observe positive and significant coefficients for the parents' *intrinsic work values*. Respondents in Denmark are also the only ones for which we obtain a significant (and negative) coefficient for female respondents. The coefficient tells us that female respondents have lower values than men do, if their parents scored low on *intrinsic work values*.

The regression results of the fourth outcome variable as shown in Table 1 confirm our reasoning that intergenerational transmission matters for explaining the values of the variable *gender-role work values*. However, gender now also produces significant and negative coefficients for respondents from all four countries: young women have lower scores on that outcome variable than young men. This is the first time we can confirm the reasoning underlying H2. Yet it should be noted that in the models that include the interaction terms the coefficients of *female* are insignificant, and so are the coefficients of the interaction terms themselves. This means that the effect of gender is direct, and it also does not moderate the effect of intergenerational value transmission. The lack of a systematic difference across countries with varying levels of collectivism and traditionalism suggest a micro-level, individual difference effect rather than a macro-level contextual effect. It is interesting that male respondents (in all four countries) rather than females reported higher gender-role work values.

Table 2 summarizes the findings of our analysis, broken down by hypotheses and work values. We obtained the most consistent and compelling results for H1, which was confirmed for all countries for three out of four measurements of work values. H2 was confirmed once for the UK; in addition, we found some evidence for H2 for the determinants of *extrinsic work values* in the UK and *intrinsic work values* in Denmark. Only for *work centrality*—and, to a weaker degree, for *extrinsic work values* in the UK—did we find support for H3. Overall, however, cross-country variation seemed much less marked than we anticipated. Most remarkably, the effect of intergenerational transmission of work values is robust across different measurements of work values and across countries with marked cultural differences regarding the participation of women in the labor market.

As we can infer from Tables A2–A5 in the online appendix, some of the control variables have significant effects on work values. *Age* has a negative effect on work centrality and extrinsic work values for respondents in Denmark. As they age, people are less likely to place work in the center of their lives (hence are likely to also value other domains of life, such as family or leisure activities), and

TABLE 2
Summary of Findings

Hypothesis	Work Centrality	Extrinsic Work Values	Intrinsic Work values	Gender-Role Work Values
H1	All	All	Germany, UK, Turkey	All
H2	UK	(UK)	(Denmark, Germany)	All
H3	UK	(UK)		
RQ1	Country differences H2–H3	Weak country differences H2–H3	Country differences H1–H2	No country differences

NOTE: Countries in parentheses indicate that the coefficients were significant at the 10-percent-level only.

are less likely to seek a secure and high paying job. *Living with parents* has a positive effect on the work centrality and intrinsic work values of respondents in the UK. On the other hand, the same control variable has a negative effect for work-centrality and gender-role work values of respondents in Turkey. *Financial satisfaction* decreases the level of work values, with a significant effect for work-centrality for respondents in the UK, extrinsic work values in Denmark and the UK, and intrinsic work values in Germany. Finally, respondents in Turkey with *caring responsibilities* are less likely to have higher intrinsic work values and respondents in Germany and the UK with caring responsibilities agree more with a traditional understanding of the division of work between men and women. Yet it is possible that many of these control variables signify the direct or indirect effects of other background variables (such as parenting style, living conditions while growing up) that may impede upon young individuals work values. Furthermore they are likely to call for the remaining portion of variance to be explained in understanding how young people acquire work values.

Conclusion

Are the work values of young people determined by the work values of their parents? Is the transmission of work values conditioned by the young adults' gender? Having run a series of analyses in four European countries, we are in a position to answer these questions. First, in the countries we studied, young adults' work values are strongly influenced by the work values of their parents. We found this for three measurements of work values, regardless of the country context.

Turning to our second research question, we found some evidence of a gender effect—both direct and indirect—but our results did not reveal a clear pattern that is robust across the different measurements of work values or country contexts. The effect of gender is less prominent than we anticipated, even in a country such as Turkey, where gender differences are most marked. Having said that, though, we did find gender effects in all countries for the fourth measurement of work values—women being responsible for the household and men being the breadwinners. Finding a gender effect for that measurement is plausible since it also represents the most gendered of all outcome variables used for the analyses.

Our findings revealed that women hold views on their roles in labor markets that are more modern than men's; that is, they are less likely to agree with the statement that women should be primarily responsible for looking after the home, regardless of the country context. Overall, though, individuals in countries that are more "gender-defamilized" (Saxonberg 2013), that is, where economic independence of females from the family unit is secured, do not hold markedly different attitudes on work values than individuals in countries that are "gender-familized" (on the concept, see Esping-Andersen 1999), that is, where the family unit plays an important role for securing the economic situation of females. The work values of individuals in countries as different as Denmark and Turkey, for instance, do not vary as much as one would have anticipated. This suggests that the intergenerational transmission is a powerful mechanism in the formation of work values and functions regardless of the characteristics of the youth welfare regimes in place in the countries (on this concept, see Chevalier 2016).

What are the broader implications of our findings? First, as prior research suggests, work values play a role in determining whether individuals are partially or fully economically independent. This means that work values are relevant for explaining the socioeconomic status of individuals. However, it is also possible that gender and country contexts matter when using work values as explanatory variables in models that seek to predict labor market outcomes. Second, having learned about the robust effect of socialization within families (see also Evans and Shen 2010), policy approaches and public service aiming to promote the (self-)employment of young people need to take into consideration the family context and include the parents in their outreach activities. However, designing such a policy is not straightforward for multiple reasons. One of them is the question of how and when to reach out to parents in an attempt to influence educational and career choices of their children. Another is the risk of stigmatizing certain families by inviting them to collaborate with state institutions in an attempt to improve their children's chances in the labor market. Policy interventions seeking to bring in parents to motivate their children concerning education and career choices (e.g., Harackiewicz et al. 2012) need to be aware of both the chances and challenges such an approach entails.

In closing, we want to stress the value of comparative empirical research on work values. At first glance, the countries selected for this study look very different from each other, suggesting that other mechanisms might be at work with the intergenerational transmission of work values and how gender plays a role in it. Yet our analysis revealed that in terms of the underlying mechanisms of intergenerational transmission, these countries are remarkably similar. Drawing from that observation, we invite future research to build on our methodological approach and to compare seemingly different countries to learn more about causality. Future research should also replicate this study by using longitudinal data, ideally for respondents in a greater number of countries, for that allows for a harder empirical test of hypothesized causal relationships. Thus, despite the growing body of literature on the intergenerational transmission of work values, there still exists numerous research perspectives to be addressed by future research.

References

Arslan, Mahmut. 2001. The work ethic values of Protestant British, Catholic Irish and Muslim Turkish managers. *Journal of Business Ethics* 31 (4): 321–39.

Blanchflower, David G., and Andrew J. Oswald. 2011. International happiness: A new view on the measure of performance. *The Academy of Management Perspectives* 25 (1): 6–22.

Boehnke, Klaus, Andreas Hadjar, and Dirk Baier. 2007. Parent-child value similarity: The role of zeitgeist. *Journal of Marriage and Family* 69 (3): 778–92.

Busemeyer, Marius R., and Carsten Jensen. 2012. The impact of economic coordination and educational institutions on individual-level preferences for academic and vocational education. *Socio-Economic Review* 10 (3): 525–47.

Cemalcilar, Zeynep, Ekin Secinti, and Nebi Sumer. 2018. Intergenerational transmission of work values: A meta-analytic review. *Journal of Youth and Adolescence* 47 (8): 1559–1579.

Cieciuch, Jan, Schalom H. Schwartz, and Eldad Davidov. 2015. The social psychologx of values. In *International encyclopedia of the social & behavioral sciences*, ed. James D. Wright, 41–46. Oxford: Elsevier.

Chevalier, Tom. 2016. Varieties of youth welfare citizenship: Towards a two-dimension typology. *Journal of European Social Policy* 26 (1): 3–19.

Crompton, Rosemary, Michaela Brockmann, and Clare Lyonette. 2005. Attitudes, women's employment and the domestic division of labour: A cross-national analysis in two waves. *Work, Employment and Society* 19 (2): 213–33.

Döring, Anna K., Elena Makarova, Walter Herzog, and Anat Bardi. 2017. Parent–child value similarity in families with young children: The predictive power of prosocial educational goals. *British Journal of Psychology* 108 (4): 737–56.

Eagly, Alice H., and Wendy Wood. 2013. The nature-nurture debates: 25 years of challenges in understanding the psychology of gender. *Perspectives on Psychological Science* 8 (3): 340–57.

Esping-Andersen, Gøsta. 1999. *Social foundations of postindustrial economies*. Oxford: Oxford University Press.

Evans, Jonathan, and Wei Shen, eds. 2010. *Youth employment and the future of work*. Strasbourg: Council of Europe Publishing.

Gallie, Duncan. 2019. Research on work values in a changing economic and social context. *The ANNALS of the American Academy of Political and Social Science* (this volume).

Gallie, Duncan, and Susanne Alm. 2000. Unemployment, gender and attitudes to work. In *Welfare regimes and the experience of unemployment in Europe*, eds. Duncan Gallie, and Serge Paugam, 109–33. Oxford: Oxford University Press.

Grusec, Joan E., and Maayan Davidov. 2007. Socialization in the family: The roles of parents. In *Handbook of socialization: Theory and research*, eds. Joan E. Grusec and Paul D. Hastings, 284–308. New York, NY: Guilford Press.

Harackiewicz, Judith M., Christopher S. Rozek, Chris S. Hulleman, and Janet S. Hyde. 2012. Helping parents to motivate adolescents in mathematics and science: An experimental test of a utility-value intervention. *Psychological Science* 23 (8): 899–906.

Hitlin, Steven. 2006. Parental influences on children's values and aspirations: Bridging two theories of social class and socialization. *Sociological Perspectives* 49 (1): 25–46.

Hofstede, Geert, Gert Jan Hofstede, and Michael Minkov. 2010. *Cultures and organizations: Software of the mind*. New York, NY: McGraw-Hill.

Hult, Carl, and Stefan Svallfors. 2002. Production regimes and work orientations: A comparison of six western countries. *European Sociological Review* 18 (3): 315–31.

Jaeger, Mads Meier. 2006. Welfare regimes and attitudes towards redistribution: The regime hypothesis revisited. *European Sociological Review* 22 (2): 157–70.

Kandler, Christian, Juliana Gottschling, and Frank M. Spinath. 2016. Genetic and environmental parent-child transmission of value orientations: An extended twin family study. *Child Development* 87 (1): 270–84.

Kraaykamp, Gerbet, Zeynep Cemalcilar, and Jale Tosun. 2019. Transmission of work attitudes and values: Comparisons, consequences, and implications. *The ANNALS of the American Academy of Political and Social Science* (this volume).

Kraaykamp, Gerbert, and Koen Van Eijck. 2010. The intergenerational reproduction of cultural capital: A threefold perspective. *Social forces* 89 (1): 209–31.

Kraaykamp, Gerbert, Jochem Tolsma, and Maarten H.J. Wolbers. 2013. Educational expansion and field of study: Trends in the intergenerational transmission of educational inequality in the Netherlands. *British Journal of Sociology of Education* 34 (5–6): 888–906.

Krahn, Harvey J., and Nancy L. Galambos. 2014. Work values and beliefs of "Generation X" and "Generation Y." *Journal of Youth Studies* 17 (1): 92–112.

Lips, Hilary, and Katie Lawson. 2009. Work values, gender, and expectations about work commitment and pay: Laying the groundwork for the "motherhood penalty"? *Sex Roles* 61 (9–10): 667–76.

Norris, Pippa. 2013. Women's legislative participation in Western Europe. In *Women and politics in Western Europe*, ed. Sylvia Bashevkin, 98–112. London: Routledge.

Oyserman, Daphna. 2002. Values, psychological perspectives. In *International encyclopedia of the social & behavioral sciences*, eds. Neil J. Smelser, and Paul B. Baltes, 16150–16153. New York, NY: Elsevier.

Roest, Annette M. C., Judith Semon Dubas, and Jan R. M. Gerris. 2009. Value transmissions between fathers, mothers, and adolescent and emerging adult children: The role of the family climate. *Journal of Family Psychology* 23 (2): 146–55.

Ros, Maria, Shalom H. Schwartz, and Shoshanna Surkiss. 1999. Basic individual values, work values, and the meaning of work. *Applied Psychology: An International Review* 48 (1): 49–71.

Rupasingha, Anil, Stephan J. Goetz, and David Freshwater. 2006. The production of social capital in U.S. counties. *The Journal of Socio-Economics* 35 (1): 83–101.

Saxonberg, Steven. 2013. From defamilialization to degenderization: Toward a new welfare typology. *Social Policy & Administration* 47 (1): 26–49.

Schönpflug, Ute. 2001. Intergenerational transmission of values: The role of transmission belts. *Journal of Cross-Cultural Psychology* 32 (2): 174–85.

Schwartz, Shalom H. 1999. A theory of cultural values and some implication for work. *Applied Psychology: An International Review* 48 (1): 23–47.

Sparrow, Paul R., Anil Chadrakumara, and Nelson Perera. 2010. Impact of work values and ethics on citizenship and task performance in local and foreign invested firms: A test in a developing country context. Paper presented at the 11th International Human Resource Management Conference.

Steiber, Nadia, and Barbara Haas. 2012. Advances in explaining women's employment patterns. *Socio-Economic Review* 10 (2): 343–67.

Tosun, Jale, José Arco-Tirado, Maurizio Caserta, Zeynep Cemalcilar, Markus Freitag, Felix Hörisch, Carsten Jensen, Bernhard Kittel, Levente Littvay, and Martin Lukes, et al. 2018. Perceived economic self-sufficiency: A country- and generation-comparative approach. *European Political Science*. DOI: 10.1057/s41304-018-0186-3.

Trommsdorff, Gisela. 2008. Intergenerational relations and cultural transmission. In *Cultural transmission: Psychological, developmental, social, and methodological aspects*, ed. Ute Schönpflug, 126–60. Cambridge: Cambridge University Press.

Vedder, Paul, John Berry, Colette Sabatier, and David Sam. 2009. The intergenerational transmission of values in national and immigrant families: The role of Zeitgeist. *Journal of Youth and Adolescence* 38 (5): 642–53.

Wenzelburger, Georg, Reimut Zohlnhöfer, and Frieder Wolf. 2013. Implications of dataset choice in comparative welfare state research. *Journal of European Public Policy* 20 (9): 1229–1250.

How Intergene-rational Mobility Shapes Attitudes toward Work and Welfare

BETTINA SCHUCK
and
JENNIFER SHORE

Past experiences and expectations about the future shape how people think about work and welfare. Given the uncertainty many young people face when entering the labor market, we investigate whether 1) young peoples' experiences of social mobility and 2) their future mobility expectations impact their attitudes regarding the meaning of work and welfare. Drawing on the concepts of self-interest and deservingness, we examine how both the experiences and expectations of intergenerational social mobility influence the ways in which young adults view the so-called moral dimension of work and welfare. Results of logistic regression analyses of around 11,000 young adults in eleven countries suggest that the relationship between mobility and individuals' views on work and welfare varies depending on the dimension of mobility (economic and social origins, for example), with expected future mobility exerting a stronger effect on attitudes than past mobility experiences. We find that self-interest, not empathy with one's social origins, appears to be the primary driver of these attitudes.

Keywords: social mobility; welfare attitudes; mobility effects; self-interest; deservingness

Work and welfare attitudes have many antecedents, including the crucial role that one's economic position and social origin plays in shaping opinions and preferences. The experiences people have throughout their lifetimes, and particularly in their younger years, shape how they view the meaning of work. Today we face a situation in which intergenerational upward mobility (i.e., achieving a higher socioeconomic status than one's parents) is no longer a given for many young people: economic circumstances remain challenging after the economic crisis, and an increase in university graduates has led to fierce competition on

Bettina Schuck is a postdoctoral researcher at the Institute of Political Science at Heidelberg University, Germany. Her research focuses on social inequality and stratification in a country-comparative perspective.

Correspondence: bettina.schuck@ipw.uni-heidelberg.de

DOI: 10.1177/0002716218822457

the job market (Eurofound 2017). In light of this situation, characterized by both real and threatened downward mobility, we are interested in how the experiences and expectations of social mobility, both upward and downward, impact young people's attitudes toward work and welfare.

Our work here addresses the following research questions: 1) How does intergenerational social mobility (upward/downward) impact young people's attitudes regarding the meaning of work? 2) Do future mobility expectations matter for young people's normative attitudes regarding work and welfare? By adopting a differentiated approach to the study of social mobility and its consequences, we offer new insights into the formation of work and welfare attitudes. While there are broad literatures covering both how social position as well as the prospects of moving up or down the socioeconomic ladder impact redistributive preferences, we know much less about how social mobility can shape the so-called moral aspects of welfare states. These moral or normative dimensions go beyond pure redistributive preferences and rather tap into beliefs about deservingness (Mau 2003) and the normative conceptions of work. A multidimensional conceptualization of welfare state support enables us to consider sources of support beyond material self-interest, such as normative concerns and preferences (Roosma, Gelissen, and van Oorschot 2013; Sihvo and Uusitalo 1995; van Oorschot 2010). Such a conceptualization furthermore allows for the possibility that individuals may hold a differentiated set of views. By focusing on the so-called moral dimension of the work-welfare nexus, in particular the receipt of welfare benefits and the influence on work values, we investigate the effects of intergenerational mobility beyond preferences for redistribution. More specifically, we provide empirical insights into how both the lived experiences and future expectations of intergenerational mobility shape young adults' attitudes about welfare and employment. When citizens do not feel recipients of social support are deserving of assistance, they will be unlikely to extend support for the maintenance or expansion of such programs and policies. In other words, social solidarity, the willingness to share social risks, and beliefs about whom should benefit from collective resources can have far-reaching consequences for elections, social policies, and even democratic legitimacy (Rothstein 1998; van Oorschot 2013). Our measures of intergenerational social mobility focus on financial status and mobility expectations in terms of standard of living. In comparison to conventional measures like occupation or education, we consider these subjective measures to have important advantages for studying young adults in contemporary Europe. Given the economic situation at the time the survey was fielded, with youth unemployment rates at nearly 50 percent in some European countries and many still struggling in the aftermath of the economic crisis, focusing on these

---

Jennifer Shore is a postdoctoral fellow at the Mannheim Centre for European Social Research at the University of Mannheim, Germany. Her research interests include political behaviors and attitudes, welfare states, comparative public policy, and survey research.

Note: This study is an outcome of the EU-funded collaborative research project CUPESSE (Cultural Pathways to Economic Self-Sufficiency and Entrepreneurship; Grant Agreement No. 613257; www.cupesse.eu).

subjective dimensions of intergenerational mobility allows us to also include young adults who are currently not employed and would therefore be hard to classify in any analysis of occupational status mobility. Finally, we illuminate mobility effects in countries where formal education may no longer be associated with the returns it once promised, such as in Spain or Greece.

Social Mobility and Normative Attitudes toward Work and Welfare

The extant literature on attitudes toward the welfare state has little to say about how social mobility shapes opinions regarding normative aspects of the welfare state and its beneficiaries. For our analysis, we formulate two sets of competing hypotheses based on two strands of literature—one that examines the effects of mobility on redistributive preferences and another that looks more specifically at welfare attitudes. Specifically, we focus on how self-interest and socialization experiences may mediate the relationship between social mobility and welfare attitudes.

The role of self-interest

The literature on welfare attitudes and redistributional preferences has grown rapidly over the last decade (Guillaud 2013; Jaeger 2005; Rehm 2009), with economic self-interest forming the basis of most studies. The origins of redistributive preferences are often traced back to income and material self-interest, with the rich seeking to minimize their tax burden and the poor hoping to benefit from redistribution. This explanation has found a great deal of traction within the political economy literature (Meltzer and Richard 1981; Romer 1975), though it is not without its critics. Accordingly, potential beneficiaries of redistribution, i.e., people with below-average incomes, are anticipated to favor redistributive measures (and therefore higher rates of income taxation), whereas those with higher incomes—the potential contributors and bearers of the burden of income taxation—will oppose redistribution. More generally, the association between material self-interest and redistributional preferences is expected to hold not only for current income, but also for other indicators of socioeconomic position, such as social class or educational level (Armingeon 2006).

Whereas the predictive power of an individual's socioeconomic position has been widely documented, it does not fully account for the role of one's past socioeconomic position, which might equally influence preferences and attitudes (Alesina and Giuliano 2009; Sihvo and Uusitalo 1995). To some extent, upward or downward mobility entails processes of re-socialization. Although the family setting is an important environment for the formation of opinions and values, as children mature and encounter new economic circumstances, they may adjust their preferences and ideas about work and welfare according to their new socioeconomic situation (Abramson and Books 1971; Lown 2015; Piketty 1995).

Intergenerational mobility may lead to a "self-serving perception of the role that ascribed and attained factors play in determining success or failure" (Gugushvili 2016b, 405). These so-called internal vs. external attributions of success, in turn, influence people's perceptions of existing inequalities and the role of the state (Gugushvili 2016a; Piketty 1995). This self-serving bias in causal attribution is expected to lead those who experienced intergenerational upward mobility to be more likely to attribute their success to their own efforts, and, therefore, to be less supportive of the welfare state and people who rely on its benefits (Gaviria, Graham, and Braido 2007; Ravallion and Lokshin 2000). Similarly, people who experienced downward mobility may be more likely to attribute their situations to external sources, which may be associated with a greater welfare support and less negative views of people who receive support. As outlined in the section to follow, whether people see others as responsible for their failures shapes attitudes regarding deservingness and how they view social programs and their beneficiaries. These assumptions lead to the following hypotheses:

H1a: Intergenerational downward mobility increases the likelihood of holding positive views of receiving social support.

H1b: Intergenerational upward mobility decreases the likelihood of holding positive views of receiving social support.

In addition to past and current socioeconomic position, expectations about the future can also be expected to shape welfare state support. As illustrated by Benabou and Ok (2001) in their prospect of upward mobility hypothesis, expectations of upward mobility may lead rational actors to oppose redistribution, even if their current income would predict otherwise (Alesina and Giuliano 2009). This desire to insure against potential future losses has the potential to impact current welfare attitudes (Moene and Wallerstein 2001), as people with a stronger interest in social protection will be more likely to hold positive views of welfare programs and their recipients (van Oorschot 2010). Recent studies have found that the prospect of *downward* mobility, in particular, can drive support for redistributive measures (Buscha 2012; Lee 2016), suggesting a sensitivity to losses, which may in turn positively impact welfare support. Based on the discussion regarding the impact of experienced mobility and adding the consideration of expected mobility, we arrive at our next set of hypotheses:

H2a: Expected upward mobility decreases the likelihood of holding positive views of receiving social support.

H2b: Expected downward mobility increases the likelihood of holding positive views of receiving social support.

Socialization experiences and the role of deservingness

While self-interest appears to be an important driver of welfare attitudes, it is arguably not the only one, particularly when taking seriously the multidimensionality of welfare support (see also the contribution in this volume by Gallie on the dimensions of work values). For example, why might someone at the top of the socioeconomic ladder nevertheless hold favorable attitudes toward welfare programs and their recipients? To answer this question, it is necessary to look for answers beyond pure material self-interest (Mau 2003; Sabbagh and Vanhuysse 2006). We therefore develop a counter hypothesis, which focuses on the concept of deservingness. Whom one considers to be deserving of public support has been shown to crucially shape attitudes of welfare support for specific groups.

But what influences our evaluations of deservingness? Of the various deservingness criteria outlined by van Oorschot (2000), he finds control and identity to be the most important drivers of deservingness attitudes (Cook 1979; Will 1993). Regarding control, people tend to be supportive of benefits for individuals or groups that are perceived to be victims of circumstance. For example, both the elderly and the sick are commonly viewed as deserving groups, as both old age and poor health are regarded as life stages or situations beyond one's own control (Jensen and Petersen 2017; Petersen 2012; van Oorschot 2000, 2006). The unemployed, on the other hand, are seen as largely responsible for their own fate; in other words, unlike the elderly or the sick, they could have prevented their situation of need (Hobbins 2016). This negative image of unemployed individuals has been found to span both time and space, even in countries with generous, universalistic welfare systems such as Sweden (Furåker and Blomsterberg 2003; van Oorschot 2006). Studies have found that, compared with other groups of welfare recipients, "the unemployed are seen as having less 'character', less self-responsibility, less perseverance, and less trustworthiness" (van Oorschot 2006, 25–26).

Identity also matters, for when people identify with recipients and do not think of them in an *us vs. them* constellation, they are more likely to consider them to be deserving of social assistance (van Oorschot 2000). Danckert (2017), moreover, finds that having unemployed friends or family can weaken in-group and out-group distinctions and thereby combat negative images of the unemployed. These findings echo Rueda's (2018) finding that altruism can be identified as a reason why the well-off would support redistributive efforts: altruism is particularly relevant in cases where the recipients of benefits are seen to be similar to those financing them.

Returning to the question of why someone whose socioeconomic position would otherwise predict more conservative attitudes toward the welfare state and its recipients, the experience of social mobility, along with ideas of deservingness, can help to provide an answer. While from a rational choice perspective both the lived experience of upward intergenerational mobility and the prospects of it would predict critical assessments of the normative functions of the welfare state, we should not neglect the formative experiences of growing up less well-off: "[P]ersonal experiences with the frustrations of economic hardship or poverty ... provide a first-hand understanding of the challenges of being poor and shape beliefs regarding personal responsibility for circumstance" (Lown 2015, 6). These socialization experiences may positively shape how upwardly mobile people view welfare recipients, even those who do not work, in terms of their deservingness. For one, upwardly mobile individuals, because of their experiences growing up with less, may identify more with the less well-off. Moreover, having been socialized in an economically deprived environment, upwardly mobile people may also be less likely to attribute blame to benefit recipients, including the unemployed, for their situation. Decades-long scholarship has furthermore documented the pivotal role of childhood and adolescent socialization experiences for political attitudes well into adulthood (Campbell et al. 1960; Niemi, Craig, and Mattei 1991; Sears 1975; see also Kalleberg and Marsden, this volume).

Scholars such as Piketty (1995) argue that, even though a child grew up in an economically disadvantaged environment, he or she will update his or her economic and political attitudes in accordance with his or her destination status. There is, however, reason to believe that formative childhood and adolescent socializing experiences will continue to shape attitudes about work and welfare well into adulthood: the experience of having grown up poor may affect how upwardly mobile people think about social policies and the users of these benefits. These experiences "should serve as a counterweight to the conservative effects of upward mobility" (Lown 2015, 9). People who experienced upward intergenerational mobility have (per definition) experienced being in a lower socioeconomic status. People whose families struggled financially while they were growing up may, despite having eventually succeeded in climbing the social ladder, have feelings of empathy for or identification with lower status groups and a sense of need for a strong welfare state (Danckert 2017). Such an argument could be applied to upwardly mobile young adults, wherein the children may identify with their parents' social milieu, the one in which they also grew up. Accordingly, in light of the self-interest hypotheses, we formulate a modified and competing hypothesis on the effects of social mobility on normative attitudes toward work and welfare:

H3: Upward intergenerational mobility, both experienced and expected, increases the likelihood of holding positive views of receiving social support.

Data and Methods

Data and sample

We draw on survey data from the CUPESSE (Cultural Pathways to Economic Self-Sufficiency and Entrepreneurship) project. The CUPESSE survey is a multidisciplinary, cross-sectional, mixed-mode survey of young adults and their parents fielded in 2016 (Tosun et al. 2018). After excluding those who indicated that they are primarily in education and listwise deletion of cases with missing values on one of our explanatory or control variables, the analytical sample comprises 10,923 young Europeans aged 18 to 35 from eleven European countries (Austria, Czech Republic, Denmark, Germany, Greece, Hungary, Italy, Spain, Switzerland, Turkey, and the United Kingdom).[1]

Measures

Our dependent variables are based on respondents' responses to the following two statements: *"It's humiliating to receive money without having to work."* and *"If welfare benefits are too high, there is no incentive to find work."* These two statements are part of a battery of items on work values and were selected precisely because they tap the moral dimension of the work-welfare nexus. Answer categories range from "strongly agree" (1) to "strongly disagree" (4), and were recoded into binary outcome variables differentiating "agreement" (0) from "disagreement" (1) for the purpose of the multivariate analyses.

Our central explanatory variable is intergenerational mobility, operationalized along two key dimensions: financial mobility and expected mobility. Unlike earlier studies of the effects of mobility, we use subjective indicators of intergenerational mobility rather than relying on formal indicators such as education or occupational status. Given the high unemployment levels in some countries at the time the survey was fielded, we felt it important to also include unemployed young people. Moreover, financial status may currently be a more insightful marker of social position in countries where formal education is no longer associated with the returns it once promised.

Intergenerational financial mobility is based on respondents' assessments of their current financial situation as compared with their family's situation when growing up.[2] More specifically, we measure financial mobility as the positive (upward mobility), negative (downward mobility), or nondeviation (stability) of the respondent's current situation from one's family's situation when he or she was 14. This measurement is derived from the more general concept of economic self-sufficiency (Gowdy and Pearlmutter 1993) and taps into the degree of one's perceived financial deprivation. Despite the relatively vague reference to *"being able to afford extras"* in the survey question, we consider this measure a more favorable indicator of one's financial situation than alternative measurements such as earnings and income (that are oftentimes biased due to social desirability and recall problems if surveyed retrospectively).

Expected intergenerational mobility is calculated based on responses to the question: *"Thinking about how your standard of living will be like in the future, how does it compare to how your parents are doing today?"* Responses were recoded into three categories, indicating upward, downward, or stable expectations about the future. Standard of living is a commonly used dimension of social mobility that is closely tied to the well-being and welfare of individuals (DiPrete 2002).

We control for gender, age, first or second generation migration history, main economic activity, own and parental educational attainment, Left-Right political attitudes, religiosity, previous unemployment experience, and whether the respondent is dependent on income from unemployment or other social benefits.[3] All models furthermore include country-fixed effects to account for variation that can be traced back to differences across the eleven countries in the sample. A full description of all variables can be found in the online appendix.

Analytical approach

In a first step, we look at the distributions of intergenerational financial and expected mobility separately for all countries. We then use the pooled country sample and estimate logistic regression models with two different work-welfare support items as outcome variables.[4] For both outcomes, we first estimate separate models that include either financial or expected mobility before both effects are eventually included simultaneously in a third model.

Results

Looking at the distributions of intergenerational mobility across countries in Table 1, several between-country differences, but also differences between different dimensions of social mobility, are striking. Beginning with intergenerational financial mobility, the group of immobiles, i.e., those whose financial status is similar to their parents', constitutes the largest group in all countries except Greece and Turkey. Young Greeks report extraordinarily high rates of financial downward mobility (63 percent), which is not surprising given Greece's exceptionally poor economic situation at the time of the survey. Turkish youths show by far the lowest rates of financial downward mobility (16 percent). Beyond these two outliers, downward mobility is generally more common than upward mobility. Only in the Czech Republic, Italy, and Spain are upward mobility shares slightly higher than or equal to the shares of downwardly mobile.

Regarding young Europeans' expectations about their future standard of living compared with their parents' standard of living today, we find that most young Europeans are rather optimistic when looking toward the future. Most young Europeans expect to be able to maintain or even exceed their parents' current standard of living. However, this does not apply to the Southern European countries Greece, Italy, and Spain, where the fear of future downward mobility is rather widespread: more than one in four young people expect that they will be unable to maintain their parents' current standard of living for themselves.

Turning to the multivariate analyses, we first describe the logistic regression results for the outcome "*If welfare benefits are too high, there is no incentive to work*" and then move on to results for the second outcome "*It's humiliating to receive money without having to work.*" (see models 1–6 in Table 2). Both outcomes are phrased in such a way that disagreement indicates positive views of receiving social support and agreement indicates negative views of receiving social support. Given that disagreement is coded as 1, and agreement is coded as 0, positive coefficients represent positive views and negative coefficients represent negative views of receiving social support.

Model 1 estimates effects of intergenerational financial mobility on the moral dimension of the work-welfare nexus (outcome 1: "*If welfare benefits are too high, there is no incentive to work*"). In line with the first two hypotheses (H1a and H1b), we find that financially downward mobile people are more likely, and financially upward mobiles are less likely, to hold positive views of receiving social

TABLE 1
Intergenerational Mobility across Countries

	Financial mobility			Expected mobility		
	upward	stable	downward	upward	stable	downward
Austria	0.23	0.41	0.36	0.39	0.50	0.11
Czech Republic	0.32	0.38	0.30	0.48	0.43	0.10
Denmark	0.27	0.40	0.33	0.41	0.50	0.10
Germany	0.24	0.41	0.35	0.41	0.44	0.15
Greece	0.10	0.27	0.63	0.32	0.34	0.34
Hungary	0.25	0.47	0.27	0.45	0.49	0.05
Italy	0.31	0.38	0.31	0.33	0.38	0.30
Spain	0.30	0.41	0.30	0.38	0.36	0.26
Switzerland	0.25	0.49	0.26	0.42	0.46	0.12
Turkey	0.42	0.42	0.16	0.61	0.32	0.07
United Kingdom	0.24	0.41	0.35	0.41	0.40	0.19

NOTE: Poststratification weights used in calculations.

support than the immobiles. The latter effect is, however, not statistically significant. The findings thus support the assumption that those who succeeded in
climbing the social ladder tend to attribute their success to their own effort and
therefore show less support for the welfare state. Those who failed to maintain
parental status presumably attribute this failure externally, and therefore show
stronger support for the welfare state.

Model 2, also focusing on outcome 1, includes effects for mobility expectations, but not past mobility experience, and shows statistically significant negative
effects for upward mobility expectations and statistically significant positive
effects for downward mobility expectations. These findings are in line with the
self-interest argument underlying the second set of hypotheses (H2a and H2b),
claiming that fears of downward mobility, i.e., being a potential future beneficiary
of welfare benefits, makes people more inclined to hold positive views of receiving welfare benefits. Likewise, expecting to become a potential contributor in the
future apparently makes people less supportive of the welfare state.

Predicted probabilities for both financial and expected mobility are illustrated
in Figure 1. As the figure shows, the likelihood of disagreeing with the statement
is lower for both expected and experienced upward mobility as compared with
the immobile group. Likewise, people who expect or who have experienced
downward mobility are more likely to disagree with the statement than the
immobile group. The darker lines, representing the effects of expected mobility,
illustrate the more pronounced effects of mobility expectations, as none of the
confidence intervals (95 percent) overlap, whereas, while we see a clear distinction between the group of downwardly mobiles vs. stable and upwardly mobile,
the effects of immobility and upward mobility on this work-welfare attitude are

TABLE 2
Social mobility and work-welfare attitudes, logistic regression

	If welfare benefits are too high, there is no incentive to find work. (disagree=1; agree=0)						It's humiliating to receive money without having to work. (disagree=1; agree=0)					
	Model 1		Model 2		Model 3		Model 4		Model 5		Model 6	
	b	se	b	se	b	se	b	se	b	se	b	se
Financial mobility, Ref.: stability												
upward mobility	-0.06	0.05			-0.04	0.05	0.06	0.04			0.08*	0.04
downward mobility	0.16**	0.05			0.13*	0.05	-0.03	0.04			-0.05	0.05
Mobility expectation, Ref.: stability												
upward mobility			-0.13***	0.03	-0.11***	0.03			-0.08*	0.03	-0.10**	0.03
downward mobility			0.32***	0.08	0.30***	0.08			0.11	0.06	0.12	0.07
Constant	-0.33	0.17	-0.27	0.17	-0.31	0.17	0.38*	0.17	0.41**	0.16	0.41*	0.16
N	10923		10923		10923		10923		10923		10923	
Pseudo R²	0.098		0.100		0.101		0.046		0.047		0.047	

NOTE: * p<0.05, ** p<0.01, *** p<0.001. Models 1 to 6 display logit coefficients. Control variables and country-fixed effects included, but not shown (see online appendix Table A3 for full models).

FIGURE 1
Predicted Probability Plot

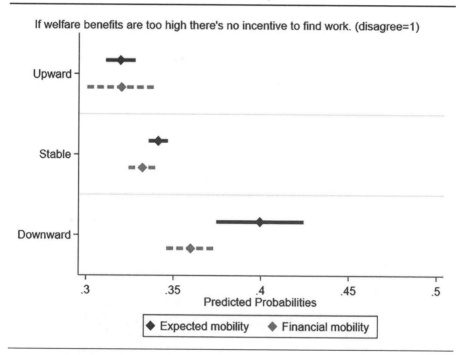

NOTE: Predicted probabilities correspond to model 1 for financial mobility and to model 2 for expected mobility (Table 2). Lines represent 95 percent confidence intervals.

not clearly distinguishable, as shown by the somewhat overlapping confidence intervals of the lighter lines.

Controlling for other status position factors such as receiving benefits oneself or being currently unemployed, mobility effects for financial and expected mobility also hold when included simultaneously in model 3. Again, the mobility effects support the self-interest argument underlying hypotheses H1 and H2, while we find no support for the competing arguments regarding deservingness. The fact that both mobility effects remain stable when included simultaneously also speaks in favor of distinct mechanisms that influence the young people's attitudes.

Models 4 to 6 are similar to models 1 to 3, but focus on our second outcome *"It's humiliating to receive money without having to work."* Model 4, which includes financial mobility, but not expected mobility, does not show statistically significant mobility effects. Though speculative, the signs of the mobility coefficients may, however, suggest a mechanism beyond self-interest, as captured by H3. We do however find statistically significant effects for upward mobility expectations in model 5, again suggesting that self-interest rather than identification with one's social origin is determining welfare support attitudes. When included simultaneously, these results hold, i.e., controlling for the effects of financial upward mobility expectations are significantly related to negative views of receiving social support.

FIGURE 2
Predicted Probability Plot

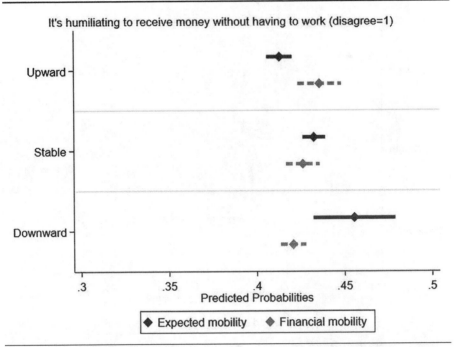

NOTE: Predicted probabilities correspond to model 4 for financial mobility and to model 5 for expected mobility (Table 2). Lines represent 95 percent confidence intervals.

Figure 2 plots the predicted probabilities of the two types of mobility for models 4 and 5, respectively. For financial mobility we can see a different pattern of agreement across mobility groups compared with Figure 1, though mobility effects are not statistically significant in this case (see also model 4 in Table 2): downwardly mobile people express a lower likelihood of disagreeing that it is humiliating to receive money without having to work compared with both stable and upwardly mobile respondents. For expected mobility, mobility effects show a pattern similar to outcome 1, with upward mobility expectations decreasing the likelihood of disagreeing that it is humiliating to receive money without having to work. Visible by the nonoverlapping confidence intervals with the remaining mobility effects, this effect is statistically significant.

Overall, our results support the assumption, *ceteris paribus*, that self-interest is a decisive driver of welfare state support, both in terms of experienced mobility and future mobility expectations. In that regard, intergenerational mobility apparently does not differ from the well-established social status effects per se. The empathy or identification with one's former social origin group is thus less influential than hypothesized earlier.

Discussion and Conclusion

We explore the impact of different types of intergenerational mobility—financial mobility and expected future mobility—on attitudes toward work and welfare. We drew on different strands of literature that remain contested in terms of the definitive effects an upward or downward shift in socioeconomic status and the role of factors beyond material self-interest for work-welfare attitudes. Using a unique cross-national dataset, we examined how different dimensions of intergenerational mobility shape attitudes about the work-welfare nexus, finding that self-interest, not empathy with one's social origin, appears to be the driver of these attitudes, both in terms of experienced mobility and future mobility expectations. While these findings align with the seminal study of Benabou and Ok (2001), not only is the prospect of *upward* mobility shown to be a significant driver of work-welfare attitudes, but *downward* mobility also matters: Those who anticipate being worse off than their parents are less likely to hold negative views of welfare recipients than people who expect to do about the same or better. These results indicate that subjective perceptions may play a relatively larger role than the objective shifts along the income distribution compared with one's parents (Bjornskov et al. 2013). This finding becomes all the more relevant when considering the very real prospects of downward mobility many young people face.

The findings regarding financial mobility generally indicate the presence of self-interest at work—that is, those who experienced upward mobility are more likely to agree with the statements *"If welfare benefits are too high, then there is no incentive to work"* and *"It's humiliating to receive money without having to work."* Our expectations in terms of empathy or identification with one's status group of origin, however, do not appear to find empirical traction. Rueda (2018) uses the concept of altruism to explain why material self-interest may not always explain preferences for redistribution, arguing that, when people identify with the less well off, in-group solidarity increases, so too does support for the welfare state. Investigating whether young people identify more with their status of origin or destination may help to elucidate our findings. Moreover, data sources that would allow the research to zoom in on the dimensions of the deservingness concept could also shed light on the mechanisms behind the relationships.

Though the present study has made inroads into further disentangling the relationships between intergenerational mobility and work-welfare attitudes, further work remains. First, and as we hinted in this article, there are certainly important country differences to be considered. For example, young people in Southern Europe faced a far more dire situation during and in the wake of the economic crisis that began to unfold in late 2007. Second, the risks of downward mobility are not equally distributed across countries nor individuals, as underscored by Moene and Wallerstein (2001). Consequently, young people in certain countries or occupational groups may simply hold different expectations about the future due to these unequally distributed risks. Therefore, future research is tasked with delving into these important country differences to provide a more complete picture of the varieties of intergenerational mobility and work-welfare attitudes.

Finally, we may be witnessing a shift in work and welfare attitudes reflecting the evolving nature of social and labor market policies. Many countries, as well as the European Union, have adopted social and labor market policies that place a greater emphasis on individual responsibility. Unemployment and training schemes, particularly those aimed at young people, are increasingly embodying concepts such as employability and responsibilization (Crisp and Powell 2017), which stress the role and even duty of the individual to make him or herself attractive to employers and to end the dependency on state support. There are also important differences between the countries in terms of welfare systems—including how benefits are allotted and administered—which also shape how the beneficiaries themselves are perceived. The findings from the current study perhaps imply that in countries with a higher incidence of downward mobility public support for unemployment programs will be higher. At the same time, this begs the question of who will fund such programs, as downward mobility is also most prevalent in countries that struggle the most economically.

Notes

1. Respondents who indicated that their current primary activity is education or training were excluded from the analyses. Since they are still in the school-to-work transition, they constitute a very distinct group and may be quite difficult to compare to young people who are, for example, in full-time employment.

2. The financial situation is captured by the question "We (I) could (can) afford extras for ourselves (myself) (such as trips, hobbies, etc.)."

3. Though political orientation is predictive of redistributive preferences (Jaeger 2008), its effect on the so-called moral dimensions of work and welfare is less clear. The inclusion of this variable could arguably be considered a particularly stringent test of the effects of mobility on work-welfare attitudes.

4. Robustness tests using ordered logit models (not shown) and linear regression models (see online appendix Table A4) revealed that mobility effects do not change substantively.

References

Abramson, Paul R., and Books, John W. 1971. Social mobility and political attitudes: A study of intergenerational mobility among young British men. *Comparative Politics* 3 (3): 403–28.

Alesina, Alberto, and Giuliano, Paola. 2009. Preferences for redistribution. NBER Working Paper Series 14825. Cambridge, MA.

Armingeon, Klaus. 2006. Reconciling competing claims of the welfare state clientele. The politics of old and new social risk coverage in comparative perspective. In *The politics of post-industrial welfare states: Adapting post-war social policies to new social risks*, ed. K. Armingeon and Giuliano Bonoli, 100–22. London: Taylor & Francis.

Benabou, Roland, and Efe A. Ok. 2001. Social mobility and the demand for redistribution: The Poum Hypothesis. *The Quarterly Journal of Economics* 116 (2): 447–87.

Bjornskov, Christian, Axel Dreher, Justina A.V. Fischer, Jan Schnellenbach, and Kai Gehring. 2013. Inequality and happiness: When perceived social mobility and economic reality do not match. *Journal of Economic Behavior & Organization* 91:75–92.

Buscha, Franz. 2012. Financial expectations and the "Left–Right" political value scale: Testing for the POUM hypothesis. *Economics letters* 115 (3): 460–64.

Campbell, Angus, Philip E. Converse, Warren E. Miller, and Donald E. Stokes. 1960. *The American voter*. Unabridged edition. Chicago, IL: The University of Chicago Press.

Cook, Fay Lomax. 1979. *Who should be helped? Public support for social services*. Beverly Hills, CA: Sage Publications.

Crisp, Richard, and Ryan Powell. 2017. Young people and UK labour market policy: A critique of "employability" as a tool for understanding youth unemployment. *Urban Studies* 54 (8): 1784–1807.

Danckert, Bolette. 2017. Facing unemployment: Personal and vicarious unemployment experiences generate favourable perceptions of unemployed people. *European Sociological Review* 33 (6): 779–90.

DiPrete, Thomas A. 2002. Life course risks, mobility regimes, and mobility consequences: A comparison of Sweden, Germany, and the United States. *American Journal of Sociology* 108 (2): 267–309.

Eurofound. 2017. *Social mobility in the EU*. Luxembourg: Publications Office of the European Union.

Furåker, Bengt, and Marianne Blomsterberg. 2003. Attitudes towards the unemployed. An analysis of Swedish survey data. *International Journal of Social Welfare* 12 (3): 193–203.

Gallie, Duncan. 2019. Research on work values in a changing economic and social context. *The ANNALS of the American Academy of Political and Social Science* (this volume).

Gaviria, Alejandro, Carol Graham, and Luis H. B. Braido. 2007. Social mobility and preferences for redistribution in Latin America [with comments]. *Economía* 8 (1): 55–96.

Gowdy, Elizabeth A., and Pearlmutter, Sue. 1993. Economic self-sufficiency: It's not just money. *Affilia* 8 (4): 368–87.

Gugushvili, Alexi. 2016a. Intergenerational objective and subjective mobility and attitudes towards income differences: Evidence from transition societies. *Journal of International and Comparative Social Policy* 32 (3): 199–219.

Gugushvili, Alexi. 2016b. Intergenerational social mobility and popular explanations of poverty: A comparative perspective. *Social Justice Research* 29 (4): 402–28.

Guillaud, Elvire. 2013. Preferences for redistribution: An empirical analysis over 33 countries. *The Journal of Economic Inequality* 11 (1): 57–78.

Hobbins, Jennifer. 2016. Young long-term unemployed and the individualization of responsibility. *NJWLS* 6 (2): 43–59.

Jaeger, Mads Meier. 2005. Welfare regimes and attitudes towards redistribution: The regime hypothesis revisited. *European Sociological Review* 22 (2): 157–70.

Jaeger, Mads Meier. 2008. Does left-right orientation have a causal effect on support for redistribution? Causal analysis with cross-sectional data using instrumental variables. *International Journal of Public Opinion Research* 20 (3): 363–74.

Jensen, Carsten, and Petersen, Michael Bang. 2017. The deservingness heuristic and the politics of health care. *American Journal of Political Science* 61 (1): 68–83.

Kalleberg, Arne L., and Peter V. Marsden. 2019. Work values in the United States: Age, period, and generational differences. *The ANNALS of the American Academy of Political and Social Science* (this volume).

Lee, Soomi. 2016. Hopeless future and the desire for welfare expansion: Testing the prospect of upward mobility hypothesis in South Korea. *The Social Science Journal* 53 (4): 545–54.

Lown, Patrick L. 2015. Understanding social mobility, economic environment, and their effects on social policy attitudes. Doctoral dissertation, State University of New York at Stony Brook.

Mau, Steffen. 2003. *The moral economy of welfare states: Britain and Germany compared*. London: Routledge.

Meltzer, Allan H., and Scott F. Richard. 1981. A rational theory of the size of government. *Journal of Political Economy* 89 (5): 914–27.

Moene, Karl Ove, and Michael Wallerstein. 2001. Inequality, social insurance, and redistribution. *American Political Science Review* 95 (4): 859–74.

Niemi, Richard G., Stephen C. Craig, and Franco Mattei. 1991. Measuring internal political efficacy in the 1988 National Election Study. *The American Political Science Review* 85 (4): 1407–13.

Petersen, Michael Bang. 2012. Social welfare as small-scale help: Evolutionary psychology and the deservingness heuristic. *American Journal of Political Science* 56 (1): 1–16.

Piketty, Thomas. 1995. Social mobility and redistributive politics. *The Quarterly Journal of Economics* 110 (3): 551–84.

Ravallion, Martin, and Michael Lokshin. 2000. Who wants to redistribute? *Journal of Public Economics* 76 (1): 87–104.

Rehm, Philipp. 2009. Risks and redistribution: An individual-level analysis. *Comparative Political Studies* 42 (7): 855–81.

Romer, Thomas. 1975. Individual welfare, majority voting, and the properties of a linear income tax. *Journal of Public Economics* 4 (2): 163–85.

Roosma, Femke, John Gelissen, and Wim van Oorschot. 2013. The multidimensionality of welfare state attitudes: A European cross-national study. *Social Indicators Research* 113 (1): 235–55.

Rothstein, Bo. 1998. Political institutions: An overview. In *A new handbook of political science*, eds. Robert E. Goodin and Hans-Dieter Klingemann, 133–67. Oxford: Oxford University Press.

Rueda, David. 2018. Food comes first, then morals: Redistribution preferences, parochial altruism, and immigration in Western Europe. *The Journal of Politics* 80 (1): 225–39.

Sabbagh, Clara, and Pieter Vanhuysse. 2006. Exploring attitudes towards the welfare state: Students' views in eight democracies. *Journal of Social Policy* 35 (04): 607–28.

Sears, David O. 1975. Political socialization. In *Handbook of political science*, eds. Fred I. Greenstein and Nelson W. Polsby, 93–153. Reading, MA. Addison-Wesley.

Sihvo, Tuire, and Hannu Uusitalo. 1995. Economic crises and support for the welfare state in Finland 1975–1993. *Acta Sociologica* 38 (3): 251–62.

Tosun, Jale, José Arco-Tirado, Maurizio Caserta, Zeynep Cemalcilar, Markus Freitag, Felix Hörisch, Carsten Jensen, Bernhard Kittel, Levente Littvay, et al. 2018 (online first). Perceived economic self-sufficiency: A country- and generation-comparative approach. *European Political Science*. doi: 10.1057/s41304-018-0186-3.

Van Oorschot, Wim. 2000. Who should get what, and why? On deservingness criteria and the conditionality of solidarity among the public. *Policy & Politics* 28 (1): 33–48.

Van Oorschot, Wim. 2006. Making the difference in social Europe: Deservingness perceptions among citizens of European welfare states. *Journal of European Social Policy* 16 (1): 23–42.

Van Oorschot, Wim. 2010. Public perceptions of the economic, moral, social and migration consequences of the welfare state: An empirical analysis of welfare state legitimacy. *Journal of European Social Policy* 20 (1): 19–31.

Van Oorschot, Wim. 2013. Globalization, the European welfare state, and protection of the poor. In *Citizenship and identity in the welfare state*, eds. Andrzej M. Suszycki and Ireneusz P. Karolewski, 37–50. Baden-Baden: Nomos.

Will, Jeffery A. 1993. The dimensions of poverty: Public perceptions of the deserving poor. *Social Science Research* 22 (3): 312–32.

What are the Effects of Attitudes Toward Work?

Work Values and the Value of Work: Different Implications for Young Adults' Self-Employment in Europe

By
MARTIN LUKEŠ,
MANUEL FELDMANN,
and
FEDERICO VEGETTI

In this study, we ask how work values impact different forms of labor market participation of young adults across Europe. We define work values as individuals' intrinsic and extrinsic motivations to work and the value of work as the importance or centrality of work in individuals' lives. We use data gathered from young adults in eleven European countries in the CUPESSE project to investigate the role of the two sets of values regarding employment and self-employment. We then replicate our analysis on a larger sample using data from the European Social Survey (ESS). Our findings suggest a high importance of nonpecuniary benefits for self-employment. Analyses based on both CUPESSE and ESS datasets clearly showed the high, positive impact that independence and creativity have on self-employment. We also show that extrinsic values, such as job security, are more important for employees than they are for the self-employed. Additionally, we find that the value of work in life does not differ between the employed and the self-employed. In sum, these findings suggest that values related to self-employment are not rooted in a general value of work, as Max Weber postulated in his *Protestant Work Ethic* nearly one hundred years ago, as much as in the aim to achieve personal satisfaction.

Keywords: employment; self-employment; career choice; work values; work centrality; young adults

Almost a decade after the onset of the Great Recession, labor markets in industrialized countries are going through a substantial change. The growing degree of flexibility required by the markets, coupled with the decrease in work protection set by policy-makers, is putting more and more workers in a

Martin Lukeš is head of the entrepreneurship department and vice-dean for research and PhD studies at the Faculty of Business Administration, University of Economics, Prague. His research focuses on psychology of entrepreneurship, evaluation of entrepreneurship policies, and entry into self-employment.

Correspondence: lukesm@vse.cz

DOI: 10.1177/0002716219828976

permanent state of training and reinvention. This is particularly salient for younger generations, who are often outsiders to the system of social protections (Skedinger 2010) and are confronted at the same time with a growing range of potential opportunities brought on by new technologies. In this scenario, entrepreneurship and self-employment are gaining centrality in the labor markets. First, entrepreneurship has been found to have a positive impact on innovation, employment, and growth (Dvouletý and Lukeš 2016). Second, labor markets are changing in such a way that some characteristics typical of self-employed work, such as independence, are becoming increasingly common (Manyika et al. 2016). Hence, because of both policy incentives and market changes, self-employment might become more the norm than the exception in future labor markets.

At the same time, studies on work values across generations show that younger individuals are less intrinsically motivated to work and see work as less central in their lives (Twenge et al. 2010); this is despite previous research suggesting that the most important motivational factors for entrepreneurs are intrinsic, nonpecuniary rewards (Burke, FitzRoy, and Nolan 2002; Schjoedt 2009). Thus, today's young adults may be less apt than their predecessors to engage in entrepreneurial activities that require time and effort (Gorgievski, Ascalon, and Stephan 2011) in a moment when labor markets appear to be more in need for them to do so.

As prior studies do not give a final answer to the question of what motivates young entrepreneurs, we suggest the following approach to bridge this gap. On one hand, *work values* are the aspects of work that individuals find desirable, the motivating factors for people to prefer one job over another (Fayolle, Liñán, and Moriano 2014; Twenge et al. 2010). Both intrinsic and extrinsic values have been found to motivate entrepreneurial careers (e.g., Douglas and Shepherd 2000; van Gelderen 2016; Stephan, Hart, and Drews 2015). On the other hand, there is the centrality that people attribute to work in their lives, a trait that we may call *value of work* (Bal and Kooij 2011; Diefendorff et al. 2002; Gallie, this volume). In his seminal work, Weber (1905) postulates that entrepreneurs have a strong work ethic, that is, they consider work as more central in their lives. We indeed see that entrepreneurs spend more hours at work than wage employees (Cardon and Patel 2015), but the answer to the "why" question is not conclusive. Moreover, research has found that both work values and centrality differ between today's young people and previous generations (Cogin 2012; Twenge et al. 2010).

Manuel Feldmann is a doctoral researcher at the University of Heidelberg in Germany, in the Department of Political Science. His research is directed at the connection of entrepreneurial psychology and policy with a focus on quantitative analyses.

Federico Vegetti is a postdoctoral research fellow at the University of Milan in Italy. His research interests lie at the intersection of political science, sociology, and psychology, which he investigates using mostly quantitative methods.

NOTE: We recognize financial support by the project Cultural Pathways to Economic Self-Sufficiency and Entrepreneurship (CUPESSE; Seventh Framework Program of the European Union; Grant Agreement No. 613257). We thank Fabian Kalleitner and one anonymous reviewer for their guidance and support, which improved this research endeavor in many ways.

Our first research question, then, is whether self-employment among young adults in Europe is determined by work values or a more general work centrality. Our second research question focuses on the differences between intrinsic and extrinsic work values and which of these is more prevalent among young employees or entrepreneurs. To answer this question, we draw on self-determination theory and its applications in management and behavioral sciences. We then move beyond both questions and ask whether employees or the self-employed are more likely to keep working if they are financially independent. To study whether and how current young entrepreneurs differ from people who choose a more conventional career path is of great importance as it may inform both policy-makers and human resource specialists about the workers' motivational profiles that are likely to be common in the future. This may help to prepare measures that tap into the real motivational profiles and are not misplaced, for example, by overestimating the importance of financial incentives.

To identify the motivational forces behind the choice between paid and self-employment, we utilize two different datasets of European young adults. First, the main dataset includes respondents aged 18 to 35 from eleven European countries and originates from the Cultural Pathways to Economic Self-Sufficiency and Entrepreneurship (CUPESSE) collaborative research project. Second, we test the results from this dataset by analyzing a larger sample of the same age drawn from the tenth round of the European Social Survey in 2010. While the former data allow for a deeper analysis and more items in the model, the latter provide broader generalizability through a tested and well-renowned methodology and a larger sample of countries.

We elaborate on the theoretical background of both constructs, investigate past research, and develop hypotheses. Then, in the following section of this article, we describe the CUPESSE and European Social Survey (ESS) datasets and our subsamples, present our research methods, discuss the results, and give concluding remarks.

Conceptual Foundations and Theoretical Framework

In this study, we compare the prevalence of two theoretical constructs among employees and self-employed individuals: *work values*, the aspects of work that people regard as desirable in their working life (Ros, Schwartz, and Surkiss 1999; Twenge et al. 2010); and *work centrality*, that is, the "value of work" in a person's life (cf. Paullay, Alliger, and Stone-Romero 1994). Both concepts belong to a general view of values as *evaluative standards*, which inform the abstract goals guiding individuals' career choices, as well as their perception of what is right and wrong in the workplace (Gallie, this volume; Parry and Urwin 2011; Smola and Sutton 2002). As such, they are central driving forces behind individuals' career prospects and their performance in the workplace (e.g., Bal and Kooij 2011; Fayolle, Liñán, and Moriano 2014; Twenge et al. 2010).

Work values

Research on entrepreneurial motivations stems from a need to mark the psychological underpinnings of entrepreneurial behavior (Carsrud and Brännback 2011). While some treat values and motivations as separate—albeit related—concepts, with values being more general than specific motivations (Fayolle, Liñán, and Moriano 2014), the majority of studies understand the concepts as equivalents, both theoretically and empirically (Bardi and Schwartz 2003). A focus on young adults arises in the literature mainly because of the incentives businesses need to offer to attract or retain younger workers (Twenge et al. 2010) and due to the high levels of youth unemployment that cause significant social pressures, especially in southern Europe (Sarfati 2013). Hence, we limit this review to the types of work values that have been pointed out as relevant for both topics.

First, we distinguish between intrinsic and extrinsic work values (Amabile 1997; Ros, Schwartz, and Surkiss 1999) as a part of self-determination theory (Ryan and Deci 2000). *Intrinsic* values (or motivations) link a person's job to her own need for self-realization, and they express themselves through valuing a job as meaningful, creative, interesting, and self-determined. *Extrinsic* values include status recognition, high income, job stability, and opportunities for career advancements, that is, they do not relate to the type of work itself. However, extrinsic values can, under some circumstances, become internal, that is, when the individual attributes value to them without external control (Gagné and Deci 2005). Even in that case, there is often a sense of pressure to engage in an action, such as "I must work to keep the job or to make enough money." While classical models of economic behavior used to focus on extrinsic rewards as the main motivational factors, self-determination theory, as well as subsequent research, has highlighted and confirmed the importance of intrinsic motivation for behavior, performance, and satisfaction in the workplace (Ryan and Deci 2000; Gagné and Deci 2005) and in entrepreneurship (Benz and Frey 2008).

Work centrality

The construct of work centrality relates directly to personal normative views on work ethic and the role of work in one's life (Dose 1997; Gallie, this volume). As such, it has its roots in Weber's (1905) original formulation of the Protestant work ethic. Yet newer studies understand the Protestant work ethic independently from personal religious affiliations (Miller, Woehr, and Hudspeth 2002) and conceptualize it as hard work, industriousness, and attitudes toward money and leisure time (Furnham 1990). Cogin (2012) refers to work ethics as a way of incorporating work as part of one's own identity. As this study contrasts specific work values with the general position of work in the respondents' lives, we use the construct of *work centrality* as the "beliefs that individuals have regarding the degree of importance that work plays in their lives" (Paullay, Alliger, and Stone-Romero 1994, 225). As socialization and prior experiences impact these beliefs, they differ among cultures, religions, and social groups. Thus, work centrality can but does not need to have roots in the Protestant work ethic, which makes it more appropriate for a cross-country study.

From a theoretical standpoint, young people value autonomy and personal growth: they prefer creative environments where they can work independently, learn marketable skills, gather experience that will serve them in the future (Martin 2005), and seek a portable career with greater degrees of personal flexibility (Glass 2007). In other words, they are expected to be driven more by intrinsic values. On the other hand, given a higher focus on family life and free time (Shaw and Fairhurst 2008) as well as a trend toward less work centrality among young adults (Smola and Sutton 2002), it remains unclear how central work is for young adults in the twenty-first century.

A link to career choice

How do work values and centrality affect people's career choices? In general terms, values as motivational constructs are the driving force of various behaviors, entrepreneurial behavior included. It is natural for an individual to pursue important values by behaving accordingly (Bardi and Schwartz 2003). However, the relationship between values and entrepreneurship warrants enhanced scholarly attention (Fayolle, Liñán, and Moriano 2014). Existing research identifies three values as particularly relevant for distinguishing self-employment from paid employment as a career choice: independence, creativity, and a low need for security (Amabile 1997; Jaén and Liñán 2013; Schjoedt 2009). Additionally, financial motivation is said to be a crucial factor for starting an entrepreneurial activity (Douglas and Shepherd 2000; Hessels, van Gelderen, and Thurik 2008). While independence and creativity are regarded as intrinsic values, a need for security and a high income are genuinely extrinsic factors.

It is important to point out that existing research on values and entrepreneurship does not focus on young people. However, research on generational differences of work values shows that today's young adults—defined as those born in the 1980s and 1990s—are less motivated by intrinsic factors than previous generations (e.g., Twenge et al. 2010). At the same time, labor market changes and the rise of the "gig economy" are reducing the relevance of extrinsic rewards such as security for a multitude of jobs (Manyika et al. 2016). Hence, it is crucial to assess whether intrinsic and extrinsic values are still associated with self-employed work among younger individuals in the way they used to be for previous generations.

Independence is the best-confirmed value of entrepreneurs (Burke, FitzRoy, and Nolan 2002; van Gelderen 2016; Rauch and Frese 2007; Stephan, Hart, and Drews 2015). By running their own firm, entrepreneurs have autonomy in organizing their own time, in determining procedures to carry out their work tasks, and in general decision-making. Independence is thus a major driver of entrepreneurship (Carter et al. 2003; Hessels, van Gelderen, and Thurik 2008; Schjoedt 2009; Shane, Locke, and Collins 2003; Benz and Frey 2008) and entrepreneurs' job satisfaction (Benz and Frey 2008; Hundley 2001). *Need for creativity* captures the interest to look for novel ways of action, the importance of developing one's own ideas and accomplishing something new (Edelman et al. 2010; Rauch and Frese 2007). Empirically, the importance of this trait for entrepreneurship is more controversial than is the case for independence (see, e.g., Carter et al. 2003). However, Rauch and Frese (2007) link entrepreneurial behavior to other creativity-related values, such as innovativeness. Hence, we would expect the need for creativity to have an impact on people's career choices. These two expectations lead to our first hypothesis:

H1a: *Intrinsic work values, expressed through valuing creativity and independence, will be higher for self-employed individuals than for employees.*

Intrinsic values place the source of reward within individuals' psychological satisfaction, be it due to self-expression or personal freedom, rather than external, pecuniary benefits. These are the kinds of rewards that, according to previous research, appeal to entrepreneurs the most (Burke, FitzRoy, and Nolan 2002; Hamilton 2000). A general implication of intrinsic values is that entrepreneurs should be willing to continue working even if they do not have an immediate economic need for it. In other words, if an entrepreneurial career is driven by such values, we would expect self-employed individuals to be more willing than employees to continue working even if they are not financially obligated to do so. Indeed, a study on lottery winners by Arvey, Harpaz, and Liao (2004) found that 10 percent of winners started their own business, even though they had no economic need to do so. Thus, we hypothesize,

H1b: *Intrinsic work values, expressed through the willingness to continue working even if not needed, will be higher for the self-employed than for employees.*

Looking at extrinsic factors, *job security* correlates significantly with paid employment (Burke, FitzRoy, and Nolan 2002; Tyszka et al. 2011). Individuals valuing security may find the challenges of entrepreneurship threatening and unattractive (Jaén and Liñán 2013). It is important to emphasize that this value negatively affects the self-employed career choice. Yet in the literature it is often entangled with other financial incentives. Stephan, Hart, and Drews (2015) note that most of the existing studies of entrepreneurial motivation ignore the distinction among income security, personal wealth, and significant financial success (e.g., Edelman et al. 2010). Tyszka et al. (2011), in one of the rare studies to differentiate these constructs, find that the most important motive in the group of nonentrepreneurs is job security, which is not important for opportunity-driven entrepreneurs. Hence, it is important to distinguish between the value of *security* and the value of *high income* or wealth. Whereas high income and wealth creation are often suggested as key values of entrepreneurs (Douglas and Shepherd 2000; Hessels, van Gelderen, and Thurik 2008), previous research shows that the self-employed in general are willing to work for lower wages (Hamilton 2000; van Praag and Versloot 2007). The high-income motive seems to be essential only for a small group of growth-oriented entrepreneurs (Hessels, van Gelderen, and

Thurik 2008). Most entrepreneurs start and run firms, even if it means lower earnings in the earlier stages of the entrepreneurial life cycle and no certainty of higher earnings in the later stages (Hamilton 2000). In their review, van Praag and Versloot (2007) concluded, contrary to the common view of superstar entrepreneurs, that most entrepreneurs have lower income levels than nonentrepreneurs. In other words, when starting an entrepreneurial career, personal fulfillment is expected to be valued more than making money (Hemingway 2005). Thus, we hypothesize,

H2: *Extrinsic values, expressed through valuing high income and job security, will be lower for the self-employed than for employees.*

Finally, entrepreneurship often requires significant effort, hard work, and long hours (Douglas and Shepherd 2000). Hyytinen and Ruuskanen (2007) find that self-employed individuals, in comparison with employees, work longer hours, work more in the evenings and on weekends, have less leisure time, and are less frequently absent from work. All these behaviors are indicators of an underlying ethic that places work at the center of the individual's life (Miller, Woehr, and Hudspeth 2002). Indeed, Weber's seminal essay on the Protestant work ethic explicitly links the greater sense of dedication and leisure avoidance of Puritans to a heightened sense of self-reliance that ultimately gave a boost to individual enterprise in early capitalism (Weber 1905). In line with this theory, we expect entrepreneurs to hold normative views that place work at the center of life (i.e., work centrality; cf. Diefendorff et al. 2002). People who attribute great value to work will more likely choose self-employment due to its potential to position work at the center of one's life. Thus, we hypothesize,

H3: *Work centrality in one's life will be higher for the self-employed than for employees.*

The Database

We base our analyses on two different data sources: data from the CUPESSE research project (Tosun et al. 2018) collected in 2016[1] and from the fifth round of the ESS collected in 2010. We use the ESS5 data because they are the most recent round that includes questions on work values from the module "Family, work and well-being." Given our interest in young adults, we select only individuals within the age range 18 to 35 in ESS5 data as well. While we are aware of possible differences in value preferences due to the different time of data collection in the two datasets, we maintain that comparing two data sources of this size provides a remarkably high external validity to our results.

Given our focus on career choice between self-employment and paid employment, we exclude from both datasets the respondents who are unemployed; in full-time education; doing training, household work, full-time caring, or military service; or those who selected "other." Moreover, in the CUPESSE sample, we exclude all those who are self-employed in the family business, as succession represents its own career path including very distinct job value sets (cf. Feldmann, Lukeš, and Uhlaner 2018). After some adjustments due to listwise deletion of missing values in the explanatory variables (no imputation was conducted), the final samples on which we base our analyses are 10,774 young adults in eleven countries in the CUPESSE data and 9,163 young adults in twenty-eight countries in the ESS data.[2]

Operationalization and Methodology

Operationalization

Our dependent variable, *career choice*, is a binary indicator taking value 1 if the respondent is *self-employed* and 0 if she or he works as an employee. As for the independent variables, we group them as follows: the first group comprises demographic controls, whose impact on self-employment has been widely demonstrated in entrepreneurship literature; the second group captures respondents' work values; and the third group adds two variables related to work centrality.

The control variables include a basic set of demographic indicators. They describe *age* (a continuous numerical variable ranging in both samples from 18 to 35, centered on the median age of 28); *gender* (a dummy variable for male respondents); and *education* (an ordinal variable based on the International Standard Classification of Education [ISCED] 2011, recoded in three categories, and centered around middle education).[3] Further, we use two dummy variables to indicate whether the respondent belongs to an *ethnic minority* and whether the respondent has *caring responsibilities*. We capture *entrepreneurial role models in the family* by a variable that takes a value of 1 if one parent was self-employed when the respondent was 14, 2 if both parents, and 0 if there was no entrepreneurial role model. Additionally, to control for idiosyncratic differences between countries, we include *country dummies*, 10 in the CUPESSE data and 27 in the ESS data. The baseline category is Germany in both data sources, as it is the largest national sample in both datasets.

The second group of indicators comprises variables describing the respondents' work values: how much they value *creativity, independence, job security*, and *high income* in a job. In the CUPESSE dataset, the variables are coded from 1 (*very unimportant*) to 4 (*very important*) and were retrieved from a specific job-related item battery (see Table 1 for exact wording). In the ESS dataset, the variables *creativity* and *independence* are coded from 1 (*not like me at all*) to 6 (*very much like me*) and were retrieved from the Schwartz item battery of basic human values; the values *job security* and *high income* are coded from 1 (*very unimportant*) to 5 (*very important*) and stem from a battery of job-related items.

The third group of predictors contains the variables *lottery* and *work centrality*. In the CUPESSE dataset, the *lottery* variable describes whether respondents would continue to work or would stop working if they were to get enough money

TABLE 1
List of Questionnaire Items in CUPESSE and ESS 2010

Variable	CUPESSE Questionnaire	ESS 2010 Questionnaire
Creativity	"How important: job allowing me to develop my creativity"	"Important to think new ideas and be creative"
Independence	"How important: job allowing me to work independently"	"Important to make own decisions and be free"
Security	"How important: secure job"	"Important if choosing job: secure job"
High Income	"How important: high income"	"Important if choosing job: high income"
Lottery	"If you were to get enough money to live as comfortably as you would like for the rest of your life, would you continue to work or would you stop working?"	"I would enjoy working in my current job even if I did not need the money."
Work centrality	Index of agreement with (1) "To fully develop your talents you need to have a job," (2) "Work is a duty towards society," and (3) "Work should always come first even if it means less spare time."	—

to live comfortably. It is categorical with the values of –1 for those who would cease to work, 0 for those who do not know, and 1 for those who say they would keep working nonetheless. The variable *work centrality* represents an index of three items, to which respondents are asked to express their degree of agreement. All indicators range from 1 (*strongly disagree*) to 4 (*strongly agree*). Cronbach's alpha for this index is .61, and the average interitem correlation is .35. As this is a small three-item scale and Cronbach's alpha grows with the number of items, such reliability may be considered as satisfactory (Cortina 1993) given that prior factor analysis suggested one underlying dimension for these variables. In the ESS dataset, the *lottery* item is retrieved from the similar question coded from 1 (*strongly disagree*) to 5 (*strongly agree*). Unfortunately, in the ESS data there are no equivalent items to calculate the *work centrality* index. Exact questions are listed and compared in Table 1.[4]

We treat all items with Likert-type response formats as quasi-continuous interval data that allow parametric statistical analysis in line with the recommendations of Carifio and Perla (2007).

Model specification

As our dependent variable is a binary indicator, we conduct a binomial logistic regression. The coefficients display how a unit change in the independent variables affects the log of the odds to be self-employed compared to having a paid employment. For the CUPESSE models (1–3), we include the variable groups incrementally: first, we include only controls and country dummies; second, we add the different work values; and finally, we add the predictors concerning work centrality. Then, we model the regression of the ESS data (4–5), first including control variables only, then all variables. In line with the recommendations of Angrist and Pischke (2008), we do not apply any weights to the model estimation.

Results and Discussion

In the CUPESSE model (see Table 2), our expectations concerning work values receive partial support. Hypothesis 1, on the intrinsic work values, creativity, and independence, is fully supported: self-employed individuals are more likely than employees to value creativity ($\beta = .222$; $p < .001$) and independence ($\beta = .224$; $p < .001$) in CUPESSE data. Both our results for creativity and independence clearly confirm the findings of previous studies (e.g., Benz and Frey 2008; Burke, FitzRoy, and Nolan 2002) and underlie the importance of both values under different economic circumstances. Hypothesis 1b on the *lottery* indicator also receives full support ($\beta = .102$; $p < .05$). This finding further confirms the importance of nonpecuniary benefits of entrepreneurship as suggested by previous studies (Burke, FitzRoy, and Nolan 2002; Hamilton 2000).

Hypothesis 2 about extrinsic work values, income, and job security is also fully supported: self-employed individuals are less likely to value high income ($\beta = -.146$; $p < .05$) and job security ($\beta = -.54$; $p < .001$) than employees (cf. Tyszka et al. 2011; Hamilton 2000). Last, we must reject hypothesis 3 on work centrality. Self-employed individuals do not score significantly higher than employees with respect to the index ($\beta = -.086$; $p > .1$). In other words, self-employed people do not attribute a higher value to work in their lives than do employees. This result is surprising, especially in relation to the lottery question. These combined findings suggest that the willingness of the self-employed to continue working, even if they do not need to, is due not to the position of work in their lives and morals but to nonpecuniary benefits of entrepreneurship and satisfaction of their own intrinsic needs. Thus, in this regard, self-employment represents an attractive career choice that promises work as an enjoyable pastime.

Moreover, the ESS model supports almost all results derived above. Hypothesis 1 is fully supported: self-employment correlates with independence ($\beta = .236$; $p < .001$) and with creativity ($\beta = .296$; $p < .001$). Also, hypothesis 1b on the lottery indicator receives full support ($\beta = .185$; $p < .001$). Hypothesis 2 on extrinsic work values, however, is not fully supported. In the ESS model, only security value ($\beta = -.123$; $p < .1$) significantly and negatively correlates with self-employment; the income variable is not significant. We suggest that the economic recession, which in 2010 was still around the peak stage, may have played a role in shifting the determinants of individual career choices: the value of high income may be lower during economic crises when unemployment is high and wages are under pressure. Indeed, some previous studies found that the higher rates of unemployment brought about by the economic crisis increased the

TABLE 2
Logistic Regression: Self-Employed vs. Employed

SE vs. Employed	(CP1)	(CP2)	(CP3)	(ESS1)	(ESS2)
Age	0.0316°°°	0.0329°°°	0.0326°°°	0.0783°°°	0.0800°°°
	(3.48)	(3.57)	(3.53)	(7.29)	(7.78)
Gender (Male)	0.201°°	0.193°°	0.198°°	0.861°°°	0.853°°°
	(2.77)	(2.63)	(2.69)	(9.91)	(9.69)
Education	0.00986	–0.0428	–0.0469	0.0826	–0.0175
	(0.18)	(–0.76)	(–0.83)	(1.31)	(–0.27)
Minority	0.109	0.0595	0.0644	0.0980	0.103
	(0.83)	(0.43)	(0.47)	(0.64)	(0.66)
Caring resp.	0.266°°°	0.290°°°	0.297°°°	0.237°	0.313°°
	(3.33)	(3.57)	(3.64)	(2.47)	(3.24)
Parental SE	0.430°°°	0.405°°°	0.409°°°	0.677°°°	0.645°°°
	(7.46)	(6.98)	(7.03)	(9.77)	(9.07)
Motive: Creativity		0.229°°°	0.222°°°		0.296°°°
		(3.87)	(3.53)		(6.44)
Motive: Independence		0.221°°°	0.224°°°		0.236°°°
		(3.75)	(3.80)		(4.66)
Motive: Job security		–0.540°°°	–0.528°°°		–0.123+
		(–8.39)	(–8.15)		(–1.91)
Motive: High income		–0.146°	–0.138°		–0.00897
		(–2.23)	(–2.11)		(–0.14)
Lottery		0.0919°	0.102°		0.185°°°
		(2.05)	(2.24)		(4.67)
Work centrality index			–0.0860		
			(–1.26)		
Constant	–3.706°°°	–3.584°°°	–3.438°°°	–3.717°°°	–6.457°°°
	(–27.59)	(–11.38)	(–10.19)	(–17.00)	(–13.80)
Observations	10,774	10,774	10,774	9,163	9,163
Log likelihood	–2,916.1	–2,827.9	–2,827.0	–2,280.8	–2,212.5
Chi-squared	447.4	630.4	629.5	503.2	593.6
AIC	5,866.1	5,699.8	5,700.0	4,627.6	4,501.0
R^2-McFadden	.0771	.105	.105	.102	.129

NOTE: SE = Self-employed; AIC = Akaike information criterion.
+p<.1. °p<.05. °°p<.01. °°°p< .001.

chance that individuals started a business against their own preference, but by necessity (Vegetti and Adăscăliței 2017).

Considering prior studies, these results confirm the importance of intrinsic work values for self-employment as well as lesser importance of extrinsic values. Surprisingly, the self-employed score much higher in the lottery indicator, which suggests—in line with prior results—that they do not work for pecuniary

FIGURE 1
Covariate Effects on Self-Employment

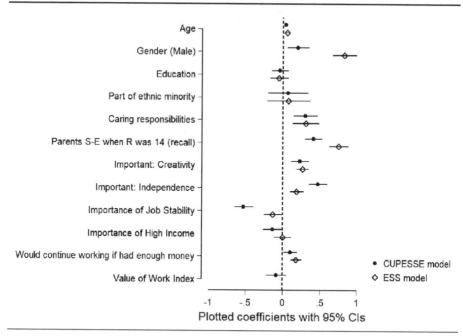

benefits, but at the same time work does not take a more central position in their lives. One approach to address this finding could be that young adults do not understand work by itself as a duty or as central in their lives, but much more their current job with its specific benefits (cf. discussion of work centrality and job involvement in Paullay, Alliger, and Stone-Romero 1994).

Yet it remains unclear when and where these policy suggestions can enter political manifestos. Debus, Tosun, and Maxeiner (2017) discuss under which circumstances which parties tend to adopt these entrepreneurship-friendly policies in their political manifestos: with somewhat different implications for countries with a socialist heritage, parties are more prone to adapt entrepreneurship-friendly policies in times of economic hardship.

Conclusion

This study provides an empirical assessment of how different values attributed to work relate to different career paths among young adults. Previous literature shows that today's youth regard work as less central in their lives and appear to value less both intrinsic and extrinsic factors (Cogin 2012; Twenge et al. 2010). Given the economic relevance of entrepreneurship for innovation and employment, policy-makers increasingly strive to support it (Dvouletý and Lukeš 2016). To tailor this support effectively, there is a need to understand motivational patterns behind entrepreneurship because such patterns predict the career choice of becoming and remaining self-employed.

Despite many studies inquiring about entrepreneurial motivation, none has so far differentiated work values and work centrality between employees and the self-employed. This study fills this gap with a specific analysis of young adults between 18 and 35 in thirty different countries in 2010 and 2016. Results provide mixed evidence for our expectations. One robust pattern emerging from the data is that intrinsic values, such as independence, creativity, and the willingness to continue working even if not needed, correlate positively with the probability of being self-employed. Thus, we support the link between self-determination theory and self-employment. On the other hand, we find that extrinsic factors such as valuing a secure job correlate more strongly with paid employment. For valuing high income, another extrinsic value, the negative association with self-employment holds in only one of the two samples used. Finally, we do not find any correlation between work centrality and self-employment.

This study contributes to the literature on young adults' behavior in the labor market, the literature on entrepreneurial motivation, and last, to policy-makers' understanding of the entrepreneurial mind. While work centrality has been found to decline among young adults (Twenge et al. 2010), the current study shows that this decline does not affect young adults' choice to start their own business. Moreover, extrinsic work values and the prospect of high and secure income do not lead young people into self-employment; quite the contrary, it motivates them to become wage employees. Based on self-determination theory (Gagné and Deci 2005), one may even expect the opposite, namely, that various pecuniary subsidies offered to entrepreneurs may replace their intrinsic values and inhibit efforts to establish an entrepreneurial culture. This stands in contrast to classical economic views that extrinsic factors such as high income motivate entrepreneurs. Thus, political programs to boost entrepreneurship should not merely focus on such levers but rather provide as many opportunities for intrinsically meaningful self-employment as possible; political decisions regarding self-employment should not underestimate the importance of intrinsic values. Policies focused on reducing the red tape and bureaucracy may prove to be more efficient drivers of entrepreneurial activity as they enable entrepreneurs to enjoy more independence and creativity. Likewise, these findings suggest a new paradigm for entrepreneurship education: while many educational policies define entrepreneurial skills as key capabilities to be studied (including grading and testing), creating an atmosphere where students may freely develop self-determination, creativity, and independence may be a more promising avenue. Our study suggests that among younger individuals, the choice to become self-employed is driven largely by genuinely intrinsic values.

Notes

1. For an overview of the project, see www.cupesse.eu.

2. For the countries in the CUPESSE study, see Tosun et al. (2018); and for the countries in the ESS study, see http://www.europeansocialsurvey.org/about/participating_countries.html.

3. For the respondents who are still in part-time education, the highest achieved level was used. For easier interpretation, the seven ISCED levels were translated into a three-level ordinal index with ISCED levels 1 and 2 grouped together (coded as –1), 3 to 5 grouped together and coded as 0 and levels 6 and 7 grouped together and coded as +1.

4. See Tables A1 and A2 in the online appendix for an overview on all variables and correlations in the two data sources. We calculated the variance inflation factors (VIF), which provide a mean value of 1.12 in the CUPESSE data and 1.16 in ESS data, and found no hints at multicollinearity.

References

Amabile, Teresa M. 1997. Entrepreneurial creativity through motivational synergy. *Journal of Creative Behavior* 31 (1): 18–26.

Angrist, Joshua D., and Jörn-Steffen Pischke. 2008. *Mostly harmless econometrics*. Princeton, NJ: Princeton University Press.

Arvey, Richard D., Itzhak Harpaz, and Hui Liao. 2004. Work centrality and post-award work behavior of lottery winners. *Journal of Psychology* 138 (5): 404–20.

Bal, Matthijs P., and Dorien Kooij. 2011. The relations between work centrality, psychological contracts, and job attitudes: The influence of age. *European Journal of Work and Organizational Psychology* 20 (4): 497–523.

Bardi, Anat, and Shalom H. Schwartz. 2003. Values and behavior: Strength and structure of relations. *Personality & Social Psychology Bulletin* 29 (10): 1207–20.

Benz, Matthias, and Bruno S. Frey. 2008. The value of doing what you like: Evidence from the self-employed in 23 countries. *Journal of Economic Behavior & Organization* 68 (3): 445–55.

Burke, Andrew E., Felix R. FitzRoy, and Michael A. Nolan. 2002. Self-employment wealth and job creation: The roles of gender, non-pecuniary motivation and entrepreneurial ability. *Small Business Economics* 19 (3): 255–70.

Cardon, Melissa S., and Pankaj C. Patel. 2015. Is stress worth it? Stress-related health and wealth trade-offs for entrepreneurs. *Applied Psychology* 64 (2): 379–420.

Carifio, James, and Rocco J. Perla. 2007. Ten common misunderstandings, misconceptions, persistent myths and urban legends about Likert scales and Likert response formats and their antidotes. *Journal of Social Sciences* 3 (3): 106–16.

Carsrud, Alan, and Malin Brännback. 2011. Entrepreneurial motivations: What do we still need to know? *Journal of Small Business Management* 49 (1): 9–26.

Carter, Nancy M., William B. Gartner, Kelly G. Shaver, and Elizabeth J. Gatewood. 2003. The career reasons of nascent entrepreneurs. *Journal of Business Venturing* 18 (1): 13–39.

Cogin, Julie. 2012. Are generational differences in work values fact or fiction? Multi-country evidence and implications. *International Journal of Human Resource Management* 23 (11): 2268–94.

Cortina, Jose M. 1993. What is coefficient Alpha? An examination of theory and applications. *Journal of Applied Psychology* 78 (1): 98–104.

Debus, Marc, Jale Tosun, and Marcel Maxeiner. 2017. Support for policies on entrepreneurship and self-employment among parties and coalition governments. *Politics & Policy* 45 (3): 338–71.

Diefendorff, James M., Douglas J. Brown, Allen M. Kamin, and Robert G. Lord. 2002. Examining the roles of job involvement and work centrality in predicting organizational citizenship behaviors and job performance. *Journal of Organizational Behavior* 23 (1): 93–108.

Dose, Jennifer J. 1997. Work values: An integrative framework and illustrative application to organizational socialization. *Journal of Occupational and Organizational Psychology* 70 (3): 219–40.

Douglas, Evan J., and Dean A. Shepherd. 2000. Entrepreneurship as a utility maximizing response. *Journal of Business Venturing* 15 (3): 231–51.

Dvouletý, Ondrej, and Martin Lukeš. 2016. Review of empirical studies on self-employment out of unemployment: Do self-employment policies make a positive impact? *International Review of Entrepreneurship* 14 (3): 361–76.

Edelman, Linda F., Candida G. Brush, Tatiana S. Manolova, and Patricia G. Greene. 2010. Start-up motivations and growth intentions of minority nascent entrepreneurs. *Journal of Small Business Management* 48 (2): 174–96.

Fayolle, Alain, Francisco Liñán, and Juan A. Moriano. 2014. Beyond entrepreneurial intentions: Values and motivations in entrepreneurship. *International Entrepreneurship and Management Journal* 10 (4): 679–89.

Feldmann, Manuel, Martin Lukeš, and Lorraine Uhlaner. 2018. Have it made or make it yourself: Why do young Europeans enter their family's business or strive to found their own? Paper presented at the European Academy of Management Conference, Reykjavik.

Furnham, Adrian F. 1990. A content, correlational, and factor analytic study of seven questionnaire measures of the protestant work ethic. *Human Relations* 43 (4): 383–99.

Gagné, Marylène, and Edward L. Deci. 2005. Self-determination theory and work motivation. *Journal of Organizational Behavior* 26 (4): 331–62.

Gallie, Duncan. 2019. Research on work values in a changing economic and social context. *The ANNALS of the American Academy of Political and Social Science* (this volume).

Glass, Amy. 2007. Understanding generational differences for competitive success. *Industrial and Commercial Training* 39 (2): 98–103.

Gorgievski, Marjan J., M. Evelina Ascalon, and Ute Stephan. 2011. Small business owners' success criteria, a values approach to personal differences. *Journal of Small Business Management* 49 (2): 207–32.

Hamilton, Barton H. 2000. Does entrepreneurship pay? An empirical analysis of the returns to self-employment. *Journal of Political Economy* 108 (3): 604–31.

Hemingway, Christine A. 2005. Personal values as a catalyst for corporate social entrepreneurship. *Journal of Business Ethics* 60 (3): 233–49.

Hessels, Jolanda, Marco van Gelderen, and Roy Thurik. 2008. Entrepreneurial aspirations, motivations, and their drivers. *Small Business Economics* 31 (3): 323–39.

Hundley, Greg. 2001. Why and when are the self-employed more satisfied with their work? *Industrial Relations* 40 (2): 293–316.

Hyytinen, Ari, and Olli-Pekka Ruuskanen. 2007. Time use of the self-employed. *Kyklos* 60 (1): 105–22.

Jaén, Inmaculada, and Francisco Liñán. 2013. Work values in a changing economic environment: The role of entrepreneurial capital. *International Journal of Manpower* 34 (8): 939–60.

Manyika, James, Susan Lund, Jacques Bughin, Kelsey Robinson, Jan Mischke, and Deepa Mahajan. 2016. Independent work: Choice, necessity, and the gig economy. McKinsey Global Institute Report. Available from https://www.mckinsey.com.

Martin, Carolyn A. 2005. From high maintenance to high productivity: What managers need to know about Generation Y. *Industrial and Commercial Training* 37 (1): 39–44.

Miller, Michael J., David J. Woehr, and Natasha Hudspeth. 2002. The meaning and measurement of work ethic: Construction and initial validation of a multidimensional inventory. *Journal of Vocational Behavior* 60 (3): 451–89.

Parry, Emma, and Peter Urwin. 2011. Generational differences in work values: A review of theory and evidence. *International Journal of Management Reviews* 13 (1): 79–96.

Paullay, Irina M., George M. Alliger, and Eugene F. Stone-Romero. 1994. Construct validation of two instruments designed to measure job involvement and work centrality. *Journal of Applied Psychology* 79 (2): 224–28.

Rauch, Andreas, and Michael Frese. 2007. Let's put the person back into entrepreneurship research: A meta-analysis on the relationship between business owners' personality traits, business creation, and success. *European Journal of Work and Organizational Psychology* 16 (4): 353–85.

Ros, Maria, Shalom H. Schwartz, and Shoshana Surkiss. 1999. Basic individual values, work values, and the meaning of work. *Applied Psychology* 48 (1): 49–71.

Ryan, Richard M., and Edward L. Deci. 2000. Self-determination theory and the facilitation of intrinsic motivation, social development, and well-being. *American Psychologist* 55 (1): 68–78.

Sarfati, Hedva. 2013. Coping with the unemployment crisis in Europe. *International Labour Review* 152 (1): 145–56.

Schjoedt, Leon. 2009. Entrepreneurial job characteristics: An examination of their effect on entrepreneurial satisfaction. *Entrepreneurship Theory and Practice* 33 (3): 619–44.

Shane, Scott, Edwin A. Locke, and Christopher J. Collins. 2003. Entrepreneurial motivation. *Human Resource Management Review* 13 (2): 257–79.

Shaw, Sue, and David Fairhurst. 2008. Engaging a new generation of graduates. *Education + Training* 50 (5): 366–78.

Skedinger, Per. 2010. *Employment protection legislation: Evolution, effects, winners and losers*. Cheltenham, UK: Edward Elgar Publishing.

Smola, Karen Wey, and Charlotte D. Sutton. 2002. Generational differences: Revisiting generational work values for the new millennium. *Journal of Organizational Behavior* 23 (4): 363–82.

Stephan, Ute, Mark Hart, and Cord-Christian Drews. 2015. *Understanding motivations for entrepreneurship: A review of recent research evidence*. Birmingham, UK: Enterprise Research Centre.

Tosun, J., J. Arco, M. Caserta, Z. Cemalcilar, M. Freitag, F. Hörisch, C. Jensen, B. Kittel, L. Littvay, M. Lukeš, W. Maloney, et al. 2018. Perceived economic self-sufficiency: A country-and generation-comparative approach. *European Political Science*.

Twenge, Jean M., Stacy M. Campbell, Brian J. Hoffman, and Charles E. Lance. 2010. Generational differences in work values: Leisure and extrinsic values increasing, social and intrinsic values decreasing. *Journal of Management* 36 (5): 1117–42.

Tyszka, Tadeusz, Jerzy Cieślik, Artur Domurat, and Anna Macko. 2011. Motivation, self-efficacy, and risk attitudes among entrepreneurs during transition to a market economy. *Journal of Socio-Economics* 40 (2): 124–31.

van Gelderen, Marco. 2016. Entrepreneurial autonomy and its dynamics. *Applied Psychology* 65 (3): 541–67.

van Praag, C. Mirjam, and Peter H. Versloot. 2007. What is the value of entrepreneurship? A review of recent research. *Small Business Economics* 29 (4): 351–82.

Vegetti, Federico, and Dragoş Adăscăliţei. 2017. The impact of the economic crisis on latent and early entrepreneurship in Europe. *International Entrepreneurship and Management Journal* 13 (4): 1289–1314.

Weber, Max. 1905. Die Protestantische Ethik und der Geist des Kapitalismus. *Archiv Für Sozialwissenschaft Und Sozialpolitik* 20, 21 (1, 1): 1–54, 1–110.

The Effect of Unemployment and Low-Quality Work Conditions on Work Values: Exploring the Experiences of Young Europeans

By
EMILY RAINSFORD,
WILLIAM A. MALONEY,
and
SEBASTIAN ADRIAN POPA

This article examines the impact that unemployment and low-quality work conditions have on young adults' work values. Academic theory suggests that harsher economic conditions will make people prize extrinsic work values (income, security) more and intrinsic work values (creative, independent working conditions, autonomy) less. We apply this reasoning to study young Europeans' response to unemployment and low-quality work conditions, expecting that those who have these experiences will value extrinsic values more and intrinsic work values less than those who do not have these experiences. Using the CUPESSE dataset of 18- to 35-year-olds in eleven European countries, we do not find support for the effect of previous unemployment experience on intrinsic or extrinsic work values. However, when it comes to the effect of low-quality work conditions, there are mixed results. We find that one dimension of low-quality work conditions—overqualification—does have a positive effect on extrinsic work values. Further, we find that age has a moderating effect: unemployment and low-quality work conditions have a larger impact on the younger workers in our sample than their older counterparts.

Keywords: work values; working conditions; CUPESSE; overqualification; precarious; unemployment; young people

S tructural changes within the labor market—including increased flexibility, high levels of unemployment, rising educational attainment levels, the changing nature of work itself (e.g., technological modernization and employment precarity), and the 2007 economic crisis—have all had a significant impact on the ways in which people experience work (Cahuc et al.

Emily Rainsford is a research associate at Newcastle University working on youth political engagement and employment.

William A. Maloney is a professor of politics and head of the School of Geography, Politics and Sociology at Newcastle University. His research interests include civil society organizations and political participation.

Correspondence: emily.rainsford@ncl.ac.uk

DOI: 10.1177/0002716219830378

2013; O'Reilly et al. 2015). These developments have had the most profound impact on those entering the labor market—the young (Dietrich 2012; Shore and Tosun 2017). Even though unemployment levels have recovered in many European countries after the crisis, youth unemployment levels remain stubbornly high (Cahuc et al. 2013; Oesingmann 2017; Tosun 2017).

Early unemployment experiences for young people can have various long-term effects both for society and the individual. Youth unemployment carries a significant economic cost, estimated at more than €50 billion in the European Union (EU) in 2011 (see Tosun 2017, 40). At the individual level, not only are young people more likely to experience unemployment "because their relative position in the queue for jobs deteriorates more easily when the growth for employment slows down" (Wolber 2007, 189), but unemployment can also have long-term scarring effects. The transition to the first sustainable job remains a critical and formative period that has consequences for the life chances of young people (Arnett 2000; Ryan 2001). Unemployment experience during this time increases the likelihood of being unemployed later in life, can decrease future salaries, send a negative signal to future employers, and lead to a loss in social networks and opportunity to develop important skills with a labor market currency (Dietrich 2012; Shore and Tosun 2017). Experience of unemployment during this formative time can directly influence young people's work values (Chow, Krahn, and Galambos 2014; Cemalcilar, Tosun, and Jensen, this volume; Gallie, this volume; Kalleberg and Marsden, this volume).

Previous research has explored how societal changes influence work values across generations (Van den Broeck et al. 2010). For example, when times are tough during an economic crisis or in its immediate aftermath, or if individuals have experienced unemployment, then people tend to value job security and high incomes—*extrinsic* work values—over independent working and opportunities for personal development and growth—*intrinsic* work values (Kalleberg and Marsden 2013). However, it is not only unemployment that shapes work values but also workplace and work-life experiences (Adkins and Naumann 2016). As Gallie (this volume) highlights, "while early socialization and education were generally important determinants of employment commitment and intrinsic reward values, differences in job quality are central for the explanation of country differences." In Europe, a growing concern for young people entering the labor market, and for policy-makers, is the *quality of work* (Cedefop 2018; Eurofound 2002).

Recent research in the UK characterized the labor market as resembling an hourglass with plenty of high quality jobs at the top, and low quality jobs at the bottom, and a hollowing out of the middle-range occupations (Sissons 2011, 4). As Sissons (2011, 4) notes, this structural change means that highly skilled

Sebastian Adrian Popa is a lecturer in comparative politics at Newcastle University and a researcher at MZES, University of Mannheim. His research focuses on political behavior in a comparative perspective.

NOTE: We recognize financial support by the project Cultural Pathways to Economic Self-Sufficiency and Entrepreneurship (CUPESSE; Seventh Framework Program of the European Union; Grant Agreement No. 613257). We thank Carolin Rapp, the guest editors, and one anonymous reviewer for their comments on earlier versions of this article.

workers may find themselves getting "bumped down" the labor market, having to take on jobs that they are overqualified for. There are similar concerns regarding the skills mismatch beyond the UK. The EU identified the skills mismatch as a critical issue following the 2007 economic crisis, with significant reductions in the number of jobs in certain sectors and employers finding it difficult to find people with the right skills for the jobs on offer (Cedefop 2018).[1] The Organisation for Economic Cooperation and Development (OECD 1996, 132–33, cited in Curtain 2001, 8) estimated that "men even up to the age of 28 may have problems in settling into stable work; for some who are early school leavers, the transition can last to age 35." The quality of work is thus a major concern for young people and policy-makers today, and it is therefore important to understand how this experience affects what contemporary young people value in work.

The concept of *quality of work* is complex and the exact definition depends on whether it is assessed from the individual or societal perspective. The United Nations Economic Commission for Europe (UNECE; 2015, 13) defined quality of work as "the conditions and ethics of employment, monetary and non-pecuniary benefits, working time arrangements and work-life balance, employment security and social protection, skills development and training as well as work motivation and employment-related relationships." In this article, we take an individual perspective and focus on the skills match and the type of contract the individual has, tapping into both the employment security and skills development aspects of the UNECE definition.[2]

We advance previous research and contribute to the policy debate on quality of work by exploring not only the impact of unemployment on contemporary young European's work values but also the effect of low-quality work. Both these experiences are highly likely to shape what young people value in work, and we aim to test the effects on intrinsic and extrinsic work values. To do this, we draw on the Cultural Pathways to Economic Self-Sufficiency and Entrepreneurship (CUPESSE) dataset of 18- to 35-year-olds in elven European countries (see Tosun et al. 2018), focusing only on the employed respondents as we are interested in the effect of working conditions on work values. Herein, *low-quality work* is defined as precarious or nonstandard jobs (casual, temporary, fractional work, or disadvantageous contracts—e.g., zero hours[3]) and/or jobs in which workers believe that their qualifications are beyond the requirements of their current position (i.e., they consider themselves to be overqualified for the job). Drawing on Kalleberg and Marsden's (2013) problematic rewards thesis that suggests that those who have secure and well-paid jobs value intrinsic values more than those who do not, we expect that people who have experience of unemployment or low-quality working conditions will value extrinsic work values more and intrinsic work values less than those who do not have these experiences.

Work Values and Young People

As Gallie (this volume) notes, the last 50 years or so have witnessed, at times, lively debates surrounding the changing nature of work and its impact on the multidimensionality of work values. Lyons, Higgins, and Duxbury (2010, 971) define work values "as generalized beliefs about the relative desirability of various aspects of work (*e.g.* pay, autonomy, working conditions), and work-related outcomes (*e.g.* accomplishment, fulfillment, prestige)." Values are fundamental beliefs that people hold about right and wrong and in "the work setting ... are the evaluative standards relating to work or the work environment by which individuals discern what is right" or assess the importance of preferences (Wey Smola and Sutton 2002, 365–66). However, while these beliefs are *normative*, they are not necessarily *positive*; that is, they relate to "what *ought to be*, rather than what *is*" (Wey Smola and Sutton, 2002, 365–66, emphasis in original). Work values are central to explanations of workers' motivations, attitudes toward material and non-material rewards, and work and career aspirations (see Kalleberg and Marsden, this volume). Following the introductory article in this volume (Kraaykamp, Cemalcilar, and Tosun), our theoretical focus centers on the main, and most extensively studied, work value classification: *intrinsic* (stimulating work, individual autonomy, helping others, making a societal contribution) and *extrinsic* (job security and pay) (also see Kuron et al. 2015). Extrinsic work values can be viewed as a compensation for the general obligatory, unpleasant character of work (see also Halman and Müller 2006), while intrinsic values reflect intangible rewards related to the process of work (Deci and Ryan 2000).

There are many institutions and experiences that can shape (young) people's work values, including the varying economic and labor market conditions that different generations face, social background, parental employment contexts, parenting styles, school, the workplace, social networks, and so on (see Kirkpatrick Johnson and Mortimer 2015; Cemalcilar, Secinti, and Sumer 2018). While early socialization is crucial in setting the foundations for values, values are not fixed or static; they can mutate as people's experiences and interactions with different institutions change. Youth is a particularly strong socialization period because it is formative, transformative, and transitional (Wyn and White 1997; Lechner et al. 2017; Sortheix, Chow, and Salmela-Aro 2015). Previous research has illustrated that the conditions and process of getting that first job after leaving education has long-term consequences for the value predispositions and life chances of young people (Ryan 2001). Because of the current challenging and precarious situation for young people in the labor market, and given the importance of youth transitions to work, it is especially important to explore how experiences during this formative period shape work values.

The Determinants of Work Values: The Quality of the Work Conditions

Kalleberg and Marsden (2013, 257) argue that the problematic rewards thesis predicts that people in highly paid and secure employment are much more likely to value *intrinsic* rewards rather than *extrinsic* rewards. Thus, the unemployed, and those in low- or unskilled employment, will value a job that is adequately remunerated and relatively secure—that is, extrinsic. The idea here is also linked to compensation. If basic material and security needs are not met or are under threat, then people's materialistic priorities are likely to increase (see Lechner et al. 2017, 54). In other words, the argument is that once workers' basic needs have been satisfied, their value preferences will shift to satisfying more aesthetic and self-actualizing needs (see also Kalleberg and Marsden, this volume).

In their study of changing work values in the United States between 1973 and 2006 Kalleberg's and Marsden's (2013, 267) results supported the problematic reward thesis. "When unemployment is high, jobs are scarce and so job security is more problematic, increasing the significance of having a job at all. Moreover, since wages are tied to jobs, attaining economic security also becomes more problematic during 'high-unemployment periods.'" Gallie, Felstead, and Green's (2012, 819) complementary findings showed that when comparing people's job preferences between 1992 and 2006 the intrinsic quality of employment clearly increased. They argued that the key explanatory factors included "higher educational levels, higher skilled jobs and greater security in terms of pay and employment … in a period of strong economic growth and rising prosperity."

For example, if young workers experience unemployment or enter the labor market in periods of economic and financial retrenchment and rising unemployment, they may tend to value more basic bread and butter aspects (*extrinsic* rewards) rather than the importance of personal development and quality of work opportunities (*intrinsic* rewards). While previous research has mainly focused on generational differences, and the effect of societal economic situations, Chow, Krahn, and Galambos (2014) illustrated in their analysis on young people in Canada that unemployment experiences early in the transition to adulthood have an immediate and long-term effect on work values. Accordingly, we examine the effects of previous unemployment experience on young people's work values. Our first hypotheses relating to the effects of unemployment on work values are:

H1a: Young people who have experienced unemployment will be more likely to value extrinsic work values compared to those who have not experienced unemployment.

H1b: Young people who have experienced unemployment will be less likely to value intrinsic work values than those who have not experienced unemployment.

As argued in the introduction to this article, the quality of working conditions is a significant issue for young people in the labor market today. However, the idea that work conditions influence work values is not new. For example, Kalleberg and Marsden (2013) and Gallie, Felstead, and Green (2012) both highlight that the conditions when an individual is seeking work and the type of employment that she or he secures—does it satisfy her or his basic needs, for example—influence individual job preferences and work values. Furthermore, Bokemeier and Lacy (1987) showed that current and past working conditions influence workers' attitudes to their current job and shape work values that, in turn, influence their behavioral patterns (Adkins and Naumann 2016). However, these scholars neither specifically addressed the position of young workers nor investigated contract type or skills match. This article directly examines young workers and the impact of the quality of their work conditions on their work values. By doing this, we make a significant and important contribution to the literature on work conditions and work values. Accordingly, we hypothesize that

H2a: Young people who have experienced low-quality work conditions will be more likely to value extrinsic work values compared to those who have not had such work conditions.

H2b: Young people who have experienced low-quality work conditions will be less likely to value intrinsic work values compared to those who have not had such work conditions.

Data, Measurement, and Methods

For this analysis, we use the CUPESSE dataset because it is a representative sample of 18- to 35-year-olds across eleven countries in Europe (for more details about the dateset, see Tosun et al. 2018). Following from our theoretical focus on the effect of working conditions, we only perform the analysis on those who are employed; thus, our sample size falls modestly from 11,989 in the full sample to 11,248 individuals in our working sample.

In line with the argument presented in the introduction to this volume, we focus on intrinsic and extrinsic values. We move slightly beyond what is outlined in the introduction (Kraaykamp, Cemalcilar, and Tosun, this volume) and build an index of extrinsic and intrinsic values using the classification presented by Kuron et al. (2015). We use valuing "job security," "high income," "having time for leisure," and "balance work and other commitments" as our measures of extrinsic work values; and "working independently," "learning new things," "developing creativity," and "self-worth" to measure intrinsic work values. In both the intrinsic and extrinsic cases, we construct an additive index (i.e., the mean of the items) of items that are measured on a 4-point scale with values between 1 (*not at all important*) and 4 (*very important*).[4]

In the case of the intrinsic values index, the Cronbach alpha is .7, confirming that the items form an internally consistent scale. Although in the case of the extrinsic value index the alpha values fall just below the accepted limits for internal consistency (.6), it is important to note that this construct is based on our theoretical propositions (Kuron et al. 2015; Kraaykamp, Cemalcilar, and Tosun, this volume). In addition to this, the correlations between each item and the extrinsic values index are very strong (between .65 and .7), pointing toward an acceptable level of internal consistency. Finally, in both cases, the distributions of the indices are highly skewed to the right (extrinsic mean = 3.4, SD = 0.44; intrinsic mean = 3.4, SD = 0.5).

Turning to our main independent variable, we measure the effect of previous unemployment experience on work values by using a dichotomous variable that is given the value of 1 if respondents answered yes to the question, "Have you ever been unemployed for a period longer than 6 months?" and 0 otherwise. We conceptualize the quality of work using two indicators. The first captures job insecurity and is assigned the value 1 for those who do not have a permanent contract and 0 for those who have a permanent contract. The second variable captures the self-assessed match between the respondent's qualifications and their current job; this variable has three values: (1) those who consider themselves overqualified for their current job, (2) those who believe they are under-qualified for their current job, and (3) those who consider their job to be a good match with their qualifications. We use the latter as the reference category in our analysis.

We further control for a number of characteristics including the type of employment (being self-employed or not), the current economic situation of the respondents (being able to cover the basic costs of living, having moved out from the parental home, having responsibilities to care for others, or receiving financial support from parents), family financial background (if their family could afford extras beyond basic needs when the respondent was aged 14, for example, going on vacation), and a number of sociodemographic characteristics (age, education, gender, and migration background).

For the analysis, we rely on a pooled regression model with fixed country effects.[5] All the independent variables are standardized and have values between 0 and 1 so that the coefficients can be easily compared and interpreted.

Results and Discussion

Table 1 summarizes the results of the analysis used to test our main theoretical expectations.[6] Surprisingly, we do not find support for the effect of previous unemployment experience on intrinsic or extrinsic work values. However, when it comes to the effect of low-quality work conditions, there are mixed results. On one hand, as expected, those who experience a mismatch between their qualifications and their current job, (i.e., believe they are overqualified) tend to place greater emphasis on extrinsic values (see model 1 in Table 1). On the other hand, contrary to our expectations, those who do not have a permanent contract place less weight on extrinsic values than those who have a permanent contract (see model 1 in Table 1).

While all the findings outlined above are statistically significant, the effects are nevertheless relatively small. This is not surprising given the distribution of the dependent variables. However, the low variation of the dependent variables increases the chances of Type II errors, making the detection of statistically significant effects more difficult. Thus, we are confident that the effects are robust and not an artifact.

Given our surprising but interesting findings, we further explore why the effects of experiencing unemployment and not having a permanent contract differ from our theoretical expectation. In this regard, the explanation could be that the analysis is based on a sample of young adults. To be more specific, our general expectation is that the effects of both variables are substantially different for the younger respondents in our sample—remember our age range of 18 to 35 is more extensive than many other studies on young people. In other words, we

TABLE 1
Predicting Extrinsic and Intrinsic Work Values, Main Effects

	Model 1: Extrinsic Values	Model 2: Extrinsic Values
Intercept	3.212 (0.032)°°	3.271 (0.037)°°
No permanent contract	−.042 (.010)°°	.012 (.011)
Experienced unemployment	.016 (.010)	−.000 (.012)
Overqualified	.024 (.010)°	.004 (.012)
Underqualified	.025 (.020)	.008 (.023)
Born in the country	.007 (.018)	.054 (.020)°°
Can afford basics	−.001 (.010)	−.005 (.012)
Moved out	−.002 (.019)	−.028 (.022)
Age	.027 (.010)°°	.000 (.012)
Caring responsibilities	.042 (.006)°°	.018 (.007)°
Self-employed	−.077 (.014)°°	−.093 (.017)°°
Parent support	.017 (.013)	.014 (.015)
Parents afforded extras	.004 (.014)	.031 (.016)
Secondary education	.028 (.015)	.016 (.018)
Tertiary education	.012 (.015)	.057 (.018)°°
Female	.034 (.008)°°	.050 (.010)°°
Adj. R^2	.097	.054
Num. obs.	9,971	9,971

NOTE: Ordinary least squares (OLS) regression coefficients with standard errors in parenthesis; country fixed-effects are included in the models but not reported in Table 1 (for full models, see online appendix).
°$p < .05$. °°$p < .01$.

suspect that age acts as a moderator for the effect of our independent variables on work values. In Table 2, we examine how the interactions between these two variables that do not behave as we expected with age can help to explain the level of extrinsic and intrinsic values.

We find that age has a statistically significant interaction with not having a permanent contract for extrinsic values (see Table 2, model 3) and with unemployment experience in the case of intrinsic values (see Table 2, model 4). For ease of interpretation, we plot these effects. Thus, we note that that the difference in extrinsic work values between those who have and those who do not have a permanent contract diminishes with age (see Figure 1).[7] This outcome is mostly because extrinsic values are more important for older individuals who are in precarious work situations compared to their younger counterparts. At the same time, those who have a permanent contract have the same level of extrinsic values irrespective of their age. However, for individuals who are around 35 years old, the difference in the level of extrinsic values depending on the type of contract is close to zero.

In the case of intrinsic values (see Figure 2), we can see that the difference between those who have experienced unemployment and those who have not

TABLE 2
Predicting Extrinsic and Intrinsic Work Values, Interactions Effects

	Model 3: Extrinsic Values (interactions)	Model 4: Intrinsic Values (interactions)
Intercept	3.239 (0.033)°°	3.297 (0.039)°°
No permanent contract	−.083 (.022)°°	−.011 (.026)
Experienced unemployment	−.024 (.025)	−.063 (.029)°
Overqualified	.023 (.010)°	.003 (.012)
Underqualified	.026 (.020)	.008 (.023)
Born in the country	.008 (.018)	.055 (.020)°°
Can afford basics	.041 (.006)°°	.018 (.007)°
Moved out	−.001 (.010)	−.005 (.012)
Age	−.042 (.023)	−.068 (.027)°
Caring responsibilities	.027 (.010)°°	.002 (.012)
Self-employed	−.077 (.014)°°	−.093 (.017)°°
Parent support	.018 (.013)	.015 (.015)
Parents afforded extras	.003 (.014)	.030 (.016)
Secondary education	.027 (.015)	.015 (.018)
Tertiary education	.011 (.015)	.056 (.018)°°
Female	.033 (.008)°°	.049 (.010)°°
Not permanent × age	.069 (.034)°	.038 (.040)
Unemployment × age	.062 (.036)	.100 (.042)°
Adj. R^2	.098	.055
Num. obs.	9,971	9,971

NOTE: Ordinary least squares (OLS) regression coefficients with standard errors in parenthesis; country fixed-effects are included in the models but not reported in Table 2 (for full models, see online appendix).
°$p < .05$. °°$p < .01$.

dissipates as people get older. In this case, there are two driving forces. On one hand, intrinsic values are more important for older individuals who have not experienced unemployment in comparison to their younger peers. At the same time, these values have become less important for older individuals who have experienced unemployment. Overall, these results confirm our main intuition that our sample of young workers is the main reason for our findings differing from previous research. In summary, in both the cases of intrinsic and extrinsic values, the differences depending on previous unemployment experience or current low-quality work conditions (i.e., having no permanent contract) dissolve for individuals who are older.

Conclusion

We set out to evaluate the extent to which previous unemployment experience and current work conditions influence the work values of young adults in Europe.

FIGURE 1

Effect of Not Having a Permanent Contract on Extrinsic Values, Conditional on Age

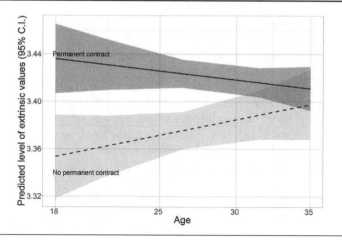

FIGURE 2

Effect of Experiencing Unemployment on Intrinsic Values, Conditional on Age

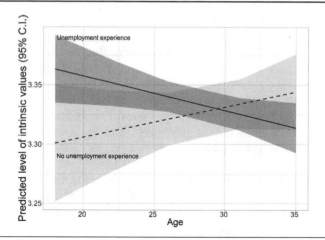

Previous research addressed the impact of unemployment on work values (Kalleberg and Marsden 2013), but we argue that by solely focusing on unemployment, we fail to capture the full extent to which working conditions and experiences influence the development of work values for young people transitioning into the labor market. Given the important socializing experience of the workplace and its role in helping to shape work values (Adkins and Naumann 2016), and given the challenges young people face when entering the labor market (Cedefop 2018), we further argue that it is crucial to consider the *quality of work conditions*, in terms of precarious or nonstandard contracts and the skills match, as important to shaping work values. We are also well aware that other profound contextual factors will play an important role in the development of young people's work values—for example, the differential impact of the 2007 economic crisis on young people in terms of both high youth unemployment and the diminishing quality of work.

In formulating our hypotheses, our datum was the problematic rewards thesis. This theoretical proposition argues that under conditions of economic hardship, people tend to place greater emphasis on extrinsic work values and are less concerned with intrinsic values (Kalleberg and Marsden 2013). Once we factor in the long-term scaring effect of unemployment experiences on young people (Chow, Krahn, and Galambos 2014), this led us to hypothesize that past unemployment experiences are associated with an increased emphasis on extrinsic values (H1a), while they would have a negative impact on the level of intrinsic values (H1b). Furthermore, we also expected the quality of working conditions to shape work values (Bokemeier and Lacy 1987), that is, low-quality work conditions lead to higher levels of extrinsic values (H2a) and lower levels of intrinsic values (H2b). We chose to test our second hypothesis by focusing on the effect of not having a permanent contract or having a job that does not match our respondents' educational attainment and skills levels. These two indicators have been underresearched, but contemporaneously they represent a significant challenge for young adults transitioning into the labor market (Curtain 2001; Sissons 2011). They are also increasingly of concern for policy-makers (Cedefop 2018).

Our analysis offers mixed evidence in support of our hypotheses, while also opening up further questions. We find support for the positive effect on extrinsic work values from one dimension of low-quality work conditions, overqualification (H2a). Contrary to the same hypothesis (H2a), the other facet of low-quality working conditions, not having a permanent contract, has a negative and statistically significant effect on the level of extrinsic values. Even more puzzling is the fact that in the case of unemployment experience, which has previously been found to be an important explanatory factory for both intrinsic and extrinsic work values, we do not find any statistically significant effects for either type of work value.

These contradictory findings and the lack of effect in the case of the unemployment experience leads us to believe that this pattern of results is specific to young adults. In fact, once we consider the possible moderating effect of age, we notice that the effects do indeed relate directly to the younger segment of our sample and start to dissipate in their older peers. To be more precise, for the older part of our sample, the type of contract has no statistically significant effect on extrinsic values. At the same time, the effect of unemployment experience is more in line with previous studies for the older individuals in the sample. In their case, we note that those who experienced unemployment do indeed seem to have lower levels of intrinsic values (H1b), while in the case of younger adults, we see the opposite pattern. The problematic rewards of work and need for satisfaction of material needs (Kalleberg and Marsden 2013) thus seem to be more or less problematic depending on the age of the worker.

To conclude, this article has illustrated two important points. First, we see a significant moderating effect for age, where the effect of unemployment and precarious working conditions works differently depending on the age of the respondent. This effect of age could be something related to characteristics of being that age specifically, or we are observing a change in this cohort of young people, who are growing up at this particular point in time. We do not have the capacity with our dataset to disentangle whether we are observing an age or cohort effect, but what we have illustrated is the importance of understanding age as more than a control variable, especially when researching young people's lives. Second, for young workers today, the quality of the working conditions does shape their work values. They are more concerned with extrinsic work values, such as pay and security, if they consider themselves overqualified for their current job. Overqualification is an issue for policy-makers and employers alike (Cedefop 2018). So far, the policy concern has primarily been the loss in productivity that overqualification leads to (Eurofound 2002). Our research illustrates that overqualification also has consequences for individuals and how they approach work, and this should be taken into consideration in the debate on overqualification. We also find, contrary to our expectation, that precarious working conditions are associated with a higher emphasis on intrinsic work values, such as personal development and independent working conditions. We must acknowledge that this pattern could be a consequence of self-selection effects. To be more specific, it could be the case that those who consider extrinsic values of security and pay to be less important are more likely to self-select into precarious jobs where they might satisfy their intrinsic needs to work independently and be creative. Both causal mechanisms are plausible, and future research should test which causal path is more likely. We argue that in this case, for young adults who are in the early stage of their "work" socialization process, it is more likely their conditions of work that shape their values.

Notes

1. The European Skills Jobs Survey found that four in ten adult employees consider themselves overqualified for their work, and the same proportion of employers said that it was difficult to find employees with the appropriate skills for the job (Cedefop 2018).

2. We acknowledge that our concept of *quality of work* is similar to the concept of underemployment, another very important concept in the youth labor market. However, underemployment relates to, on one hand, the skills match, or overqualification, that overlaps with our concept; and on the other hand, whether the employee has the opportunity to work as many hours as they like, for example, they work part time and they want to work full time. This is a more economic concept relating to the productivity of the worker; we are interested in the experience of work and how the quality of this experience affects what the worker values in work.

3. Zero hour contracts are a kind of casual contract that is increasingly common in Europe, which means a contract with no hours (or zero) specified for work, but the worker is "on call" when the employer needs him or her to work but may also not get any work for periods of time.

4. This theoretical distinction is also confirmed by a factor analysis using promax rotation. Nevertheless, adopting a restrictive conceptualization that only identifies high income and job security as reflecting extrinsic values, while intrinsic values are only reflected by working independently and developing creativity (Cemalcilar, Tosun, and Jensen, this volume), yields the same substantive conclusions.

5. Using clustered standard errors is not necessary given that we do not have any variables that are at the country level. Still, using such a model yields the exact same conclusions.

6. Due to item nonresponse, the number of cases drops from 11,284 to 9,971.

7. For all figures predicted values and the confidence intervals associate with them are computed using R "effect" function with the values for the fixed predictors set at default.

References

Adkins, Cheryl L., and Stefanie E. Naumann. 2016. The value of achievement and responses to the work environment. *Journal of Behavioral and Applied Management* 3 (2): 141–58.

Arnett, Jeffery Jensen. 2000. Emerging adulthood: A theory of development from the late teens through the twenties. *American Psychologist* 55 (5): 469–80.

Bokemeier, Janet L., and William B. Lacy. 1987. Job values, rewards, and work conditions as factors in job satisfaction among men and women. *Sociological Quarterly* 28 (2): 189–204.

Cahuc, Pierre, Stéphane Carcillo, Ulf Rinne, and Klaus F. Zimmermann. 2013. Youth unemployment in old Europe: The polar cases of France and Germany. *IZA Journal of European Labor Studies.* Available from http://ftp.iza.org/dp7490.pdf.

Cedefop. 2018. *Insights into skill shortages and skill mismatch: Learning from Cedefop's European skills and jobs survey.* Luxembourg: Publications Office. Available from http://data.europa.eu/doi/10.2801/645011.

Cemalcilar, Zeynep, Ekin Secinti, and Nebi Sumer. 2018. Intergenerational transmission of work values: A meta-analytic review. *Journal of Youth and Adolescence* 47 (8): 1559–79.

Cemalcilar, Zeynep, Jale Tosun, and Carsten Jensen. 2019. Gendered intergenerational transmission of work values? A country comparison. *The ANNALS of the American Academy of Political and Social Science* (this volume).

Chow, Angela, Harvey J. Krahn, and Nancy L. Galambos. 2014. Developmental trajectories of work values and job entitlement beliefs in the transition to adulthood. *Developmental Psychology* 50 (4): 1102–15.

Curtain, Richard. 2001. Youth and employment: A public policy perspective. *Development Bulletin* 56 (October): 7–10.

Deci, Edward L., and Richard M. Ryan. 2000. The "what" and "why" of goal pursuits: Human needs and the self-determination of behavior. *Psychological Inquiry* 11 (4): 227–68.

Dietrich, Hans. 2012. *Youth unemployment in Europe: Theoretical considerations and empirical findings.* Berlin: Friedrich-Ebert-Stiftung.

Eurofound. 2002. *Quality of work and employment in Europe: Issues and challenges.* Luxembourg: Office for Official Publications of the European Communities. Available from https://www.eurofound.europa.eu.

Gallie, Duncan. 2019. Research on work values in a changing economic and social context. *The ANNALS of the American Academy of Political and Social Science* (this volume).

Gallie, Duncan, Alan Felstead, and Francis Green. 2012. Job preferences and the intrinsic quality of work: The changing attitudes of British employees 1992–2006. *Work, Employment and Society* 26 (5): 806–21.

Halman, Loeck, and Hans Müller. 2006. Comparing orientations to work in African and European societies. *International Journal of Comparative Sociology* 47 (2): 117–43.

Kalleberg, Arne L., and Peter V. Marsden. 2013. Changing work values in the United States, 1973–2006. *Social Science Research* 42:255–70.

Kalleberg, Arne L., and Peter V. Marsden. 2019. Work values in the United States: Age, period and generational differences. *The ANNALS of the American Academy of Political and Social Science* (this volume).

Kirkpatrick Johnson, Monica, and Jeylan T. Mortimer. 2015. Reinforcement or compensation? The effects of parents' work and financial conditions on adolescents' work values during the Great Recession. *Journal of Vocational Behavior* 87:89–100.

Kraaykamp, Gerbert, Zeynep Cemalcilar, and Jale Tosun. 2019. Transmission of work attitudes and values. Comparisons, consequences and implications. *The ANNALS of the American Academy of Political and Social Science* (this volume).

Kuron, Lisa K. J., Sean T. Lyons, Linda Schweitzer, and Eddy S. W. Ng. 2015. Millennials' work values: Differences across the school to work transition. *Personnel Review* 44:991–1009.

Lechner, C. M., F. M. Sortheix, R. Göllner, and K. Salmela-Aro. 2017. The development of work values during the transition to adulthood: A two-country study. *Journal of Vocational Behavior* 99:52–65.

Lyons, Sean T., Chris A. Higgins, and Linda Duxbury. 2010. Work values: Development of a new three-dimensional structure based on confirmatory smallest space analysis. *Journal of Organizational Behavior* 31:969–1002.

Oesingmann, Katrin. 2017. Youth unemployment in Europe. *ifo DICE Report, ISSN* 2511-7823, 15 (1): 52–55.

O'Reilly, Jacquieline, Werner Eichhorst, András Gábos, Kari Hadjivassiliou, David Lain, Janine Leschke, Seamus McGuinness, Lucia Mýtna Kureková, Tiziana Nazio, Renate Ortlieb, Helen Russell, and Paola Villa. 2015. Five characteristics of youth unemployment in Europe: Flexibility, education, migration, family legacies, and EU Policy. *SAGE Open* (January–March): 1–19.

Ryan, Paul. 2001. The school-to-work transition: A cross-national perspective. *Journal of Economic Literature* 39 (1): 34–92.

Shore, Jennifer, and Jale Tosun. 2017. Assessing youth labour market services: Young people's perceptions and evaluations of service delivery in Germany. *Public Policy and Administration.* https://doi.org/10.1177/0952076717722192.

Sissons, Paul. 2011. *The hourglass and the escalator: Labour market change and mobility.* London: The Work Foundation. Available from https://www.researchonline.org.uk.

Sortheix, Florencia M., Angela Chow, and Katariina Salmela-Aro. 2015. Work values and the transition to work life: A longitudinal study. *Journal of Vocational Behavior* 89:162–71.

Tosun, Jale. 2017. Promoting youth employment through multi-organizational governance. *Public Money and Management* 37 (1): 39–46.

Tosun, Jale, José Arco-Tirado, Maurizio Caserta, Zeynep Cemalcilar, Marcs Freitag, Felix Hörisch, Carsten Jensen, Bernhard Kittel, Levente Littvay, Martin Lukes, et al. 2018. Perceived economic self-sufficiency: A country-and generation-comparative approach. *European Political Science.* https://doi.org/10.1057/s41304-018-0186-3.

United Nations Economic Commission for Europe (UNECE). 2015. *Handbook on measuring quality of employment.* New York, NY: United Nations. Available from https://www.unece.org/stats/publications/stat_qua_emp.html.

Van den Broeck, Anja, Maarten Vansteenkiste, Willy Lens, and Hans De Witte. 2010. Unemployed individuals' work values and job flexibility: An explanation from expectancy-value theory and self-determination theory. *Applied Psychology* 59 (2): 296–317.

Wey Smola, Karen, and Charlotte D. Sutton. 2002. Generational differences: Revisiting generational work values for the new millennium. *Journal of Organizational Behavior* 23:363–82.

Wolber, Maarten H. J. 2007. Patterns of labour market entry: A comparative perspective on school-to-work transitions in 11 European countries. *Acta Sociologica* 50 (3): 189–210.

Wyn, Johanna, and Rob White. 1997. *Rethinking youth.* London: Sage Publications.

Work Values and Political Participation: A Cross-National Analysis

MARK VISSER,
MAURICE GESTHUIZEN,
and
GERBERT KRAAYKAMP

This study examines to what extent extrinsic and intrinsic work values are associated with nonelectoral political participation, such as signing a petition and taking part in a public demonstration. We examine whether individualism and economic factors at the country level moderate the relation between work values and political participation. Using data from two rounds of the European Social Survey covering thirty-one countries ($N = 55,927$), results show that people who are extrinsically motivated are less politically active, while people who are intrinsically motivated are more politically active. Comparatively low national wealth weakens these relations. Findings also reveal that people who highly value extrinsic job rewards are even less politically active in individualist countries, whereas people who highly value intrinsic job aspects are more politically engaged in those countries. Overall, this study adds to understanding who is politically active and under which conditions.

Keywords: extrinsic; individualism; intrinsic; political participation; work values

Contemporary societies face major challenges, such as aging populations, mass migration, climate change, and severe economic crises. Governments and politicians are expected to deal with such problems, thereby acquiring legitimation for their role in democratic political systems (Dahl 1971). Citizens may express dissatisfaction with how governments deal with major social problems through conventional or electoral political participation. Radical ideologies and parties have, for instance, gained support in many countries (Rooduijn et al. 2017; Visser et al. 2014). Citizens may also consider unconventional or nonelectoral ways to take

Mark Visser is an assistant professor in the Department of Sociology at Radboud University in the Netherlands. His major research interests include older workers, political sociology, social inequality, and the welfare state. He has published widely on these topics in both national and international scientific journals.

Correspondence: m.visser@ru.nl

DOI: 10.1177/0002716219830961

political action. One can think of joining the Occupy movement, signing a petition against the bio-industry, or taking part in mass demonstrations against global warming. These kinds of political protest are often viewed as a reaction to the (perceived) inaction or inadequate response of governments (Barnes and Kaase 1979). Connecting citizens to the state by political participation and civic involvement, however, is considered crucial for a vibrant and well-functioning democracy (Putnam 1993). As Van Deth (2014, 350) puts it, "participation is the elixir of life for democracy."

In this contribution, we examine citizens' nonelectoral political participation and its relation to work values. Specifically, we are interested in the associations between extrinsic work values (e.g., valuing job security or a high income) and intrinsic work values (e.g., valuing a job that enables the use of own initiative) and political participation. Prior studies on the influence of work values predominantly focused on consequences for work-related outcomes, such as job aspirations (Gallie, Felstead, and Green 2012), job mobility (Gesthuizen and Dagevos 2008), and job satisfaction (Kalleberg 1977). At the same time, previous studies on political participation have not considered work values as a predictor (e.g., Brady, Verba, and Schlozman 1995; Dalton 2008; Linssen et al. 2014; Norris, Walgrave, and Van Aelst 2005; Van Aelst and Walgrave 2001; Verba, Nie, and Kim 1977). We argue that people's work values reflect socialization processes and outcomes related to working under specific conditions (see also the contribution by Gallie, this volume). Looking at features of a person's job or work place to explain involvement in nonelectoral political action may thus add to our understanding of the complex interplay between motives and resources that are decisive for who becomes politically engaged. Moreover, the work domain seems especially important as jobs and work contracts are increasingly precarious as a result of globalization and labor market flexibilization, which are guided by political processes (Kalleberg 2009). This could be conducive to people taking political action. Empirical evidence suggests that workplaces act as "pools" rather than "schools" of democracy (Ayala 2000; Van der Meer and Van Ingen 2009), yet work values have not been closely scrutinized.

The relation between work values and political participation has also not been examined comparatively. To deal with the variety in economic and political constellations in which work values could be relevant for people's political participation, we propose a cross-national approach. More specifically, we expect that cultural (i.e., individualism) and structural country characteristics (i.e., wealth, unemployment, and income inequality) may strengthen or weaken

Maurice Gesthuizen is an assistant professor in the Department of Sociology at Radboud University in the Netherlands. His major research interests include educational inequality, economic vulnerability, social capital, and their interrelations. He has published widely on these subjects in international scientific journals.

Gerbert Kraaykamp is a professor of empirical sociology in the Department of Sociology at Radboud University in the Netherlands. His major research interests include educational inequality, partner effects, and health inequality. He has published widely on these subjects in international scientific journals.

the relation between work values and political participation. Hence, we formulate the following research questions: (1) *to what extent are people's extrinsic and intrinsic work values associated with nonelectoral political participation,* and (2) *to what extent are these relations moderated by a country's level of individualism and by macroeconomic conditions?* We employ data from two rounds of the European Social Survey (ESS), gathered in 2004 and 2010. The ESS is a high-quality survey that is particularly suitable for the purpose of our study, because it includes valid measurements of both work values and nonelectoral political participation. By this, we mean that the sample size is large and covers a broad and diverse population within countries, and the survey questions have been tested in a way that ensures they actually measure what they intend to measure. To answer our research questions, we conduct multilevel regression analysis on a sample of more than 55,000 individuals across thirty-one countries.

Theoretical Framework and Hypotheses

Much research has been done on unconventional political participation (Inglehart 1997; Norris 2002; Opp 2009; Theocharis and Van Deth 2017). We will not discuss all possible theoretical explanations for individual differences in nonelectoral participation but focus on the unique contribution of people's work values and rigorously control for confounding explanations in our analysis. Furthermore, we theoretically elaborate on factors at the country level that possibly moderate the relation between work values and political participation.

Work values and political participation

People's sociopolitical ideologies and values seem more important than self-interest in determining whether they are politically active (Inglehart 1997). Researchers generally acknowledge that such values are the result of socialization processes (Grusec and Hastings 2014). People's work values are established along the life course, and several socializing agents play a role in this process (Gallie 2007; Kalleberg and Marsden 2013). First, growing up with higher-educated and well-to-do parents likely nurtures values of autonomy and self-expression (primary socialization). Second, a person's own schooling (secondary socialization) supports the development of more liberal work attitudes (Hyman and Wright 1979). Most importantly for this study, we expect work place characteristics to affect the way people feel about their work. The work domain can thus also be seen as a socializing agent through which people internalize work values (e.g., Gallie, this volume). Thus, one could say, this tertiary socialization process contributes to the formation of political opinions, which in turn may affect political participation. This seems especially relevant because the work domain is important in politics—wage systems, company regulations, and labor market laws are directly affected by political decision-making.

In general, involvement in associations is theoretically thought of as training for democracy (Van der Meer and Van Ingen 2009). Being active in nonpolitical organizations would have a positive effect on political participation as people obtain the civic skills, mindset, and social network needed to participate politically. These capabilities and competencies can be directly acquired in the workplace and transferred to the political domain (Brady, Verba, and Schlozman 1995; Schur 2003). This spillover hypothesis assumes that work offers opportunities to learn how to participate in politics and to develop an ideological position that is required for political participation (Sobel 1993). However, Ayala (2000) demonstrated that civic skills learned in voluntary, nonpolitical associations are more decisive for a person's level of political participation than skills learned in involuntary or at least less voluntary settings such as that of the workplace. What is more, studies thereafter have shown that the commonly found relation between active involvement in voluntary associations and political participation is likely due to a selection effect instead of a socialization effect, implying that individual resources and personality traits stimulate both civic and political engagement (Van der Meer and Van Ingen 2009; Van Ingen and Van der Meer 2016).

Although the supposed participation-enhancing effect of the workplace has been examined, we know of no studies that have looked specifically at work values. Two distinct but related dimensions are often distinguished regarding attitudes toward work. Extrinsic work values are largely driven by monetary incentives, such as a high income, bonuses, or fringe benefits. Jobs are thus mostly valued for their material rewards (Gallie 2007). Intrinsic work values stress the importance of job autonomy and personal development (Ester, Braun, and Vinken 2006). It then seems most important for people to make use of their talents and capabilities (Gallie 2007). It is important to acknowledge that nonelectoral political participation, such as taking part in demonstrations or working in a political party or action group, is occasionally considered as individualized collective action or responsibility-taking (Stolle and Micheletti 2013). We expect that people who put more emphasis on intrinsic work values and who highly value a job that enables them to take initiative would be more prone to take political action as a way to contribute to the common good. People who subscribe more to extrinsic work values and appreciate monetary benefits would be considered more self-centered and therefore less prone to collective action. People with high extrinsic work values may also refrain from taking political action because they are afraid of losing their job when they do so or because they might fear their employer's reaction if it becomes known that they are politically engaged. The fear of losing material job rewards thus hampers political participation, particularly among extrinsically motivated people. This leads to the following individual-level hypotheses: (H1) *The higher people value extrinsic job rewards, the less they participate in nonelectoral political activities*; and (H2) *The higher people value intrinsic job rewards, the more they participate in nonelectoral political activities*. To test these hypotheses, we rigorously control for individual characteristics and resources, human values, political interest, and social origin with the aim of ruling out selection effects.

The role of individualism and macroeconomic conditions

Next to individual-level expectations, we argue that both cultural and structural country characteristics may influence the association between work values and political participation. Research on unconventional political participation has scarcely examined such cross-level interaction effects and did not do so for work values (Dalton, Van Sickle, and Weldon 2010; Rapp and Ackermann 2016; Welzel and Deutsch 2012). We first derive hypotheses about the moderating role of individualism.

Based on the seminal work of Inglehart (1997), we expect that people are affected by the cultural makeup of a country. Hofstede, Hofstede, and Minkov (2010) differentiate national cultures according to their collectivist and individualist nature. In collectivist countries, individuals are stimulated to regard personal goals as subordinate to collective ones. By contrast, people are less bound to collective norms in individualist countries, where they mostly take care of themselves and more often pursue their own interests. With respect to nonelectoral political participation, we expect that valuing extrinsic work rewards has stronger consequences for taking political action in more individualist countries. In such environments, less attention is paid to the creation of collective goods. As a consequence, people who mainly value extrinsic job rewards will be supported in their self-centered attitude and will refrain even more from politically participating for a greater good. People who hold intrinsic work attitudes, with generally more attention given to collective goods, might also be affected by individualism in society. In those societies, where the breeding ground for collective action is weak and opposition toward it might be stronger, it could be more difficult to organize collective action. People who highly value intrinsic job aspects are thus also expected to be less prone to take part in political activities due to the attenuating influence of individualism. We hypothesize: (H3) *The more individualized a country, (a) the stronger the negative relation between extrinsic work values and participation in nonelectoral political activities and (b) the weaker the positive relation between intrinsic work values and participation in nonelectoral political activities.*

We also expect structural macroeconomic conditions to affect the relation between work values and political action. Earlier studies showed that macroeconomic conditions affect support for extrinsic and intrinsic work values (Gallie 2007; Gesthuizen and Verbakel 2011). Research has also shown that people are less politically active in countries with greater income inequality (Dubrow, Slomczynski, and Tomescu-Dubrow 2008). However, comparative research that examines how the association between work values and political participation is affected by macroeconomic conditions is lacking.

Our expectation is that adverse macroeconomic circumstances stimulate people with high extrinsic work values to take part in nonelectoral political activities. Under these conditions, especially extrinsic aspects of work and acquiring a good income are threatened. For extrinsically motivated citizens, poor economic circumstances might be a motive to engage in political activism to advance their point of view and to act upon labor market insecurity, which

FIGURE 1
Theoretical and Analytical Framework

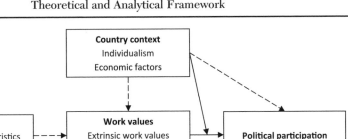

might hit them personally. As we expect to find a negative relation between extrinsic work values and political participation, this relation will likely be less negative (weaker) in countries with worse macroeconomic conditions. For people with high intrinsic work values, we predict the opposite. We expect them to be less politically active in countries that perform worse economically. In situations of economic hardship, expressing intrinsic work values will likely be less important, and simply having sufficient financial means may prevail. Even people who highly value intrinsic job rewards might be worried about losing their job and making ends meet. Therefore, they are more often forced to refrain from action to protect collective goods. This leads to our final hypotheses: (H4) *The poorer the economic performance of a country*, (a) *the weaker the negative relation between extrinsic work values and participation in nonelectoral political activities, and* (b) *the weaker the positive relation between intrinsic work values and participation in nonelectoral political activities.* Figure 1 graphically summarizes our theoretical and analytical framework. Dashed arrows reflect nonhypothesized effects.

Methods

Data

We use data from rounds two and five of the ESS, collected in 2004 and 2010. The target population consisted of persons aged 15 and older who live in private households. Respondents are selected for face-to-face interviews based on strict random probability sampling. Response rates for round two range from 44 percent in France to 79 percent in Estonia. For round five, response rates vary between 30 percent in Germany and 77 percent in Bulgaria.[1]

We pooled the data from both rounds. The initial sample was made up of 99,995 respondents. We selected adults age 18 to 64, as 65 was the state pension age in most European countries at the time. This means that we excluded retirees. The main reason for doing so is that retired people are likely a selective group with regard to work values. We also removed first-generation migrants because they are a selective group as well, especially regarding political participation. These selections reduced the sample to 61,680 respondents.[2] Finally, we removed respondents with missing values. The analytical sample comprises 55,927 individuals across thirty-one countries.[3]

Nonelectoral political participation

Individual nonelectoral political participation refers to people who participate voluntarily with the objective of influencing political decisions (Van Deth 2014). Unlike for politicians, the political activities citizens undertake are not part of their job. The question was asked as follows: "There are different ways of trying to improve things in [country] or help prevent things from going wrong. During the last 12 months, have you done any of the following?" Respondents had to answer whether they (1) contacted a politician, government, or local government official; (2) worked in a political party or action group; (3) worn or displayed a campaign badge/sticker; (4) signed a petition; and (5) took part in a lawful public demonstration.[4] A confirmatory factor analysis (enforcing a single-factor structure) of the total sample of countries confirmed that these items measure one underlying construct. The factor accounts for nearly 38 percent of the total variance. Confirmatory factor analyses for each country separately also support unidimensionality with explained variances ranging from 30 percent in Finland to 47 percent in Turkey. The dependent variable is constructed by the sum score of the five dichotomous items, which is a common operationalization in the literature (e.g., Ayala 2000; Van Ingen and Van der Meer 2016). On average, respondents score 0.572 on the political participation scale, which ranges from participating in none of the activities to participating in all five. There are substantial cross-national differences. Average political participation is lowest in Hungary (0.207) and Portugal (0.220) and highest in Iceland (1.464) and Norway (1.100).

Work values

Work values are measured by the following question: "How important do you think each of the following would be if you were choosing a job?" Respondents could answer on a scale ranging from 0 (*not important at all*) to 4 (*very important*). The items "a secure job" and "a high income" were averaged to measure extrinsic work values. The Pearson correlation between both items is .465 ($p <$ .001). Intrinsic work values are measured by a single item: "a job that enables you to use your own initiative." The correlation between extrinsic and intrinsic work values across all countries is .244 ($p < $ .001), which is in line with previous cross-national studies that reported a positive association (e.g., Gesthuizen and Verbakel 2011). The relation is strongest in Turkey (.589, $p <$ .001) and weakest in Norway (.029, $p = $ .183).

Country-level variables

We added five variables at the country level. First, we included a measure of individualism, which is one of six dimensions to compare the cultures of countries in Hofstede's 6D model (Hofstede, Hofstede, and Minkov 2010). According to this model, individualism is the degree of interdependence among members of a society. In highly individualist countries, people predominantly look after themselves and their direct family. In contrast, in highly collectivist countries, people also take care of others. Second, we added three variables to capture macroeconomic conditions: gross domestic product (GDP) per capita, unemployment rates, and Gini coefficients. Figures on GDP were derived from the World Bank to measure the level of national wealth. We logged this variable to minimize the impact of countries with high GDP. Unemployment rates are taken from the online database of the United Nations Economic Commission for Europe (UNECE). Gini coefficients are obtained from the Standardized World Income Inequality Database (SWIID), ensuring comparability across time and space (Solt 2016). Finally, we included a control variable indicating whether a country has been known to be an authoritarian regime since 1945.[5] The highest correlation at the country level (between authoritarian regime and GDP) is –.762 ($p <$ .001), which does not directly indicate multicollinearity.

Control variables

Based on previous research (e.g., Opp 2009; Theocharis and Van Deth 2017), we controlled for a battery of relevant variables to deal with alternative explanations of work values and political participation and to take into account compositional differences between countries. We control for an individual's openness to change (a higher-order group of basic human values) and universalism, as developed by Schwartz (1992). We also control for the extent to which people are politically interested. Educational attainment of respondents and their parents refers to the highest level of education completed based on the International Standard Classification of Education (ISCED). For parental educational level, we also included a dummy variable for missing values. Occupational status of respondents and their parents is measured by the International Socio-Economic Index of occupational status (ISEI), which ranges from 16 to 90 (Ganzeboom, De Graaf, and Treiman 1992). We also added dummy variables for respondents who are unemployed, students, and inactive; and a dummy variable for missing values on parental occupational status. Finally, we included age, gender, marital status, and number of children living in the household. Table 1 provides descriptive statistics of all variables.

Analysis

We applied multilevel linear regression analysis to take into account that individuals are nested within countries.[6] We first estimated a random intercept model without covariates to calculate the intraclass correlation (M0). In the next

TABLE 1
Descriptive Statistics ($N_1 = 55{,}927$; $N_2 = 31$)

	Min.	Max.	Mean	SD
Political participation	0	5	0.572	0.936
Extrinsic work values	0	4	3.207	0.694
Intrinsic work values	0	4	3.007	0.879
Political interest	0	3	1.343	0.880
Openness to change	0	5	3.166	0.884
Universalism	0	5	3.772	0.779
Educational level				
ISCED 1–2	0	1	0.230	
ISCED 3–4	0	1	0.478	
ISCED 5–6	0	1	0.292	
Parental educational level				
ISCED 1–2	0	1	0.407	
ISCED 3–4	0	1	0.351	
ISCED 5–6	0	1	0.198	
Missing	0	1	0.044	
Occupational status				
ISEI 16–34	0	1	0.233	
ISEI 35–55	0	1	0.271	
ISEI 56–90	0	1	0.165	
Unemployed	0	1	0.118	
Student	0	1	0.091	
Inactive	0	1	0.122	
Parental occupational status				
ISEI 16–34	0	1	0.405	
ISEI 35–55	0	1	0.316	
ISEI 56–90	0	1	0.209	
Missing	0	1	0.071	
Age category				
18–34 years	0	1	0.369	
35–54 years	0	1	0.479	
55–64 years	0	1	0.152	
Male	0	1	0.467	
Marital status				
Married/cohabiting	0	1	0.516	
Divorced	0	1	0.100	
Widowed	0	1	0.023	
Single	0	1	0.337	
Missing	0	1	0.024	
Number of children in household	0	14	0.865	1.095
ESS round 5	0	1	0.527	
Individualism	25.0	89.0	56.000	17.818
GDP per capita (logged)	8.8	11.2	10.190	0.488
Unemployment rate	4.0	16.5	8.965	3.390
Income inequality (Gini)	24.2	42.8	29.765	4.878
Authoritarian legacy	0	1	0.520	

SOURCE: European Social Survey (2004 and 2010).

model (M1), we added all variables in Table 1 to test H1 and H2. We also controlled for ESS round in this model and onward. In the following model (not shown), we allowed the effects of the work values to vary across countries. The random slope variance components are significant, meaning that the effects of extrinsic and intrinsic work values vary cross-nationally and that country characteristics should be able to explain this variation. To this end, we ran four models (M2–M5) that test H3 and H4. Interval variables are centered on their mean value in all models.

Results

The results of the multivariate analysis are shown in Tables 2 (M1) and 3 (M2–M5) and present unstandardized coefficients. Based on the null model, the intraclass correlation is $(.087/[.087 + 0.809=]) .097$. This means that almost one-tenth of the total variance in political participation is situated at the country level. The country-level variance is also highly significant $(p < .001)$, confirming that multilevel analysis is appropriate.

Model 1 shows that extrinsic and intrinsic work values are both significantly associated with political participation, controlled for individual and country characteristics. The higher people value extrinsic job aspects, the less they participate politically. The results show the opposite for intrinsic work values. The higher people value intrinsic job aspects, the more they participate politically. We find these relations over and above the influence of a wide range of potential confounders, strengthening our confidence that we are able to avoid selection effects. If extrinsic work values increases with its range, political participation decreases by .240 (4 × –.060); and if intrinsic work values increases with its range, political participation increases by .152 (4 × .038). These findings support H1 and H2.

We briefly pay attention to the effects of the control variables. As can be seen in Table 2, people who are more interested in politics, more open to change, and more universalist in nature are more politically active. The same holds true for higher-educated people and those who have higher occupational status as they are politically more active than their counterparts. Similar effects are found for parental educational level and occupational status. We also observe that students, people aged 35 to 54 years, and divorced people exhibit more political behavior. Men take less political action than do women. At the country level, GDP per capita is positively and marginally significantly related to political participation. All in all, the variables in Model 1 account for 10 percent of the individual-level and 61 percent of the country-level variance.

Table 3 contains the results with regard to the cross-level interactions. The main effects of extrinsic and intrinsic work values apply to countries with average levels of individualism (M2), wealth (M3), unemployment (M4), and income inequality (M5). Starting with individualism, we find support for H3a: the more individualized a country, the stronger the negative association between extrinsic

TABLE 2
Linear Multilevel Regression Analysis of Political Participation

	M1
Extrinsic work values	−.060°°°
Intrinsic work values	.038°°°
Political interest	.251°°°
Openness to change	.047°°°
Universalism	.054°°°
Educational level	
ISCED 1–2	ref.
ISCED 3–4	.052°°°
ISCED 5–6	.163°°°
Parental educational level	
ISCED 1–2	ref.
ISCED 3–4	.024°
ISCED 5–6	.063°°°
Occupational status	
ISEI 16–34	ref.
ISEI 35–55	.033°°
ISEI 56–90	.073°°°
Unemployed	.019
Student	.102°°°
Inactive	−.024†
Parental occupational status	
ISEI 16–34	ref.
ISEI 35–55	.012
ISEI 56–90	.029°
Age category	
18–34 years	ref.
35–54 years	.020°
55–64 years	.005
Male	−.016°
Marital status	
Married/cohabiting	ref.
Divorced	.055°°°
Widowed	−.008
Single	.016
Number of children in household	.019°°°
ESS round 5	−.033°°°
Individualism	−.003
GDP per capita (logged)	.219†
Unemployment rate	.016
Income inequality (Gini)	−.012
Authoritarian legacy	−.203
Intercept	.555°°°
Individual-level variance	.728°°°
Country-level variance	.034°°°

SOURCE: European Social Survey (2004 and 2010).
†$p < .10$. °$p < .05$. °°$p < .01$. °°°$p < .001$.

TABLE 3
Random Slopes Work Values and Cross-Level Interaction Effects

M2		M3	
Intercept	.519°°°	Intercept	.518°°°
Extrinsic work values	−.052°°°	Extrinsic work values	−.054°°°
Extrinsic × Individualism	−.001°	Extrinsic × GDP per capita (logged)	−.038°
Intrinsic work values	.035°°°	Intrinsic work values	.038°°°
Intrinsic × Individualism	.001°°	Intrinsic × GDP per capita (logged)	.060°°°
M4		M5	
Intercept	.521°°°	Intercept	.522°°°
Extrinsic work values	−.054°°°	Extrinsic work values	−.053°°°
Extrinsic × Unemployment rate	.003	Extrinsic × Income inequality (Gini)	.000
Intrinsic work values	.036°°°	Intrinsic work values	.036°°°
Intrinsic × Unemployment rate	−.004	Intrinsic × Income inequality (Gini)	−.004°

SOURCE: European Social Survey (2004 and 2010).
NOTE: Models are controlled for all variables in Table 2.
°$p < .05$. °°$p < .01$. °°°$p < .001$.

work values and political participation (−.052 − .001). The positive relation between intrinsic work values and political participation also becomes stronger if individualism increases (.035 + .001), which rejects H3b.

Moving on to the macroeconomic variables, the results with regard to GDP per capita are clear and in accordance with H4a and H4b. The lower a country's GDP per capita, the weaker the negative effect of extrinsic work values (−.054 + .038) and the weaker the positive effect of intrinsic work values on political participation (.038 − .060). Unemployment does not moderate the effects of extrinsic and intrinsic work values, which refutes H4a and H4b for this macroeconomic indicator. Last, and in support of H4b, the higher the level of income inequality, the weaker the relation between intrinsic work values and political participation (.036 − .004).

We present predicted scores on political participation across the range of extrinsic and intrinsic work values as well as the range of individualism and the macroeconomic factors in Figure 2. The figure sheds light on the strength of the cross-level interaction effects. First, note that the direct effect of GDP on political participation is visible in Figure 2 as the two lines are farthest apart, regardless of looking at the minimum or maximum scores on work values. GDP also seems to play the strongest moderating role, particularly in affecting the effect of intrinsic work values given that the lines are strongly diverging. Finally, unemployment and income inequality seem to be of the least importance, especially with regard to extrinsic work values because the lines run virtually parallel or slightly diverge.

FIGURE 2
Predicted Scores on Political Participation (Y-Axis) for Minimum and Maximum Scores
on Work Values (X-Axis) and Minimum and Maximum Scores on Country Characteristics

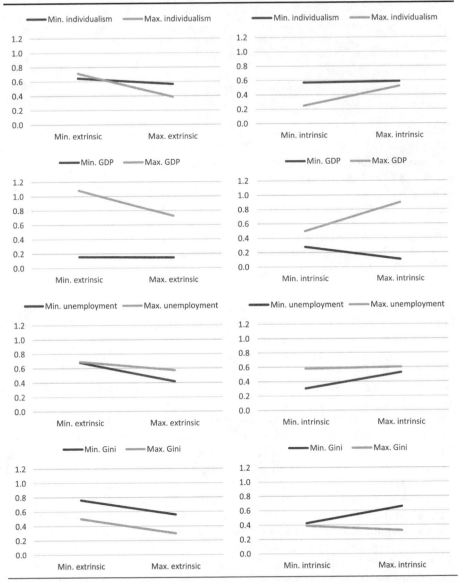

NOTE: The moderated effects of extrinsic work values are shown on the left, those of intrinsic work values on the right. The top panel displays the moderating effect of individualism, while the panels below represent the moderating effects of GDP per capita, unemployment, and income inequality.

Conclusion and Discussion

Citizens exert influence over government policies by taking political action. This study assessed the relation between people's extrinsic and intrinsic work values and their nonelectoral political participation—activities such as signing petitions, contacting a (local) government official, or taking part in a public demonstration. We took a cross-national approach and assessed whether the effects of both types of work values are moderated by cultural and structural country characteristics, using data from two rounds (2004 and 2010) of the methodologically rigorous ESS.

Starting with the first research question, the results clearly showed that people who highly value extrinsic job rewards are less prone to take part in political activities, whereas people who hold more intrinsic job attitudes are more politically active. We argued that these associations likely reflect socialization processes in the workplace that either hamper or promote one's inclination to contribute to the common good. On one hand, individuals with extrinsic work values have been subject to socializing forces that emphasize self-interest, attach less importance to collective goals, and do not foster the development of skills useful for taking political action. On the other hand, individuals who find intrinsic aspects of work important have been socialized at work in "intrinsic" environments. Personal development, autonomy, and the common good are generally held to be important in those environments, which may subsequently translate into increasing political action. People who are intrinsically motivated may also be more motivated to use their acquired civic skills to politically participate (e.g., Schur 2003).

Our findings are inconsistent with previous studies that show that the workplace does not seem to matter as much (Ayala 2000) and that voluntary associations do not socialize people to be politically active, but bring politically active people together (Van der Meer and Van Ingen 2009; Van Ingen and Van der Meer 2016). Although these studies did not examine work values and although our cross-sectional research design cannot completely rule out selection effects, we took into account a wide range of factors that are related to both work values and political participation. By doing this, we found robust associations between work values and political activity.

Both nonelectoral political participation rates and their relation to work values differ considerably across countries, rendering our cross-national approach plausible. Building on works by Inglehart (1997) and Hofstede, Hofstede, and Minkov (2010), we expected individualist national cultures—as opposed to collectivist ones—to weaken the effect of extrinsic and intrinsic work values. Indeed, individuals primarily concerned with extrinsic work values are even less likely to take political action in individualist countries, suggesting that such a cultural makeup supports a self-centered work attitude.

Contrary to our expectations, individuals who value intrinsic job factors show more political involvement in individualist countries than in collectivist countries. This finding perhaps implies that in individualist countries the necessity to take political action is felt stronger because the breeding ground to solve collective problems is less well developed. This might stimulate individuals who recognize the greater good to achieve change through unconventional political participation.

In accordance with our expectations, findings revealed that in countries with lower GDP per capita, people who have extrinsic work values take more political action, whereas people who hold intrinsic work attitudes are politically less active. GDP was also the only economic factor that directly affected political participation rates. For extrinsically motivated people, the role of lower national wealth can be understood in terms of self-interest: (the fear of) being hit by an economic downturn might motivate them to act. For intrinsically motivated people, (the fear of) economic decline might result in a lower prioritization of taking collective action. This could be the case because poor economic performance of a country might mean that taking political action is directed at personal, material goals, coinciding less with their values and more with the values of extrinsically motivated individuals. The empirical evidence with regard to the moderating role of unemployment and income inequality was less univocal.

For our cross-national comparison, the ESS rounds of 2004 and 2010 provided high-quality and tailored data: sufficient countries, valid measures—the items pertaining to extrinsic and intrinsic work values, and their intercorrelations, nicely fit into previous work on these dimensions (Gesthuizen and Verbakel 2011; Kalleberg 1977)—and ample opportunity to control for confounding factors. This enabled us to advance current knowledge as we demonstrated the relation between work values and nonelectoral political participation, as well as the moderating role of cultural and structural characteristics of European countries. Future comparative research could benefit from multiple-item measurements of extrinsic and, in particular, intrinsic work values; and from extending the scope to other work dimensions, such as values related to workload and preferred supervision style. It would also be interesting to examine whether the politic climate of countries affects the association between work values and political participation. Finally, taking a longitudinal perspective would provide the opportunity to more adequately deal with possible selection effects and reciprocal causal relations and may get a grip on what precisely is driving the effect of work values on political participation (Van Ingen and Van der Meer 2016). For example, under which conditions do work values change from extrinsic to intrinsic and vice versa, and to what extent does that influence (un)conventional political participation?

To conclude, this study underlines the importance of collective action, as do many other studies (e.g., Putnam 2000). An intrinsic (work) motivation favors autonomy, own initiative, and personal development over material rewards; and socially flourishing (work) places over "bowling alone." Unconventional political participation exemplifies the willingness to take action to contribute to the collective good and to invest time and effort in achieving collective gains. Our findings showed that a person's intrinsic work motivation is strongly associated with taking collective action. What is more, people with a stronger self-centered work motivation contribute more to the collective good when cultural values and norms regard personal goals as subordinate to collective ones. Intrinsically motivated individuals also seem to feel a stronger need to take political action in individualist countries. As ever more empirical evidence underscores that cohesive and inclusive societies are better protected from collective ills (Fukuyama 1995; Putnam 2000), governments face the challenge to nourish and stimulate collective awareness and the collective good.

Notes

1. More detailed information about the ESS is available at www.europeansocialsurvey.org.

2. We performed a robustness analysis on employed people only. The results regarding our hypotheses do not change.

3. The list of countries is Austria, Belgium, Bulgaria, Croatia, Cyprus, the Czech Republic, Denmark, Estonia, Finland, France, Germany, Greece, Hungary, Iceland, Ireland, Israel, Lithuania, Luxembourg, the Netherlands, Norway, Poland, Portugal, Russia, Slovakia, Slovenia, Spain, Sweden, Switzerland, Turkey, Ukraine, and the United Kingdom.

4. Two additional items—"worked in another organization or association" and "boycotted certain products"—were excluded from the political participation scale. By looking at face validity, these items are not strictly political. Nevertheless, the findings with regard to our hypotheses are not substantially different when we include these items.

5. Although our interest lies in the moderating effect of cultural and structural country characteristics, we tested if an authoritarian legacy moderates the relation between work values and political participation. Results show that the negative effect of extrinsic work values and the positive effect of intrinsic work values are weaker in countries with a history of authoritarianism.

6. More than 60 percent of all respondents do not participate politically at all. Because of this skewed distribution, we considered multilevel Poisson regression analysis. The results of this alternative analysis are similar to the effects in model 1 of Table 2. Unfortunately, a model with a random slope for either extrinsic or intrinsic work values is unable to converge.

References

Ayala, Louis J. 2000. Trained for democracy: The differing effects of voluntary and involuntary organizations on political participation. *Political Research Quarterly* 53 (1): 99–115.

Barnes, Samuel H., and Max Kaase. 1979. *Political action: Mass participation in five Western democracies*. Beverly Hills, CA: Sage Publications.

Brady, Henry E., Sidney Verba, and Kay L. Schlozman. 1995. Beyond SES: A resource model of political participation. *American Political Science Review* 89 (2): 271–94.

Dahl, Robert A. 1971. *Polyarchy: Participation and opposition*. New Haven, CT: Yale University Press.

Dalton, Russell J. 2008. Citizenship norms and the expansion of political participation. *Political Studies* 56 (1): 76–98.

Dalton, Russell J., Alix Van Sickle, and Steven Weldon. 2010. The individual-institutional nexus of protest behaviour. *British Journal of Political Science* 40 (1): 51–73.

Dubrow, Joshua K., Kazimierz M. Slomczynski, and Irina Tomescu-Dubrow. 2008. Effects of democracy and inequality on soft political protest in Europe: Exploring the European Social Survey data. *International Journal of Sociology* 38 (3): 36–51.

Ester, Peter, Michael Braun, and Henk Vinken. 2006. Eroding work values? In *Globalization, value change, and generations: A cross-national and intergenerational perspective*, eds. Peter Ester, Michael Braun, and Peter Mohler, 89–113. Leiden: Brill.

Fukuyama, Francis. 1995. *Trust: The social virtues and the creation of prosperity*. New York, NY: Free Press.

Gallie, Duncan. 2007. Welfare regimes, employment systems and job preference orientations. *European Sociological Review* 23 (3): 279–93.

Gallie, Duncan. 2019. Research on work values in a changing economic and social context. *The ANNALS of the American Academy of Political and Social Science* (this volume).

Gallie, Duncan, Alan Felstead, and Francis Green. 2012. Job preferences and the intrinsic quality of work: The changing attitudes of British employees 1992–2006. *Work, Employment and Society* 26 (5): 806–21.

Ganzeboom, Harry B. G., Paul M. De Graaf, and Donald J. Treiman. 1992. A standard International Socio-Economic Index of occupational status. *Social Science Research* 21 (1): 1–56.

Gesthuizen, Maurice, and Jacob Dagevos. 2008. Mismatching of persons and jobs in the Netherlands: Consequences for the returns to mobility. *Work, Employment and Society* 22 (3): 485–506.

Gesthuizen, Maurice, and Ellen Verbakel. 2011. Job preferences in Europe. Tests for scale invariance and examining cross-national variation using EVS. *European Societies* 13 (5): 663–86.

Grusec, Joan E., and Paul D. Hastings. 2014. *Handbook of socialization: Theory and research*. New York, NY: Guilford Press.

Hofstede, Geert, Gert J. Hofstede, and Michael Minkov. 2010. *Cultures and organizations: Software of the mind*. New York, NY: McGraw-Hill.

Hyman, Herbert H., and Charles R. Wright. 1979. *Education's lasting influence on values*. Chicago, IL: University of Chicago Press.

Inglehart, Ronald. 1997. *Modernization and postmodernization: Cultural, economic and political change in 43 societies*. Princeton, NJ: Princeton University Press.

Kalleberg, Arne L. 1977. Work values and job rewards: A theory of job satisfaction. *American Sociological Review* 42 (1): 124–43.

Kalleberg, Arne L. 2009. Precarious work, insecure workers: Employment relations in transition. *American Sociological Review* 74 (1): 1–22.

Kalleberg, Arne L., and Peter V. Marsden. 2013. Changing work values in the United States, 1973–2006. *Social Science Research* 42 (2): 255–70.

Linssen, Rik, Hans Schmeets, Peer Scheepers, and Manfred Te Grotenhuis. 2014. Trends in conventional and unconventional political participation in Europe, 1981–2008. In *Political trust and disenchantment with politics: International perspectives*, eds. Christina Eder, Ingvill C. Mochmann, and Markus Quandt, 31–58. Leiden: Brill.

Norris, Pippa. 2002. *Democratic phoenix: Reinventing political activism*. Cambridge: Cambridge University Press.

Norris, Pippa, Stefaan Walgrave, and Peter Van Aelst. 2005. Who demonstrates? Antistate rebels, conventional participants, or everyone? *Comparative Politics* 37 (2): 189–205.

Opp, Karl-Dieter. 2009. *Theories of political protest and social movements. A multidisciplinary introduction, critique, and synthesis*. New York, NY: Routledge.

Putnam, Robert D. 1993. *Making democracy work: Civic traditions in modern Italy*. Princeton, NJ: Princeton University Press.

Putnam, Robert D. 2000. *Bowling alone: The collapse and revival of American community*. New York, NY: Simon & Schuster.

Rapp, Carolin, and Kathrin Ackermann. 2016. The consequences of social intolerance on non-violent protest. *European Political Science Review* 8 (4): 567–88.

Rooduijn, Matthijs, Brian Burgoon, Erika J. Van Elsas, and Herman G. Van de Werfhorst. 2017. Radical distinction: Support for radical left and radical right parties in Europe. *European Union Politics* 18 (4): 536–59.

Schur, Lisa. 2003. Employment and the creation of an active citizenry. *British Journal of Industrial Relations* 41 (4): 751–71.

Schwartz, Shalom H. 1992. Universals in the content and structure of values: Theoretical advances and empirical tests in 20 countries. *Advances in Experimental Social Psychology* 25:1–65.

Sobel, Richard. 1993. From occupational involvement to political participation: An exploratory analysis. *Political Behavior* 15 (4): 339–53.

Solt, Frederick. 2016. The Standardized World Income Inequality Database (version 6.0). *Social Science Quarterly* 97 (5): 1267–81.

Stolle, Dietlind, and Michele Micheletti. 2013. *Political consumerism: Global responsibility in action.* Cambridge: Cambridge University Press.

Theocharis, Yannis, and Jan W. Van Deth. 2017. *Political participation in a changing world: Conceptual and empirical challenges in the study of citizen engagement.* New York, NY: Routledge.

Van Aelst, Peter, and Stefaan Walgrave. 2001. Who is that (wo)man in the street? From the normalisation of protest to the normalisation of the protester. *European Journal of Political Research* 39 (4): 461–86.

Van der Meer, Tom, and Erik Van Ingen. 2009. Schools of democracy? Disentangling the relationship between civic participation and political action in 17 European countries. *European Journal of Political Research* 48 (2): 281–308.

Van Deth, Jan W. 2014. A conceptual map of political participation. *Acta Politica* 49 (3): 349–67.

Van Ingen, Erik, and Tom Van der Meer. 2016. Schools or pools of democracy? A longitudinal test of the relation between civic participation and political socialization. *Political Behavior* 38 (1): 83–103.

Verba, Sidney, Norman H. Nie, and Jae-On Kim. 1977. *The modes of democratic participation: A cross-national comparison.* Beverly Hills, CA: Sage Publications.

Visser, Mark, Marcel Lubbers, Gerbert Kraaykamp, and Eva Jaspers. 2014. Support for radical left ideologies in Europe. *European Journal of Political Research* 53 (3): 541–58.

Welzel, Christian, and Franziska Deutsch. 2012. Emancipative values and non-violent protest: The importance of "ecological" effects. *British Journal of Political Science* 42 (2): 465–79.

I Want to Be a Billionaire: How Do Extrinsic and Intrinsic Values Influence Youngsters' Well-Being?

By
ANJA VAN DEN BROECK,
BERT SCHREURS,
KARIN PROOST,
ARNE VANDERSTUKKEN,
and
MAARTEN VANSTEENKISTE

Values guide our attitudes and behavior, but to what extent and how do individual values determine our overall well-being? Self-determination theory holds that particular types of values (i.e., intrinsic or extrinsic) matter most, but the person-environment fit perspective argues that any values can be beneficial as long as they align with values prevalent in one's environment. The evidentiary support for these competing claims is inconclusive. We use the World Value Survey to see how these perspectives do in predicting life satisfaction, happiness, and health in youngsters aged 18 to 30 around the world. Our results generally confirm hypotheses derived from self-determination theory, showing that the type of values held by youngsters and the type of values prevailing in their environments account for significant variation in young peoples' life satisfaction, happiness, and health. The pattern of evidence suggests that youngsters benefit from attaching greater importance to intrinsic values related to affiliation and community contribution rather than to extrinsic values that relate to financial success and accumulation of power.

Keywords: values; materialism; person-environment fit; self-determination theory; well-being; health; World Value Survey

People may hold a myriad of different values in various domains of life such as work, schooling, or sports. While some attach high importance to material wealth, other people attach more importance to building good relationships and making a contribution to society. The types of values people pursue matter: values direct our thoughts, determine

Anja Van den Broeck is an associate professor of work and organizational studies in the Faculty of Economics and Business at KU Leuven. She specializes in work and motivation psychology. Her research goal is to examine how, and under which circumstances, individuals may thrive at work. She focuses on job design; well-being, including burnout and work engagement; and motivation in terms of needs, values, and qualitatively different types of motivation.

Correspondence: Anja.vandenbroeck@kuleuven.be

DOI: 10.1177/0002716219831658

our actions, and thus guide us through our lives (Schwartz 1992). To date, however, there is inconclusive evidence about what kinds of values matter most to individuals' long-term well-being.

Two contrasting views have emerged in the scientific literature. On one hand, self-determination theory (SDT; Kasser and Ryan 1993; Deci and Ryan 2000) maintains that particular types of values (i.e., intrinsic or extrinsic) matter when predicting variations in individuals' well-being. On the other hand, the person-environment fit perspective (Kristof-Brown, Zimmerman, and Johnson 2005; Kristof 1996) argues that any type of values can yield potential benefits to well-being, depending on whether one's personal values are aligned with the values stressed in one's environment. Although both views have empirical support (see Dittmar et al. 2014; Kristof-Brown, Zimmerman, and Johnson 2005, among others) and some studies have even begun addressing these contradicting perspectives (e.g., Sagiv and Schwartz 2000; Vansteenkiste et al. 2008), no conclusive answers have been given about whether the type or the fit of values matters most.

This study adds to this literature by testing the validity of both perspectives in a large sample of youngsters (aged 18 to 30 years) across the globe (i.e., the World Value Survey [WVS]; Inglehart et al. 2014). SDT or person-environment fit theory makes general assumptions, regardless of people's age. However, understanding how values relate to youngsters' well-being is particularly important because experimentation and forming of values is an integral aspect of youngsters' identity formation (Erikson 1968), and their well-being is increasingly at risk due to growing poverty, increased migration, and technological evolutions worldwide (see Call et al. [2002] for a review among adolescents). Additionally, environments become increasingly materialistic (Edmunds and Turner 2005), as do the youngsters, aged 17 to 18 years, living in those environments (Twenge and Kasser 2013). The

Bert Schreurs is an associate professor in the Faculty of Social Sciences and Solvay Business School, Vrije Universiteit Brussel, Belgium. His research focuses on work stress and motivation, proactive work behaviors, and HRM/careers. He currently serves as an associate editor of Career Development International *and is the immediate past division chair of the Academy of Management Careers Division.*

Karin Proost is an assistant professor in the Faculty of Economics and Business at KU Leuven and in the Faculty of Psychology and Educational Sciences at the Open University of the Netherlands. Her research focuses on work stress and anxiety and on person-organization fit in the work context as well as the selection and recruitment context.

Arne Vanderstukken is a senior researcher at the HIVA Research Institute for Work and Society. His main interests lie in HRM, work psychology, and cognitive psychology. He focuses on how people think about their goals at work and how they get a sense of the possibilities in their (future) work context to pursue those goals.

Maarten Vansteenkiste is a full professor in the Department of Developmental, Personality and Social Psychology at Ghent University. Through his research, he aims to expand self-determination theory, a broad theory on human motivation. He specifically links the theory with other well-established motivation theories and studies individuals' motivational dynamics and their supportive and thwarting conditions in a variety of life domains, including education, parenting, work, and sports and exercise.

present research provides insights into whether we should be worried about the latter trends. Based on SDT, it can be assumed that youngsters' well-being may be increasingly at risk, which would warrant actions renewing the focus on intrinsic values. Based on the fit perspective, in contrast, the evolution toward more materialistic values may optimize the fit with the social environment, thereby safeguarding youngsters' well-being.

Values and Well-Being from the Perspective of Self-Determination Theory

SDT is a broad theory on human motivation, well-being, and integrity and the factors promoting or derailing individuals' optimal functioning (Deci and Ryan 2000; Ryan and Deci 2017). One key factor of SDT concerns the type of values people hold in terms of intrinsic or extrinsic values (Kasser 2016; Kasser and Ryan 1993). Intrinsic values are closely aligned with people's growth-oriented nature and include the pursuit of self-development, affiliation, and community contribution. Youngsters who find it important to extend their skills, to build strong bonds with peers, and to take up responsibility by contributing to the community act on values that are predominantly intrinsic. Extrinsic values, in contrast, include striving for financial success, status, and power. Youngsters who dream of earning a lot of money and who want to obtain social status or gain power and prestige in social networks have extrinsic values. These type of values are said to emerge especially when individuals' growth gets actively blocked or undermined; they (extrinsic values) emerge when people feel the need to compensate for negative experiences (Deci and Ryan 2000).

Whether youngsters have intrinsic or extrinsic values thus matters for their well-being. While some studies have examined the impact of intrinsic and extrinsic values separately, others have examined the effect of the pursuit of extrinsic relative to intrinsic values. Meta-analytic evidence shows that people having extrinsic rather than intrinsic values suffer from poor psychological and physical health (Dittmar et al. 2014): They are less satisfied with their life, experience less positive and more negative emotions, and have a negative self-image. They also report more symptoms of anxiety and depression, have more somatic complaints (e.g., headaches), and engage more in risk behaviors (e.g., compulsive shopping, smoking, and alcohol misuse). This pattern of findings has emerged in diverse countries and cultures across the globe (Chen et al. 2015; Unanue et al. 2017) and among both adults and youngsters. For example, a study by Tang, Wang, and Zhang (2017) showed that valuing extrinsic values caused Chinese youngsters, aged 17 to 23 years, to become less satisfied with their lives and more depressed over the course of one and a half years.

Not only can individuals differ in the type of values they hold, environments may also stress or promote intrinsic and extrinsic values to different degrees (Vansteenkiste, Lens, and Deci 2006). Such environmental intrinsic and extrinsic values may yield parallel effects on people's well-being as those being observed for personal pursuit. Research in diverse life domains such as education (Vansteenkiste et al. 2008), parenting (Duriez 2011; Mouratidis et al. 2013), and work (Van den Broeck et al. 2014; Schreurs et al. 2014) provides evidence that an environment promoting the pursuit of intrinsic values is better for one's well-being than a context in which extrinsic values prevail.

Person-Environment Fit Perspective

The person-environment fit perspective has been prevalent in the motivation literature for almost 100 years (e.g., Murray 1938). It assumes that people thrive when their personal characteristics (i.e., needs and values) are compatible with the environmental characteristics (i.e., supplies and values). Rather than assuming that individual and environmental values impact well-being separately, this perspective considers their interplay, thereby suggesting that a fit or correspondence in personal and environmental values—regardless of the type of values—is the most critical predictor of individuals' well-being (see van Vianen [2018] for an overview).

In line with this perspective, several meta-analyses in the work domain have shown that employees who fit with their organization are more satisfied with their job, committed, and willing to stay in the organization (Kristof-Brown, Zimmerman, and Johnson 2005; Verquer, Beehr, and Wagner 2003). They also perform better and help their colleagues more often (Hoffman and Woehr 2006). Such results have been found when people report their feelings of "fitting in," as well as when fit is calculated based on the separate assessment of individual and environmental values. The benefits of fit have been documented across the globe (Oh et al. 2014) and also emerge outside work. A fit in values between consumers and online sellers, for example, has been shown to increase consumers' trust in the seller, purchase intentions, and the price they want to pay for a product (Cazier, Shao, and Louis 2017); and people have been found to be happier when their values match with the culture of their country in terms of individualistic (Musiol and Boehnke 2013) and transcendence values (van Vianen et al. 2004).

Conflicting Hypotheses

Because SDT and the fit perspective collide, a number of studies have begun contrasting both. Specifically, a series of questionnaire studies examined whether students majoring in psychology or business benefit more from having intrinsic or extrinsic values, respectively, assuming that psychology students find themselves in an intrinsic environment, whereas business students study in an environment that promotes extrinsic values (Sagiv and Schwartz 2000; Kasser and Ahuvia 2002; Vansteenkiste et al. 2006). Two of these studies (Kasser and Ahuvia 2002; Vansteenkiste et al. 2006) indicated that both students majoring in psychology and business felt less good when they acted upon extrinsic values and benefited from acting upon intrinsic values, as suggested by SDT. Sagiv and Schwartz (2000), in contrast, reported that valuing power, for example, was associated with life satisfaction among business students, but proved detrimental for psychology students, suggesting evidence for the fit-perspective. However, none of these studies measured students' environmental values, instead assuming that different values were salient in these different environments, thereby failing to allow for a fair test of the fit perspective. To overcome this limitation, Vansteenkiste et al. (2008) examined the impact of intrinsic and extrinsic values in the context of a fundraising activity among elementary school children aged 11 to 12 years old. They manipulated the activity as instrumental for attaining intrinsic (i.e., helping the community) versus extrinsic (i.e., making a good impression on others) goals and assessed children's perspective of the activity independently from this manipulation. Framing the activity in intrinsic terms proved to stimulate children's motivation and performance, as did holding intrinsic values. Again, no evidence for the fit perspective was found. Finally, in a more recent study, Vanderstukken, Van den Broeck, and Proost (2016) reported that business students pursuing extrinsic values were more attracted to potential employers conveying extrinsic values, yet such a value-congruent effect was not observed in the case of intrinsic values. Yet choosing to apply for an employer who holds a similar value-profile as oneself does not necessarily guarantee that one will thrive in the job.

Current Study

The question whether intrinsic and extrinsic values relate to individuals' well-being depending on or irrespective of those being promoted in the social environment deserves further investigation given the paucity of previous studies on this topic. This study seeks to add novel data to this debate by, first, drawing upon a large, international, and hence culturally diverse sample, compromising fifty-four countries. As such, we expand the study of the environmental values to the country level. Studies in the framework of Hofstede (Hofstede and Bond 1984), the Globe project (Dorfman et al. 2012), or Schwartz (1992) suggest that people in different countries may pursue different values and therefore create a different context (Gallie, this volume). Grouzet and colleagues (2005) were the first to study intrinsic and extrinsic values at the country level. We add to this line of research by documenting mean levels of intrinsic and extrinsic values for fifty-four countries involved in the WVS and, most importantly, study the associations of these country-level values with youngsters' well-being in conjunction with their individual values.

We make use of multilevel analyses to examine whether the contribution of individuals' personal intrinsic and extrinsic values to their well-being depends on the values prevailing within their country. Finally, instead of creating a composite score that pits intrinsic against extrinsic values and masks whether observed effects are carried by the benefits associated with intrinsic values or the poor outcomes associated with extrinsic values, both sets of values are studied separately here (see also Unanue et al. 2014, 2017). Based on SDT, we expect independent effects of personal and environmental intrinsic and extrinsic values such that

Hypothesis 1a: Pursuing intrinsic values associates positively with life satisfaction, happiness, and health.

Hypothesis 1b: Pursuing extrinsic values associates negatively with life satisfaction, happiness, and health.

Hypothesis 2a: Contexts that promote intrinsic values associate positively with individuals' life satisfaction, happiness, and health.

Hypothesis 2b: Contexts that promote extrinsic values associate negatively with individuals' life satisfaction, happiness, and health.

Based on the fit perspective, however, we expect the combination of personal and environmental intrinsic and extrinsic values to matter most such that

Hypothesis 3a: A fit between the intrinsic values of youngsters with the intrinsic values of their environment associates positively with their life satisfaction, happiness, and health.

Hypothesis 3b: A fit between the extrinsic values of youngsters with the extrinsic values of their environment associates positively with their life satisfaction, happiness, and health.

Method

Procedure and participants

To study our hypotheses, we combined data from the sixth wave of the WVS and the World Bank's Databank. The WVS has conducted face-to-face, nationally representative surveys in a multitude of different countries since 1981 and is the largest noncommercial survey in the world. The sixth wave was collected over the period 2010–2014.[1] For the purpose of this study, we studied the associations of individual value pursuit with well-being among individuals aged 18 to 30. This sample consisted of 25,442 individuals from fifty-eight countries. The list of countries included in our analyses and country-specific descriptives can be found in the online appendix.

Measures

Individual values. To measure individual values, respondents were asked to indicate on a scale from 1 (*very much like me*) to 6 (*not at all like me*) the extent to which they resemble person descriptions presented by the interviewer. We reversed the items so that higher scores reflected greater similarity. We used the following items to measure *intrinsic values*: "It is important to this person to do something for the good of society" and "Looking after the environment is important to this person; to care for nature and to save life resources." The inter-item correlation was .45. *Extrinsic values* were measured using the following items: "It is important to this person to be rich; to have a lot of money and expensive things" and "Being very successful is important to this person; to have people recognize one's achievements." The interitem correlation was .28.

Environmental values at country level. The intrinsic and extrinsic values fostered in the youngsters' environment were derived from the total samples of each of the countries including 88,754 individuals in total. We assessed within-country agreement by calculating r_{wg}, using the expected variance of a 6-point scale with a uniform null distribution (James, Demaree, and Wolf 1984). The mean r_{wg} across countries was .65 for intrinsic values and .62 for extrinsic values. Next, we computed the intraclass correlation coefficient ICC(1) to examine the relative consistency of responses among nationals. ICC(1) was .14 for intrinsic values and .18 for extrinsic values. This suggests that people within one country share, at least to some extent, the same values (LeBreton and Senter 2008). These indices provide justification for aggregating individual-level values to the country level.

Individual well-being. We included three common indicators of individual well-being: happiness, life satisfaction, and perceived health. *Happiness* was measured via the question, "Taking all things together, would you say you are [very happy, quite happy, not very happy, not at all happy]?" We reversed the item so that higher scores reflected higher levels of happiness. *Life satisfaction* was measured via the question, "All things considered, how satisfied are you with your life as a whole these days?" measured on a scale from 1 to 10, with 1 representing *completely dissatisfied* and 10 *completely satisfied*. *Perceived health* was measured via the question, "All in all, how would you describe your state of health these days? Would you say it is [very good, good, fair, poor]?" We reversed the item so that higher scores reflected better health. The three-item well-being aggregate had a Cronbach's alpha of .44, well below the recommended cutoff of .70. We therefore decided to treat the indicators as separate outcomes.

Covariates. As country wealth associates with individual well-being (Diener, Diener, and Diener 1995), we included *gross domestic product (GDP) per capita* (current US$) and *GDP growth* (annual percent) for the year in which the survey was conducted as country-level covariates in the analyses (Dittmar et al. 2014). In addition, to account for the effect of socioeconomic status on health and well-being (Adler and Rehkopf 2008), we included the following three individual-level covariates: educational level (from 1 = *no formal education* to 9 = *university-level education, with degree*), social class (from 1 = *lower class* to 5 = *upper class*), and household income (from 1 = *lowest income group in country* to 10 = *highest income group in country*).

Data analyses

Data are structured such that the measurements at the individual level (level 1) are nested within countries (level 2). To account for the dependent nature of the measurements at level 1, we conducted multilevel analysis using Stata/SE 14.2. Level-2 predictor variables were centered around the grand mean, and level-1 predictor variables were centered around the country mean to rule out interpretations referring to stable between-country differences (Enders and Tofighi 2007).

We conducted separate analyses for each of the dependent variables and did so in a stepwise manner (see the online appendix). First, we estimated the unconditional means model (model 1), including the intercept as the only predictor. In the second step, we added the level-1 covariates (model 2). In step 3, intrinsic and extrinsic values were added to the equation to test SDT's Hypotheses 1a and 1b (model 3). We treated level-1 intrinsic and extrinsic values as random effects at level 2. In the fourth step, we entered the level-2 variables (model 4). We added the covariates GDP per capita and GDP growth, together with country-level intrinsic and extrinsic values, to test SDT's hypotheses 2a and 2b. In the fifth and final step (model 5), we entered the cross-level interaction terms individual-level × country-level intrinsic values and individual-level × country-level extrinsic values to examine the hypothesis of the fit perspective (hypotheses 3a and 3b) that corresponding levels of values would yield higher levels of individual well-being.

We estimated the models using the full maximum likelihood estimation method (the mle Stata command). We calculated pseudo-R^2s after each step indicating the within- and between-country variance explained by the variables in that step (Snijders and Bosker 2012). The improvement of each model over the previous one was tested using the difference between the respective likelihood ratios. This difference follows a chi-square distribution (degree of freedom equal to the number of new parameters added to the model).

Results

Descriptive statistics and correlations among the study variables are shown in Table 1. At the individual level, the three indicators of well-being are positively associated. Intrinsic and extrinsic values are also positively correlated. Further, having intrinsic values is positively correlated with all three well-being indicators, while having extrinsic values related positively with perceived health and happiness yet negatively with life satisfaction. At the country level, intrinsic values are positively correlated with GDP growth, and extrinsic values are negatively correlated with GDP per capita and positively correlated with GDP growth and intrinsic values.

Test of hypotheses

The results of the multilevel analyses for happiness, life satisfaction, and perceived health are presented in Table 2. We first ran intercept-only models to

TABLE 1
Correlations between Study Variables

		M	SD	2	3	4	5	6	7	8	9	10	11
Country-level variables													
1	GDP per capita	12,966.05	16,287.36	−.09	−.25	−.27	—	—	—	—	—	—	—
2	GDP growth	4.86	3.44	—	.26	.37	—	—	—	—	—	—	—
3	Intrinsic values	4.52	0.39	—	—	.42	—	—	—	—	—	—	—
4	Extrinsic values	4.02	0.49	—	—	—	—	—	—	—	—	—	—
Individual-level variables													
5	Educational level	6.24	2.12	—	—	—	—	—	—	—	—	—	—
6	Social class	2.78	1.02	—	—	—	.26	—	—	—	—	—	—
7	Household income	5.17	2.05	—	—	—	.20	.44	—	—	—	—	—
8	Intrinsic values	4.52	1.08	—	—	—	.00	.03	.02	—	—	—	—
9	Extrinsic values	4.02	1.16	—	—	—	−.01	.06	.10	.27	—	—	—
10	Happiness	3.23	0.73	—	—	—	.05	.12	.16	.09	.02	—	—
11	Life satisfaction	6.98	2.20	—	—	—	.12	.16	.23	.08	−.03	.42	—
12	Perceived health	3.20	0.76	—	—	—	.04	.07	.13	.10	.11	.35	.23

NOTE: Numbers below the diagonal represent individual-level correlations ($N_{individual}$ = 25,442); numbers above the diagonal represent country-level correlations ($N_{country}$ = 58). At country-level: $r \geq .43$, $ps < .001$; $r \geq .34$, $ps < .01$; $r \geq .26$, $ps < .05$. At individual-level: $r \geq .021$, $ps < .001$; $r \geq .016$, $ps < .01$; $r \geq .013$, $ps < .05$.

examine whether there was systematic variance in the dependent variables. ICC(1) was used as an indicator of nonindependence for the dependent variables and can be interpreted as the proportion of total variance that can be explained by group (i.e., country) membership (Bliese 2000). For happiness, the ICC(1) was .11 [95 percent confidence interval [CI]: .08; .15], $F(57, 25,384) = 60.55$, $p < .001$; for life satisfaction, the ICC(1) was .09 [95 percent CI: .06; .12], $F(57, 25,384) = 49.58$, $p < .001$; for perceived health, the ICC(1) was .07 [95 percent CI: .05; .10], $F(57, 25,384) = 38.47$, $p < .001$. Although these effects are small, they are significant, and there is enough variance in the dependent variables accounted for by country level (LeBreton and Senter 2008).

We found support for hypothesis 1a: individual-level intrinsic values related positively to happiness ($B = 0.04, p < .001$), life satisfaction ($B = 0.15, p < .001$), and perceived health ($B = 0.04, p < .001$). Contrary to hypothesis 1b, individual-level extrinsic values were unrelated to happiness ($B = 0.00$, ns) and life satisfaction ($B = -0.02$, ns) and even positively related to perceived health ($B = 0.03$, $p < .001$). In support of hypothesis 2a, country-level intrinsic values were positively associated with youngsters' happiness ($B = 0.16, p = .06$), albeit this relationship was only marginally significant. These values were significantly positively related to life satisfaction ($B = 0.63, p < .001$) and perceived health ($B = 0.20$, $p < .001$). In line with hypothesis 2b, country-level extrinsic values were negatively related to happiness ($B = -0.14, p < .05$) and life satisfaction ($B = -0.71$,

TABLE 2
Unstandardized Regression Coefficients of Personal and Country Values Predicting
Youngsters' Well-Being and Health

Fixed Effects	Happiness (Model 5)		Life Satisfaction (Model 5)		Perceived Health (Model 5)	
	B	SE	B	SE	B	SE
Intercept	3.22°°°	0.03	7.01°°°	0.08	3.19°°°	0.02
Individual-level predictors						
Educational level	0.00°	0.00	0.03°°°	0.01	0.02°°°	0.00
Social class	0.05°°°	0.01	0.12°°°	0.02	0.04°°°	0.01
Household income	0.05°°°	0.00	0.23°°°	0.01	0.03°°°	0.00
Intrinsic values	0.04°°°	0.01	0.15°°°	0.02	0.04°°°	0.01
Extrinsic values	0.00	0.00	–0.01	0.02	0.03°°°	0.01
Country-level predictors						
GDP per capita	0.00	0.00	0.00	0.00	0.00°	0.00
GDP growth	0.02°	0.01	0.01	0.02	0.00	0.01
Intrinsic values	0.16†	0.08	0.63°°	0.20	0.20°°	0.07
Extrinsic values	–0.14°	0.07	–0.71°°°	0.17	0.09	0.06
Cross-level interactions						
$IV_{individual} \times IV_{country}$	0.01	0.02	0.06	0.06	–0.01	0.02
$EV_{individual} \times EV_{country}$	0.02°	0.01	0.13°°°	0.04	0.01	0.01
Random parameters						
Level 2						
Var intercept	0.05		0.29		0.03	
Var slope $_{intrinsic\ values}$	0.00		0.02		0.00	
Var slope $_{extrinsic\ values}$	0.00		0.01		0.00	
Level 1						
Var intercept	0.45		4.04		0.51	
–2 × log likelihood	50232.94		103894.73		53098.30	
Δ –2 × log likelihood (df)	5.31 (2)		12.76°° (2)		1.74 (2)	
Pseudo-R^2 (level-2)	17%		30%		26%	
Pseudo-R^2 (level-1)	5%		9%		4%	

NOTE: IV = intrinsic values; EV = extrinsic values.
†p = .06. °p < .05. °°p < .01. °°°p < .001.

p < .001). However, they were unrelated to perceived health (B = 0.09, ns). Hence, hypothesis 2b was partially supported. Note that GDP per capita and GDP growth were unrelated to these outcomes, except for the positive relation between GDP growth and youngsters' happiness (B = 0.02, p < .001).

As respects the hypotheses from the fit perspective, contrary to hypothesis 3a, individual-level and country-level intrinsic values did not significantly interact to predict happiness (B = 0.01, ns), life satisfaction (B = 0.06, ns), or perceived health ($B = -0.01$, ns). Similarly individual-level and country-level extrinsic values did not significantly interact to predict perceived health ($B = 0.01$, ns), but—in line with hypothesis 3b—they interacted in predicting happiness ($B = 0.02$, $p < .05$) and life satisfaction ($B = 0.13$, $p = .001$). As seen in Figure 1, a plot of these interactions showed that increases in individual-level extrinsic values associated with more happiness ($b = 0.02$, $SE = 0.01$, $t = 2.19$, $p < .05$) and satisfaction ($b = 0.14$, $SE = 0.05$, $t = 2.93$, $p < .01$) in highly extrinsic countries, but were unrelated to happiness ($b = -0.02$, $SE = 0.01$, $t = 1.97$, ns) and negatively related to satisfaction ($b = -0.15$, $SE = 0.04$, $t = 3.53$, $p < .001$) when country-level extrinsic values were low.

Conclusion

This article set out to understand the relationship between youngsters' values and their well-being, contrasting SDT and the person-environment fit perspective. SDT assumes that intrinsic values such as community contribution support well-being and health, while extrinsic values such as materialism are detrimental, both when people hold these values as well as when these values are promoted by their environment. The person-environment fit perspective, in contrast, does not differentiate "good" from "bad" values and argues that the pursuit of all values can be beneficial as long as similar values are supported by the context.

Our results largely support SDT: youngsters are happier, more satisfied with their lives, and healthier if they have intrinsic values or live in countries where intrinsic values prevail and/or when extrinsic values are deemed less important (Kasser 2016; Ryan and Deci 2017). However, two findings contradict this overall conclusion. First, youngsters residing in a country where extrinsic values predominate were happier and more satisfied with their life when they act upon extrinsic values than when their values did not match their context. Although this may seem to fit the person-environment fit perspective, given the strong negative main effect of extrinsic country values, Figure 1 suggests that even youngsters fitting in such a context still experience less well-being than youngsters in less extrinsic environments. As such, having extrinsic values in an extrinsic environment may play a protective role but does not yield such a boost in well-being, which would require the presence of a cross-over interaction.

Second, youngsters who have extrinsic values did not experience less well-being. To the contrary, although they were not happier or more satisfied with their life, they reported being healthier. Some, albeit short-lived, benefits associated with extrinsic values have been reported before (Vansteenkiste, Lens, and Deci 2006) and may be explained by the fact that extrinsic values also provide some direction in people's life, which could be inherently satisfying (Locke and Latham 1990). However, the positive relationship of personal extrinsic values with life satisfaction and health may also be caused by the different meaning attached to these values in different countries. For some, the pursuit of money and status may yield a more ego-validating character and represent an attempt to

FIGURE 1
Interaction of Individual- and Country-Level Extrinsic Values Predicting
Happiness and Life Satisfaction

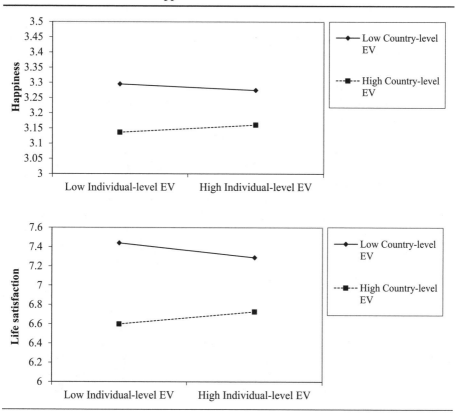

acquire approval or be a necessary mean to secure survival or support one's family and, hence, be less detrimental to their well-being (see also Chen et al. 2015; Grouzet et al. 2005; Houson, Brodbeck, and Forest 2016). Second, in the WVS only a few items tapping into intrinsic and extrinsic values were available, and not all types of intrinsic and extrinsic values could be included. For example, we did not have items tapping into personal development or power, although these are important intrinsic and extrinsic values, too. Multifaceted measures that do include all types of intrinsic and extrinsic values generally generate stronger results (Dittmar et al. 2014). Studies using such multifaceted measures could further disentangle our results, especially when such studies would explore different ways of analyzing the impact of intrinsic and extrinsic values. Specifically, we argue that much can be learned from comparing the results of different computational models to assess the values including (1) intrinsic and extrinsic values separately, as we did in this study; (2) their relative importance, for example, by subtracting intrinsic values from extrinsic values, or (3) focus on one's dominant values.

Practical implications

Despite this need for future research, our results yield practical implications, both at the individual and policy levels. First, youngsters could be stimulated to attach high importance to intrinsic values. Although values are relatively stable from childhood onward, the importance attached to particular values may still change through life experiences (Döring, Daniel, and Knafo-Noam 2016). Hence, youngsters may try to develop intrinsic values by deliberately exposing themselves to activities fitting intrinsic values such as engaging in community service (Horn 2012) or be stimulated by others ranging from their nuclear family to the society in general to pursue intrinsic goals. For example, parents who have intrinsic values themselves (see Duriez [2011] for a study among 16-year-olds) or are autonomy supportive rather than controlling may stimulate the development of intrinsic values among their children (Lekes et al. 2010). Parents thus need to be mindful of the values they convey.

Contextual values may thus strike twice as hard in youngsters' well-being: once by influencing youngsters' values and again by impacting youngsters' well-being directly. Changing the culture of a country and the underlying values is challenging, however, as cultural values are shaped by a complex system of factors that can be changed only in the long term. For example, socioeconomic developments lead to a greater cultural emphasis on autonomy (Welzel, Inglehart, and Klingemann 2003); while social instability, disconnection, consumerism, or war leads to the development of a materialistic outlook (see Daniel et al. [2013] for a study among 14-year-olds and Twenge and Kasser [2013] for a study on 17- to 18-year-olds). Political changes such as a movement to more democratic regimes and economic changes such as industrialization and increased digitalization may be powerful tools to enable cultural change (Inglehart 1997), but policy-makers could also pay attention to the amount and tone of advertising and factors that increase insecurity, such as job insecurity, unemployment, and violence (Gallie, this volume; Kalleberg and Marsden, this volume; Twenge and Kasser 2013).

Note

1. See http://www.worldvaluessurvey.org/WVSDocumentationWV6.jsp.

References

Adler, Nancy E., and David H. Rehkopf. 2008. U.S. disparities in health: Descriptions, causes, and mechanisms. *Annual Review of Public Health* 29:235–52.

Bliese, Paul D. 2000. Within-group agreement, non-independence, and reliability: Implications for data aggregation and analysis. In *Multilevel theory, research, and methods in organizations*, 349–81. San Francisco, CA: Jossey-Bass.

Call, Kathleen Thiede, Aylin Altan Riedel, Karen Hein, Vonnie McLoyd, Anne Petersen, and Michele Kipke. 2002. Adolescent health and well-being in the twenty-first century: A global perspective. *Journal of Research on Adolescence* 12:69–98.

Cazier, Joseph, Benjamin Shao, and Robert St Louis. 2017. Value congruence, trust, and their effects on purchase intentions and reservation price. *ACM Transactions on Management Information Systems (TMIS)* 8. Available from https://doi.org/10.1145/3110939.

Chen, Beiwen, Jasper Van Assche, Maarten Vansteenkiste, Bart Soenens, and Wim Beyers. 2015. Does psychological need satisfaction matter when environmental or financial safety are at risk? *Journal of Happiness Studies* 16:745–66.

Daniel, Ella, Keren Fortuna, Sophia K. Thrun, Shaylee Cioban, and Ariel Knafo. 2013. Brief report: Early adolescents' value development at war time. *Journal of Adolescence* 36:651–55.

Deci, Edward L., and Richard M Ryan. 2000. The darker and brighter sides of human existence: Basic psychological needs as a unifying concept. *Psychological Inquiry* 11 (4): 319–38.

Diener, Ed, Marissa Diener, and Carol Diener. 1995. Factors predicting the subjective well-being of nations. *Journal of Personality and Social Psychology* 69:851–64.

Dittmar, Helga, Rod Bond, Megan Hurst, and Tim Kasser. 2014. The relationship between materialism and personal well-being: A meta-analysis. *Journal of Personality Social Psychology* 107:879–924.

Dorfman, Peter, Mansour Javidan, Paul Hanges, Ali Dastmalchian, and Robert House. 2012. GLOBE: A twenty year journey into the intriguing world of culture and leadership. *Journal of World Business* 47:504–18.

Döring, Anna K., Ella Daniel, and Ariel Knafo-Noam. 2016. Introduction to the special section value development from middle childhood to early adulthood—New insights from longitudinal and genetically informed research. *Social Development* 25:471–81.

Duriez, Bart. 2011. Adolescent ethnic prejudice: Understanding the effects of parental extrinsic versus intrinsic goal promotion. *Journal of Social Psychology* 15:441–54.

Edmunds, June, and Bryan S. Turner. 2005. Global generations: Social change in the twentieth century. *British Journal of Sociology* 56:559–77.

Enders, Craig K., and Davood Tofighi. 2007. Centering predictor variables in cross-sectional multilevel models: a new look at an old issue. *Psychological Methods* 12:121–38.

Erikson, Erik. 1968. *Identity: Youth and crisis.* New York, NY: Norton.

Gallie, Duncan. 2019. Research on work values in a changing economic and social context. *The ANNALS of the American Academy of Political and Social Science* (this volume).

Grouzet, Frederick M. E., Tim Kasser, Aaron Ahuvia, José Miguel Fernández Dols, Youngmee Kim, Sing Lau, Richard M. Ryan, Shaun Saunders, Peter Schmuck, and Kennon M. Sheldon. 2005. The structure of goal contents across 15 cultures. *Journal of Personality and Social Psychology* 89:800–816.

Hoffman, Brian J., and David J. Woehr. 2006. A quantitative review of the relationship between person-organization fit and behavioral outcomes. *Journal of Vocational Behavior* 68:389–99.

Hofstede, Geert, and Michael H. Bond. 1984. Hofstede's culture dimensions: An independent validation using Rokeach's value survey. *Journal of Cross-Cultural Psychology* 15:417–33.

Horn, Aaron S. 2012. The cultivation of a prosocial value orientation through community service: An examination of organizational context, social facilitation, and duration. *Journal of Youth and Adolescence* 41:948–68.

Houson, Dobie, Felix C Brodbeck, and Jacques Forest. 2016. Why individuals want money is what matters: Using self-determination theory to explain the differential relationship between motives for making money and employee psychological health. *Motivation and Emotion* 40:226–42.

Inglehart, Ronald. 1997. *Modernization and postmodernization: Cultural, economic, and political change in 43 societies.* Princeton, NJ: Princeton University Press.

Inglehart, Ronald, C. Haerpfer, A. Moreno, C. Welzel, K. Kizilova, J. Diez-Medrano, M. Lagos, P. Norris, E. Ponarin, and B. Puranen, et al. 2014. World Values Survey: Round six-country-pooled datafile 2010–2014. Madrid: JD Systems Institute. Available from http://www.worldvaluessurvey.org/WVSDocumentationWV6.jsp.

James, Lawrence R., Robert G. Demaree, and Gerrit Wolf. 1984. Estimating within-group interrater reliability with and without response bias. *Journal of Applied Psychology* 69:85–98.

Kalleberg, Arne, and Peter V. Marsden. 2019. Work values in the United States: Age, period and generational differences. *The ANNALS of the American Academy of Political and Social Science* (this volume).

Kasser, Tim. 2016. Materialistic values and goals. *Annual Review of Psychology* 67:489–514.

Kasser, Tim, and Aaron Ahuvia. 2002. Materialistic values and well-being in business students. *European Journal of Social Psychology* 32:137–46.

Kasser, Tim, and Richard M. Ryan. 1993. A dark side of the American dream: Correlates of financial success as a central life aspiration. *Journal of Personality and Social Psychology* 65:410–22.

Kristof, Amy L. 1996. Person-organization fit: An integrative review of its conceptualizations, measurements, and implications. *Personnel Psychology* 49:1–49.

Kristof-Brown, Amy L., Ryan D. Zimmerman, and Erin C. Johnson. 2005. Consequences of individuals' fit at work: A meta-analysis of person-job, person-organization, person-group, and person-supervisor fit. *Personnel Psychology* 58:281–342.

LeBreton, James M., and Jenell L. Senter. 2008. Answers to 20 questions and interrater agreement. *Organizational Research Methods* 11:815–52.

Lekes, Natasha, Isabelle Gingras, Frederick L. Philippe, Richard Koestner, and Jianqun Fang. 2010. Parental autonomy-support, intrinsic life goals, and well-being among adolescents in China and North America. *Journal of Youth and Adolescence* 39:858–69.

Locke, Edwin A., and Gary P. Latham. 1990. *A theory of goal setting & task performance*. Englewood Cliffs, NJ: Prentice-Hall.

Mouratidis, Athanasios, Maarten Vansteenkiste, Willy Lens, Aikaterini Michou, and Bart Soenens. 2013. Within-person configurations and temporal relations of personal and perceived parent-promoted aspirations to school correlates among adolescents. *Journal of Educational Psychology* 105:895–910.

Murray, Henry A. 1938. *Explorations in personality*. Oxford: Oxford University Press.

Musiol, Anna-lena, and Klaus Boehnke. 2013. Person-environment value congruence and satisfaction with life. *International Journal of Humanities and Social Science* 3:57–65.

Oh, In-Sue, Russell P. Guay, Kwanghyun Kim, Crystal M. Harold, Jong-Hyun Lee, Chang-Goo Heo, and Kang-Hyun Shin. 2014. Fit happens globally: A meta-analytic comparison of the relationships of person-environment fit dimensions with work attitudes and performance across East Asia, Europe, and North America. *Personnel Psychology* 67:99–152.

Ryan, Richard M., and Edward L. Deci. 2017. *Self-determination theory: Basic psychological needs in motivation, development, and wellness*. New York, NY: Guilford Publications.

Sagiv, Lilach, and Shalom H. Schwartz. 2000. Value priorities and subjective well-being: Direct relations and congruity effects. *European Journal of Social Psychology* 30:177–98.

Schreurs, Bert, I. J. Hetty Van Emmerik, Anja Van den Broeck, and Hannes Guenter. 2014. Work values and work engagement within teams: The mediating role of need satisfaction. *Group Dynamics: Theory, Research and Practice* 18:267–81.

Schwartz, Shalom H. 1992. Universals in the content and structure of values: Theoretical advances and empirical tests in 20 countries. *Advances in Experimental Social Psychology* 25:1–65.

Snijders, Tom A. B., and Roel J. Bosker. 2012. *Multilevel analysis: An introduction to basic and advanced multilevel modeling*. 2nd ed. London: Sage Publications.

Tang, Ningyu, Yumei Wang, and Kaili Zhang. 2017. Values of Chinese generation cohorts: Do they matter in the workplace? *Organizational Behavior and Human Decision Processes* 143:8–22.

Twenge, Jean M., and Tim Kasser. 2013. Generational changes in materialism and work centrality, 1976–2007. *Personality and Social Psychology Bulletin* 39:883–97.

Unanue, Wenceslao, Helga Dittmar, Vivian L. Vignoles, and Maarten Vansteenkiste. 2014. Materialism and well-being in the UK and Chile: Basic need satisfaction and basic need frustration as underlying psychological processes. *European Journal of Personality* 28:569–85.

Unanue, Wenceslao, Konrad Rempel, Marcos E. Gómez, and Anja Van den Broeck. 2017. When and why does materialism relate to employees' attitudes and well-being: The mediational role of need satisfaction and need frustration. *Frontiers in Psychology* 8, Article 1755.

Van den Broeck, Anja, Nele De Cuyper, Elfi Baillien, Els Vanbelle, Dorien Vanhercke, and Hans De Witte. 2014. Perception of organization's value support and perceived employability: Insights from self-determination theory. *International Journal of Human Resource Management* 25:1904–18.

Vanderstukken, Arne, Anja Van den Broeck, and Karin Proost. 2016. For love or for money: Intrinsic and extrinsic value congruence in recruitment. *International Journal of Selection and Assessment* 24:34–41.

Vansteenkiste, Maarten, Bart Duriez, Joke Simons, and Bart Soenens. 2006. Materialistic values and well-being among business students: Further evidence of their detrimental effect. *Journal of Applied Social Psychology* 36:2892–2908.

Vansteenkiste, Maarten, Willy Lens, and Edward L. Deci. 2006. Intrinsic versus extrinsic goal contents in self-determination theory: Another look at the quality of academic motivation. *Educational Psychologist* 41:19–31.

Vansteenkiste, Maarten, T. Timmermans, W. Lens, B. Soenens, and Anja Van den Broeck. 2008. Does extrinsic goal framing enhance extrinsic goal-oriented individuals' learning and performance? An experimental test of the match perspective versus self-determination theory. *Journal of Educational Psychology* 100:387–97.

van Vianen, Annelies E. M. 2018. Person–environment fit: A review of its basic tenets. *Annual Review of Organizational Psychology and Organizational Behavior* 5:75–101.

van Vianen, Annelies E. M., Irene E. De Pater, Amy L. Kristof-Brown, and Erin C. Johnson. 2004. Fitting in: Surface- and deep-level cultural differences and expatriates' adjustment. *Academy of Management Journal* 47:697–709.

Verquer, Michelle L., Terry A. Beehr, and Stephen H. Wagner. 2003. A meta-analysis of relations between person-organization fit and work attitudes. *Journal of Vocational Behavior* 63:473–89.

Welzel, Christian, Ronald Inglehart, and Hans Dieter Klingemann. 2003. The theory of human development: A cross-cultural analysis. *European Journal of Political Research* 42:341–79.

Reflections

Work Values in Politics: The European Union Debt Crisis as a Case Study

By
ANNA DIAMANTOPOULOU
and
KYRIAKOS PIERRAKAKIS

The European debt crisis has had significant political and economic implications throughout the Eurozone, particularly for its peripheral South. These were especially obvious for Greece, which had to face elevated levels of austerity and sign three different bailout programs within eight years to remain economically solvent and retain its position in the context of European institutions. Here, we track how the perception of the work values of Greeks by other member states—such as Germany, Slovakia or Finland—along with ensuing public debates adversely affected the bailout program design and implementation in Greece, and had significant political consequences throughout the Eurozone.

Keywords: work attitudes; work values; Greek crisis; European debt crisis; stereotyping; instrumentalizing work values; perceptions

The European sovereign debt crisis has now been formally concluded, after the successful completion of the third bailout program for Greece in August 2018, the last country within the Eurozone to be in such a program. However, the implications of this crisis, and of its overall management both at the state level and at the level of the Eurozone as a whole, have been significant and are still quite apparent (Matsaganis and Leventi 2014). Within a decade, policies, primarily in the fiscal sphere but also more broadly, changed significantly, especially as an outcome of conditionality programs in countries that were under close supervision.

Anna Diamantopoulou is president of To Diktyo, a network for reform in Greece and Europe. To Diktyo is an Athens-based independent, nonpartisan, nonprofit research and policy institute that aims to develop strong, pragmatic, and innovative policy and advocacy on all aspects of European integration, Greek domestic politics, and various international structures. Diamantopoulou has served as Minister of Education of Greece and EU Commissioner of Employment and Social Affairs, among other public appointments.

Correspondence: kyriakos.p@dianeosis.org

DOI: 10.1177/0002716219826026

ANNALS, *AAPSS*, 682, March 2019

The political implications of the crisis were also obvious, often reflected in the demise of traditional political parties and the rise of new political actors, populists and populism being particularly salient in contemporary Europe (Frieden and Walter 2017; McCoy and Somer 2019).

The aim of this reflection piece is to shed light on the tremendous political implications of work values, or, in fact, on the effects of the instrumentalization of work values and of their often skewed perceptions, in the context of the European sovereign debt crisis. Work values are defined and analyzed extensively throughout this special issue of *The ANNALS*. Our goal is to analyze how policy-makers' perceptions of work values have significant implications not only for international politics but for the policymaking process as well. The European sovereign debt crisis offers itself as an interesting case for the manifestation of how certain work value stereotypes—the most obvious one involving the work ethic of the various nations of the European Union (EU) South, especially of Greece—played in the political debates of the time, and ended up influencing policy.

The Economic and Financial Crisis: From the United States to the European Union

The European sovereign debt crisis has its origins on the other side of the Atlantic Ocean. In 2007, after the collapse of the subprime mortgage market in the United States, along with the linked bankruptcy of the New Century Financial Corporation, and the ensuing freezing of interbank markets, the crisis started its contagion in Europe, through a bank run in the United Kingdom and European Central Bank's (ECB) first emergency liquidity action (Baldwin and Wyplosz 2012). The following collapse of the investment bank Lehman Brothers triggered what was, according to many, the worst financial crisis since 1929 (Tosun, Wetzel, and Zapryanova 2014). Following these events, Hungary became the first EU member state to seek financial assistance, and, although a non-Eurozone member, the ECB provided emergency support (Tosun, Wetzel, and Zapryanova 2014; Hodson and Quaglia 2009).

As Grammatikos and Vermeulen (2012) note, the European financial markets were not insulated from what happened in the United States. The collapse of Lehman Brothers led to a series of government interventions, to bail out the banks affected, to begin with in the United States, but in the process reaching various other places, such as Iceland. European national governments started to massively inject capital to their respective financial institutions, while undertaking fiscal expansion policies. However, the single currency area proved initially vulnerable to the crisis, as it was created without a central fiscal authority, which

Kyriakos Pierrakakis is director of research of diaNEOsis, a nonprofit, nonpartisan think-tank based in Maroussi, Greece. The institute publishes academic research, policy recommendations, and investigative journalism, while aiming to actively contribute to public discourse on social and economic issues, and to promote change and meaningful political reform. Pierrakakis is also a doctoral candidate in Political Science at the University of Heidelberg.

would have been able to manage tax and spending, along with fiscal transfers between the stronger and the weaker states of the Union (Grammatikos and Vermeulen 2012). This sparked further distrust in global capital markets for certain European governments, leading to the European sovereign debt crisis.

Within Europe, the bailouts of European banks were not sufficient to stop the crisis from spreading. Budget deficits escalated as an outcome of the global financial slowdown, surpassing the 3 percent mark specified by the Stability and Growth Pact as the upper limit for deficits throughout the Union. This escalation in deficit spending was particularly prevalent in the countries of the European South—Greece, Italy, Spain, and Portugal—together with Ireland, which had its own set of problems, mainly in the banking sphere. Deficit spending, together with an economic slowdown that had just started to manifest itself globally, led to the escalation of public debts. This escalation is perceived to have been the root cause of the Eurozone debt crisis (Tosun, Wetzel, and Zapryanova 2014). The management of the crisis at the European level mandated the drafting and enactment of International Monetary Fund (IMF) conditionality programs in Greece, Portugal, Ireland, and Cyprus. It also changes EU institutions at the fiscal, banking, and monetary levels. In August 2018, Greece was the last country to complete its final—third—bailout package and formally exit the crisis.

Since 2009, Greece has been seen to be in an existential crisis for its economy and society, and is considered to be the country most severely hit by the Eurozone debt crisis. Specifically, after the Greek parliamentary elections of 2009, the newly elected government had to revise the budget deficit projection from 2.7 percent to 12.7 percent (and eventually to 15.1 percent). Concerns about the creditworthiness of the country started to grow. The rising interest rates of government bonds led to the incapacity of the country to secure adequate levels of credit on international markets, and, eventually, to the need for the first bailout, which the heads of state and government of the Euro area backed at the European summit in March 2010 (Council of the EU 2010a). Eventual agreement on the specific details of the €110 billion bilateral loan package for Eurozone members, in cooperation with IMF, was achieved two months later (Council of the EU 2010b). Overall, the severity of the crisis mandated significant levels of state aid to be provided to Greece, first in the form of bilateral loans, and, in the process, through the creation of the European Financial Stability Facility (EFSF) and the European Stability Mechanism (ESM). This bailout process involved Greece receiving aid from all other Eurozone member states, a process that often proved to have its own unique set of challenges on the technical and, mainly, political level. Namely, given the national institutional framework of every participating state, this aid had to be provided—a procedure that often nurtured fierce domestic parliamentary debates, as the following analysis showcases.

After nine years of crisis and a cumulative loss of 26 percent of GDP, the Greek economy seems to have returned to positive, albeit meager, growth rates, with an annual growth rate of 1.4 percent. At the same time, the social cost of this significant drop of economic activity was staggering (Matsaganis and Leventi 2014). In May 2008, the unemployment rate had reached its lowest point, at

TABLE 1
Stereotyping in Europe in 2012

Views in	Most Hardworking	Least Hardworking
Britain	Germany	Greece
France	Germany	Italy
Germany	Germany	Greece
Spain	Germany	Greece
Italy	Germany	Romania
Greece	Greece	Italy
Poland	Germany	Greece
Czech Republic	Germany	Greece

SOURCE: Pew Research Center, Global Attitudes Project (2012)

7.3 percent, very close to the EU average, which was 6.8 percent (Tsakloglou et al. 2016). The unemployment level for Greece peaked in July 2013, at 27.9 percent, and has been de-escalating since, reaching 20.8 percent in February 2018. Thus, during these years of crisis, wages stagnated; unemployment, specifically youth unemployment, ignited; and extreme poverty skyrocketed (Tsakloglou et al. 2016). At the same time, traditional political parties collapsed while new political powers, mostly from a populist stance, emerged.

Work Values and Political Debates during the Crisis

Given the context described above, one would have thought that work values should not have played a significant part in the equation, either in the unfolding of the crisis or during its management. Nonetheless, as this reflection piece shows, exactly the opposite proved to be true. As the crisis unfolded, it was obvious that perceptions mattered greatly, both in the broader public and among policy-makers who handled the policy responses to the crisis on the pan-European level. In the case of Greece, these perceptions were focused mostly in the realm of attitudes toward work or work values, especially with regard to how hard-working or not the Greeks were perceived to be. These perceptions affected the roll-out of the Greek crisis significantly, often leading to sub-optimal and unexpected results, and equally often undermining the significant solidarity that was otherwise exhibited in the context of the management of the crisis.

According to the Global Attitudes Project of Pew Global[1] (Pew Research Center 2012; see Table 1), in 2012 Greece was perceived to be the laziest country in Europe according to the UK, Germany, Spain, Poland, and the Czech Republic, while Italy was perceived as the laziest by France and Greece. At the same time, Greece was perceived to be the most hardworking country in Europe by its own countrymen.

However, it was obvious that these perceptions had penetrated not only the public psyche but also that of the policy-maker's. Either because policy-makers attempted not to incur political costs during the management of the European debt crisis, or because they were trying to gain political benefits, they attempted to reproduce—and often amplify—these public perceptions through their rhetoric. And, certainly, that the Greek problem was rooted in competitiveness rather than on purely fiscal issues, was also significant.

At an early stage of the Greek crisis, German Chancellor Angela Merkel proclaimed that the Greeks could not retire earlier and have longer holidays than the Germans. German magazine *Der Spiegel* interpreted this statement as follows: "We aren't going to give our hard-earned German money to lazy southern Europeans" (Boll and Bocking 2011). Most famously, the German tabloid newspaper *Bild* asked in 2011 why the Acropolis could not be sold to repay debts to Germany (Bild 2011). This line of thinking had emerged in the public discourse even before the signing of the first memorandum between Greece and its lenders. In March 2010, two German policy-makers, Josef Schlarmann, a senior member of Angela Merkel's Christian Democrats, and Frank Schaeffler, a finance policy expert in the Free Democrats, noted in the same newspaper that Greece should consider a fire sale of land, historic buildings, and artwork to cut its debts, alongside austerity measures such as cuts to public sector pay and a freeze on state pensions (Inman and Smith 2010). "Those in insolvency have to sell everything they have to pay their creditors," Schlarmann noted at *Bild* newspaper. "Greece owns buildings, companies, and uninhabited islands, which could all be used for debt redemption."

Such views unfolded in the context of a broader narrative, rooted in work values stereotyping. As the then Swedish Minister of Finance, Anders Borg, noted while on his way to an EU summit: "Obviously, Swedes and other taxpayers should not have to pay for Greeks that choose to retire in their forties. That is unacceptable" (Scocco 2015). This view became dominant quite early in the highest echelons of policymaking in the European lender states, and consequently influenced the overall management of the crisis.

It is also important to add that such statements did not only unfold at the beginning of the crisis. Even at much later stages, work values stereotypes penetrated public discourse, even at the highest levels of decision-making and policy formulation. Former Dutch Finance Minister and Former Head of the EuroGroup, the institution de facto responsible for monitoring the bailout program for Greece, Jeroen Dijsselbloem, in the context of an interview with *Frankfurter Allgemeine Zeitung* famously noted: "During the crisis of the euro, the countries of the North have shown solidarity with the countries affected by the crisis. As a Social Democrat, I attribute exceptional importance to solidarity. [But] you also have obligations. You cannot spend all the money on drinks and women and then ask for help" (McDonald 2017).

Statements such as this initiated a vicious circle of political polemic, which further aggravated the situation on both sides. Jeroen Dijsselbloem's statement specifically, picked up by the Spanish press, created significant turmoil, and led to senior political figures from the European South to ask for the resignation of the head of the EuroGroup. Gianni Pittella, the Italian MEP who led the

European Socialist group at the time, called for Mr. Dijsselbloem to resign, saying he is "not fit to be president of the Eurogroup." Spain's Finance Minister,
Luis de Guindos, led the backlash to the Dutch minister's comments, despite
sharing a seat around the Eurogroup table. "I do not think that Portugal, Greece,
Cyprus or Ireland have wasted money," he said. "Solidarity is important." "They
lent us $40 billion, but we have lent other countries a similar amount and making
such comparisons is not ideal" (McDonald 2017).

It is interesting to note that despite Greece's very significant structural problems, many of which have yet to be addressed, these views were not actually
accurate. Even in 2011, before a series of reforms in the pension sphere in the
context of the three programs that Greece had to implement, *Der Spiegel* noted:

> Greece, for example, has had no general minimum retirement age. On average, workers
> there retire at the age of 61.9 according to the Organisation of Economic Cooperation
> and Development (OECD). That's slightly older than the average age of 61.8 in
> Germany and Spain. Now there are plans to set the official Greek retirement age at 65.
> In addition, Greek citizens would have to pay into the pensions system for 40 years
> instead of the current 35 before they could draw the benefit. The reform was passed last
> year by the Greek parliament and will be implemented in 2013. (Boll and Bocking 2011)

Additionally, when taking into account both full- and part-time employment hours, according to both the OECD and to Eurostat, Greece had the
longest working week in the EU, with 42.3 hours per week, or an average of
2,035 hours per year (Smith 2018). Even when only full-time work is taken
into account, Greece still has the fourth highest working week, after the
United Kingdom, Cyprus, and Austria. Thus, the real problem that Greece
had was not sluggishness, but why these long hours did not translate into
higher rates of productivity.

Nonetheless, despite data pointing to the contrary, and significant measures of
austerity implemented in Greece leading to dire social consequences, the general
public's attitude in certain lender countries was significantly hardened as a consequence of statements acknowledging that Southern Europeans should be equally
hard working as Northern Europeans. Statements, such as the one articulated by
the leader of the Eurogroup in 2017, showcase that the work values stereotype of
the sluggish Southern Europeans in comparison to their hard-working northern
counterparts had not only affected public discourse, but had actually also penetrated, to a certain extent, the highest policy echelons. The question that naturally
arises is to what extent does such rhetoric, perceptions, and vocabulary affect
policy design. That is, to what extent did the European debt crisis unfold the way
it did because of these specific work values perceptions?

Work Values and Political Outcomes

While the degree of their influence cannot be measured with exactitude, the
instrumentalization of these perceptions did indeed have political consequences.

To begin, the domestic reaction within Greece of these negative connotations for Greeks was fierce. Negative perceptions of Greeks and Greece as a whole were widely circulated in the Greek press, and recited by anti-bailout parties to reduce the legitimacy of the bailout program and specifically of those who had voted to enact and implement it domestically. This did not only involve the reproduction of what was stated abroad, but also included the advancement of an often more vitriolic counter-narrative. For instance, after a meeting between Chancellor Angela Merkel and Prime Minister Antonis Samaras in 2012, the far-Right party Golden Dawn issued a press release stating that "[Chancellor] Merkel—as a good usurer—repeated that they have given us a lot of money and that they will be receiving even more back" (Skai 2012). However, even as late as 2017, the president of the junior partner of the coalition government "Independent Greeks" and Minister of Defense Panos Kammenos said during a TV interview that "the Germans are not functioning as allies, but as usurers" (Enikos 2017).

This phenomenon further de-legitimized the harshly austere bailout packages in the eyes of the Greek voters, and thus reduced the implementation capacity of the Greek administrations, as political costs for implementing the various program elements increased. The line of thinking that prevailed in Greek public debates for a long time was that in reality the program implemented was unfairly austere and unjust, to appeal to the prejudices of certain parts of the electorates of the lender states, and did not represent the best interests of Greece or of the Eurozone. In accordance with this view, the bailout program was rather the outcome of a moralistic and frugal approach, focused on moral hazard rather than on sound economics and solidarity. In a phrase, the argument ran that Greece's partners in the Eurozone, and specifically Germany, were not trying to bail Greece out, but rather punish her.

The political consequences of the various bailout programs in Greece were significant. The political consequences are reflected in the rise of the Golden Dawn, which was a fringe far-Right party in Greek politics that got less than 0.3 percent of the vote in the 2009 national elections, and has now become the third biggest political power in Greek politics, with almost 7 percent of the total votes. The consequences can also be seen in the decline of traditional political parties, like the Panhellenic Socialist Movement (PASOK), which fell from 40 percent of votes to single digits, or that seventy new political parties have been created in Greece since 2010. But, above all else, it was the crisis that gave rise to the current Greek government coalition, which is between a traditionally small part of the radical Left (SYRIZA) and a new party of the nationalist Right (Independent Greeks). All the new parties that emerged included as part of their rhetoric that Greece was not being helped but punished. And reports or statements of politicians from other countries accusing Greeks added fuel to the rise of these new political powers.

However, the political consequences of the instrumentalization of work values were located not only in Greece, but also in the lender states. The structure of the bailout mechanism entailed that the debate behind each one of the three bailouts had to take place in all lender countries, while certain parliaments had to hold proceedings and vote on whether their respective countries would participate in the Greek bailout.

Slovakia was one such country. The mood of the average Slovak was also not very positive toward bailing out a richer country, such as Greece. Oprita (2011) mentions the case of an anonymous Slovak citizen, who puts it very succinctly: "Life is good for those with money. Those who have to work are not living so well." This was also the mood of a large part of the policymaking apparatus of the country. In October 2011, after long hours of debates and a midnight vote, Slovakia's parliament rejected plans for the expansion of the Eurozone rescue fund—the EFSF. After the Freedom and Solidarity Party, the second largest partner in the ruling center-Right coalition, refused to support the decision, the coalition government of Iveta Radicova collapsed. While the vote passed subsequently, one could make the case that this type of friction was an outcome of populist rhetoric in the realm of work values, and not only because Greece was a richer state. As the *Financial Times* noted "while the trials of countries such as Portugal and Ireland do find sympathy in Slovakia, which is the second-poorest member of the Eurozone, there is very little feeling for Greece, which is seen by many Slovaks as having caused its own problems" (Cienski and Chaffin 2011).

A similar feeling was obvious at certain stages of the crisis in Finland. The populist party True Finns captured this statement on various occasions, with the then leader of the party, Timo Soini, famously noting "Let's not give money to the lazybones of the South" (Junkkari 2012). However, after having entered government in Finland as the second biggest party in parliament in 2015, and, after having ferociously opposed the first two Greek bailouts, the True Finns experienced a party split as an outcome of the vote on the third Greek bailout in the Finnish parliament.

After accepting what constituted a policy u-turn for his party regarding Greece, Timo Soini, in a post on his blog under the title "Greece and Rest," attempted to explain his decision: "The Finns Party believed that Greece should leave the euro, but our motion was denied. This was the motion put forward by the entire government and the Finns Party but it did not pass. We strived for something and in return received something else entirely." And then he attempted to provide an argument that had already been given by other political parties in Finland in the context of the previous bailouts: "If Greece folds it means billions of euros are lost in the process. If we support Greece, the price is high, too. Unfortunately, no other options remain at this stage. Our hope is that people will understand this." Finally, he added: "I have taken a scolding on this, mainly by those who were in charge of creating this shaky bailout for Greece. We have now entered negotiations that Finland had no way of stopping. If the Finns Party would have left the government, it wouldn't have made any difference. I have received feedback from our supporters and the message is clear. The fate of the Finns Party cannot be in the hands of communist Greeks. I am sure this will be understood" (Finland Politics 2015).

However, Germany was at the locus of this debate (Bechtel, Hainmueller, and Margalit 2014). As the largest economy in the Eurozone, Germany had the greatest influence in the design and implementation of the various Greek programs. German public opinion, and especially the German press, played a significant role through-out this process. In a year-long study, conducted by the University of Erfurt and funded by the *Konrad Adenauer Stiftung*, an attempt was made to monitor the depth of stereotypes about Greece in the German media. As *Deutsche Welle* reported, research showed that the German media was prejudiced in its portrayal of Greeks, often making references to "debt-struck Greeks"; "lazy Greeks"; "tax evad-ers"; "reimbursed by the EU"; and other similar descriptions (Proto Thema 2014).

As the full spectrum of news sources we mention showcases, such images were not only maintained in the tabloid press, but were also reproduced in high-caliber publications. Thus, stereotypes seeped across the spectrum of the German press, with adverse influence not only on public opinion, but on policy-makers as well, as such statements were often reproduced by political officials. Furthermore, according to this research, questionnaires showed that Germans were affected by the stereotypical images of Greeks regardless of their age or educational level, with most believing that Greeks are now paying the price of living above their means, effectively believing in the argument that the problematic financial man-agement on behalf of Greek governments should be perceived as reflective of the Greek people's nature.

Hence, the decision on behalf of German governments to bail out Greece, in light of this negative sentiment proved to have significant political costs. The rise of the populist far-Right party *AfD* has been attributed to Chancellor Merkel's decision to accept nearly 1 million asylum seekers in Germany in 2015. However, according to the *New York Times*,

> [the] Alternative for Germany—widely known by its German initials *AfD*—was founded in the spring of 2013 by a group of elite conservatives, many of whom had been raised in the Christian Democratic Union, the center-Right party that Ms. Merkel leads. They were frustrated with what they saw as a shift to the center on a range of policies, but especially with Ms. Merkel's decision to commit German taxpayer money to a bailout of Greece. (Eddy 2017)

In an analysis of the total content of the *AfD*'s website, Arzheimer (2015) examined the frequency of the presence of certain keywords. There, in a total of 45,990 words, "immigrants" and "immigration" were mentioned only 23 times in 2014 (equivalent to a single mention in 6 percent of all posts), while Greece and the Greeks had 297 references (Arzheimer 2015, 548).

At the same time, the former German finance minister, Wolfgang Schäuble—one of the key people in the evolution of the Greek crisis—was often accused of having a hard line regarding Greece, because he could feel the pressure from German public opinion, but also because, to a certain extent, he felt that Greece did not belong in the Eurozone in the first place, effectively agreeing with the dominant perceptions within Germany of Greeks (Wagstyl 2015; Corey 2015). As Corey (2015) notes, a poll conducted shortly after the Greek referendum of 2015 found that 60 percent of Germans supported a Greek exit from the Eurozone—a percent-age almost the same as the "No" vote in the Greek referendum. At the same time, 70 percent opposed any further concessions to Greece from the EU, while exactly the same number agreed with the hard line of Minister Schäuble (Corey 2015).

Lessons Learned from the Crisis

Almost a decade after the original manifestation of the crisis, certain institutional lessons seem to have been absorbed at the level of the EU, especially on the prevention and monitoring side of fiscal policy. The enactment of the European semester in 2010 and of the Treaty on Stability Coordination and Governance (TSCG or "the fiscal compact") in 2013, are mechanisms to control and coordinate the fiscal policies of the individual member states. However, these policies are still limited when compared with the fiscal transfers of a fully integrated economic union. This reveals that while European solidarity was apparent throughout the crisis, this solidarity has limits.

The political debates among senior policy-makers, press, and the broader public, conducted throughout the evolution of the crisis in many European states, are quite revealing. Policy-makers often seemed to be influenced by populist perceptions vis-à-vis the domestic work values of other member states of the Eurozone, affecting not only policy rhetoric but also policy design. In this context, one could make the case that this negative atmosphere played an adverse role on both sides, leading to more austere programs than the ones that should have been drafted on the one side, and to a lower willingness to enact and implement the programs on the other.

Finally, certain scholars, such as Krugman (2012), advanced the claim that the Greek bailout programs focused too much on addressing the symptoms of the Greek crisis rather than its root causes. And instead of targeting how to increase the productivity of the Greek workers and diminish the scope of "black markets" on the national level, or advancing fiscal transfer mechanisms on the EU level, the main focus of the memoranda has always been the deregulating and flexibility of work.

The extent to which this shift of focus was an outcome of work values perceptions is unclear. What is clear, however, is that work values perceptions and stereotypes, and their instrumentalization, did influence negotiations of the various bailout programs for Greece—an influence that was often adverse and problematic, and whose complete set of consequences we have probably not yet fully experienced.

Note

1. Results for the survey are based on telephone and face-to-face interviews conducted under the direction of Princeton Survey Research Associates International. Survey results are based on national samples of a 1,000-sample size or more, in the UK, Czech Republic, France, Germany, Greece, Italy, Poland, Spain, and the United States.

References

Arzheimer, Kai. 2015. The AfD: Finally a successful right-wing populist Eurosceptic party for Germany? *West European Politics* 38 (3): 535–56.

Baldwin, Richard, and Charles Wyplosz. 2012. *The economics of European integration*. London: McGraw-Hill.

Bechtel, Michael M., Jens Hainmueller, and Yotam Margalit. 2014. Preferences for international redistribution: The divide over the Eurozone bailouts. *American Journal of Political Science* 58 (4): 835–56.

Bild. 17 May 2011. EU zögert mit finanzieller Hilfe Muss Griechenland die Akropolis verkaufen?

Boll, Sven, and David Bocking. 19 May 2011. The myth of a lazy Southern Europe: Merkel's clichés debunked by statistics. *Der Spiegel*.

Cienski, Jan, and Josh Chaffin. 12 October 2011. Slovakia votes against expanded EFSF. *The Financial Times*.

Corey, Ethan. 15 July 2015. How much has public opinion driven the Greek debt negotiations? *The Nation*.

Council of the EU. 2010a. Statement by the Heads of State and Government of the Euro Area. Euro summit. Brussels, 25 March 2010.

Council of the EU. 2010b. Statement by the Heads of State or Government of the Euro Area. Press Release PCE 86/10. Brussels, 7 May 2010.

Eddy, Melissa. 25 September 2017. Alternative for Germany: Who are they and what do they want? *The New York Times*.

Enikos. 24 January 2017. Kammenos: I'm a Trump Supporter—the Germans function as usurers. Available from http://www.enikos.gr/politics/431305/kammenos-eimai-ypostiriktis-tou-trab-oi-germanoi-leitourgoun-os-tokoglyfoi-video.

Finland Politics. 23 July 2015. Timo Soini, leader of the populist party True Finns, defends his agreement on a new Greek bailout. Available from: https://finlandpolitics.org (Accessed 3 September 2018).

Frieden, Jeffrey, and Stephanie Walter. 2017. Understanding the political economy of the Eurozone crisis. *Annual Review of Political Science* 20:371–90.

Grammatikos, Theocharry, and Robert Vermeulen. 2012. Transmission of the financial and sovereign debt crises to the EMU: Stock prices, CDS spreads and exchange rates. *Journal of International Money and Finance* 31 (3): 517–33.

Hodson, Dermot, and Lucia Quaglia. 2009. European perspectives on the global financial crisis: Introduction. *Journal of Common Market Studies* 47 (5): 939–53.

Inman, Phillip, and Helena Smith. 4 March 2010. Greece should sell islands to keep bankruptcy at bay. *The Guardian*.

Junkkari, M. 24 March 2012. Finland's international image changed last year. *Helsingin Sanomat*. Available from http://www.helsinkitimes.fi.

Krugman, Paul. 18 June 2012. Greece as victim. *The New York Times*. Available from https://www.nytimes.com.

Matsaganis Manos, and Chrysa Leventi. 2014. The distributional impact of austerity and the recession in Southern Europe. *South European Society and Politics* 19 (3): 393–412.

McCoy, Jennifer, and Murat Somer, eds. 2019. Polarizing polities: A global threat to democracy. *The ANNALS of the American Academy of Political and Social Science*, 681.

McDonald, Karl. 21 March 2017. Jeroen Dijsselbloem: Southern Europeans spent the money on "drinks and women". *iNews*. Available from https://inews.co.uk (Accessed 3 September 2018).

Oprita, Antonia. 3 October 2011. Bail out Greece? Many Slovaks don't like the idea. CNBC. Available from https://www.cnbc.com/id/44752399 (Accessed 18 September 2018).

Pew Research Center. 2012. *Global attitudes project*. Washington, DC: Pew Research Center. Available from http://assets.pewresearch.org/wp-content/uploads/sites/2/2012/05/Pew-Global-Attitudes-Project-European-Crisis-Report-FINAL-FOR-PRINT-May-29-2012.pdf (accessed 3 September 2018).

Proto Thema. 19 August 2014. Germans think Greeks are "lazy", "debt-ridden", "tax evaders." Available from http://en.protothema.gr/germans-think-greeks-are-lazy-debt-ridden-tax-evaders/ (accessed 3 September 2018).

Scocco, Sandro. 5 March 2015. The tale of lazy Greeks. *Social Europe*. Available from https://www.socialeurope.eu/lazy-greeks (accessed 3 September 2018).

Skai. 24 August 2012. Party reactions after the joint interview Merkel-Samaras. Available from http://www.skai.gr/news.

Smith, Rob. 20 February 2018. This country works the longest hours in Europe. *World Economic Forum*. Available from https://www.weforum.org/agenda/2018/02/greeks-work-longest-hours-in-europe/ (accessed 3 September 2018).

Tosun, Jale, Anne Wetzel, and Galina Zapryanova. 2014. The EU in crisis: Advancing the debate. *Journal of European Integration* 36 (3): 195–211.

Tsakloglou, Panos, Giorgos Economides, Giorgos Pagoulatos, Apostolos Philippopoulos, and Christos Triantopoulos. 2016. *A roadmap to exit the crisis: A new productive model for Greece*. Athens: diaNE-Osis (in Greek).

Wagstyl, Stefan. 16 July 2015. Germany's Wolfgang Schauble puts Grexit back on the agenda. *The Financial Times*.

The Value Added of Studying Work Attitudes and Values: Some Lessons to Learn

By
JALE TOSUN,
GERBERT KRAAYKAMP,
and
ZEYNEP CEMALCILAR

Work is one of the most valued activities of individuals' lives. Attitudes toward work not only influence work-related outcomes, such as income, but also hold sway over personal well-being and satisfaction with politico-administrative institutions. Consequently, country-comparative research aimed at learning about the determinants of individuals' work attitudes and values and their consequences is worthwhile and offers insights that are relevant for many disciplines. In this epilogue, we summarize the main insights produced by the contributions to this volume on the antecedents and consequences of work attitudes and values as well as draw some broader conclusions.

Keywords: comparative analysis; mechanisms; effects; transmission; work attitudes; work values

Individuals spend a considerable share of their lives at their workplaces, where they not only fulfill their tasks but learn new skills, receive feedback on their performance, and socialize with coworkers. Therefore, it is not surprising that work attitudes and values have been the subject of sustained research interest across the behavioral and social sciences. Initial research concentrated on the impact of work attitudes and values on economic development, but contemporary research has shifted focus. As of this writing, much of it centers on how attitudes and values account for employee well-being and job satisfaction and how the rise

Jale Tosun is a professor at the Institute of Political Science at Heidelberg University, Germany. Her research focuses on comparative public policy, international political economy, and public administration.

Gerbert Kraaykamp is a professor of empirical sociology in the Department of Sociology at Radboud University in the Netherlands. His major research interests include educational inequality, intergenerational transmission, and health inequality. He has published widely on these subjects in international scientific journals.

Correspondence: jale.tosun@ipw.uni-heidelberg.de

DOI: 10.1177/0002716219831656

ANNALS, AAPSS, 682, March 2019

in female labor force participation affected work values as well as the economic and social implications of these values. The contribution by Duncan Gallie (this volume) gives a comprehensive overview of the state and development of research, which connects the study of work values to broader themes in political and social sciences, such as postmaterialism (Inglehart 1977), the "new politics" paradigm (Inglehart and Welzel 2005), and individualism versus collectivism (Hofstede 1984). Recent empirical research has concentrated on the determinants of work attitudes and values (e.g., Cemalcilar, Secinti, and Sumer 2018); changes in work attitudes and values (e.g., Lechner et al. 2017); and the effects of work values on various outcomes, such as career choices and career development (e.g., Sortheix, Chow, and Salmela-Aro 2015). In short, we draw from and contribute to a rich body of research on work values.

With this volume, we advance understandings of how work attitudes and values are formed and what their implications are in different countries. When selecting this specific analytical focus, we relied on both established (e.g., European Social Survey, General Social Survey, International Social Survey Programme, and World Value Survey) and new (e.g., the Cultural Pathways to Economic Self-Sufficiency and Entrepreneurship [CUPESSE] dataset; Tosun et al. 2018) country-comparative measurements of work attitudes and values and the factors potentially determining them. As a result, this volume is characterized by a diversity in empirical sources offering an extensive analysis of work attitudes and values.

Three research questions guide the contributions to this volume: (1) To what extent are parental qualities, individual traits, and individual resources relevant for the explanation of a person's work values? (2) To what extent do work values have consequences in the political, economic, and well-being domains? and (3) To what extent do economic and cultural qualities of countries condition (a) the determinants of work values and (b) the impact of work values on self-employment, political engagement, and well-being? Having considered the research findings reported in the contributions, we now answer those questions as best we can, summarizing and discussing the main insights produced by the individual articles. We also draw some general conclusions about the policy relevance of the

Zeynep Cemalcılar is an associate professor of social psychology at Koc University, Istanbul, Turkey. Her most recent research focuses on youth autonomy and self-sufficiency, subjective socioeconomic status, brief social psychological interventions, and technology in the social life.

NOTE: We thank all external reviewers who contributed to this volume of *The ANNALS* with thoughtful comments and suggestions on earlier versions of the articles: Nazli Baydar, Romain Boitard, Michael Gebel, Marjan Gorgievski-Duijvesteijn, Nadia Granato, Rick Hoyle, G. Tarcan Kumkale, Markus Tausendpfund, Tom van der Meer, Ellen Verbakel, Georg Wenzelburger, and Maarten Wolbers. Likewise, we acknowledge the valuable comments provided on the draft articles by the internal reviewers. This volume benefited from financial support by the collaborative research project Cultural Pathways to Economic Self-Sufficiency and Entrepreneurship (CUPESSE; Seventh Framework Programme; Grant Agreement No. 61325), the Field of Focus 3 "Cultural Dynamics in Globalised Worlds," and the Field of Focus 4 Self-Regulation and Regulation: Individuals and Organisations at Heidelberg University.

study of work attitudes and values—these may not be obvious at first glance, but we argue that the study of work attitudes and values does offer valuable insights for advancing policy studies and can be beneficial for producing better-designed public policies and bringing about policies' intended outcomes.

The remainder of this piece unfolds as follows: First, we present the empirical characteristics of work attitudes and values identified in the contributions. Then, we turn to the determinants of work attitudes and values, which is followed by a discussion of their implications for a diverse set of outcomes. Subsequently, we allude to the value added of adopting a country-comparative perspective. We conclude by discussing how our findings on work attitudes and values may inform policy studies and policymaking. Overall, we are confident that the insights presented in this volume speak to established research perspectives in different (sub)disciplines of the behavioral and social sciences. And we think that we have paved the way for novel approaches to and investigations of the study of work attitudes from a country-comparative perspective.

Empirical Characteristics of Work Attitudes and Values

We begin our integrated discussion of the individual contributions by concentrating on three articles that place great emphasis on the illustration of the empirical characteristics of work values.

First is the extensive review of the pertinent literature by Duncan Gallie, in which he points out the multidimensional nature of work attitudes and values. Gallie suggests that varied facets of work values develop differently in response to social and economic changes and consequently affect individuals and their work-related behaviors differently. The selection of studies in this volume, indeed, seeks to illuminate the dynamic nature of work attitudes and values and attempts to showcase variations in the conceptualizations, determinants, and implications of work values from a cross-national perspective.

Arne Kalleberg and Peter Marsden's in-depth analysis of how acceptance of intrinsic and extrinsic work values have changed in the United States in the past four decades uses data from multiple waves of the General Social Survey and the International Social Survey Programme. The authors show that work attitudes and values have developed in such a manner that Americans are mostly concerned with the security of jobs, followed by high income and opportunities for advancement. Some differences in work attitudes and values also seem attributable to aging or life course processes: when people become older and have family responsibilities, they tend to prioritize high income over other work values, which speaks nicely to the dynamic understanding of work values that Gallie postulates.

In contrast to studies that emphasize cohort effects (e.g., Hansen and Leuty 2012), Kalleberg and Marsden only find a few differences in work attitudes and values among members of different generations. This finding can potentially guide the design of policies on education and career choices, as it suggests that there is no need to adopt different policy measures for different cohorts. Rather, one or a set of carefully designed policy measures could bring about the intended policy outcomes for members of different generations.

While Kalleberg and Marsden use data for respondents based in one country over a 40-year period, the study by Bernhard Kittel, Fabian Kalleitner, and Panos Tsakloglou concentrates on regional patterns of work values in nine European countries as measured by the cross-national and cross-sectional CUPESSE data (Tosun et al. 2018). By examining the relative importance of work and nonfinancial employment commitment, their analysis reveals some interesting empirical patterns. For Austria, the Czech Republic, Denmark, Greece, and Spain, response patterns did not vary strongly across the regions. In contrast, the authors observe regional variation in Germany, Hungary, Italy, and the UK. Italy and the UK demonstrate a substantive cross-regional variation in nonfinancial employment commitment. Therefore, it seems that the regional level provides a valuable addition to the analysis of work values, at least in Europe. Their findings also suggest that in some countries the regional level is an adequate level of policymaking to account for the marked cross-regional variation, whereas in other countries, policymaking success or failure is best attributed to the national level because there is little cross-regional variation. In more concrete terms, this finding supports the implementation of multiple policies that address different levels of government, namely, the European, the national, and the regional (see Tosun, Unt, and Wadensjö 2017; Tosun, Treib, and De Francesco 2019).

When taken together, these three contributions provide a comprehensive and nuanced empirical picture of work attitudes and values. The complementarity among the articles is strengthened by the different analytical perspectives adopted and the different scope of the respective empirical findings.

Determinants of Work Attitudes and Values

The second set of contributions concentrates on the determinants of work values and is informed and substantiated by the literature review of Duncan Gallie and the analytical perspectives presented therein. The articles on the determinants of work attitudes and values employ the same data source as the set of articles that proceeds them (i.e., the CUPESSE data), which facilitates a set of more integrated and comparable empirical findings.

The contribution by Nebi Sümer, Daniela Pauknerová, Mihaela Vancea, and Elif Manuoğlu yields important insights into how parenting behavior leads to similarity between the work values of parents and of their children. The psychological literature in particular has alluded to the importance of parenting styles for the formation of (work) attitudes and values. Using data for the Czech Republic, Spain, and Turkey, the analyses reveal several intriguing insights. Higher levels of parental warmth are found to relate to higher work values similarity between parents and young adults in all three countries. In families with high levels of psychological control, young individuals are more gender-biased and traditional in their work attitudes, which especially held true for the respondents in Spain and the Czech Republic. More generally, a positive family climate seemed to facilitate the transmission of positive attitudes and values toward work.

Zeynep Cemalcilar, Carsten Jensen, and Jale Tosun address a similar question and ask whether work attitudes and values of young people are determined by the work attitudes and values of their parents. In contrast to Sümer et al., the authors of this contribution pay more attention to the country context and dominant cultural norms than the within-family context. Analyzing data for respondents from Denmark, Germany, Turkey, and the UK, the findings reveal that parental attitudes and work values indeed are an important determinant of the young people's work values—a result also reported by Kittel et al., who use the same data source. The second research interest of this study is whether the transmission of work values is conditioned by gender. For three of the four types of work values we examine, the effect of gender is less prominent than the authors anticipated, even for Turkey, where gender differences are more marked than in the other countries studied. The fourth outcome variable taps into a traditional understanding of women being responsible for the household and men being the primary breadwinners, and for that one a gender effect is found for all countries examined.

How does intergenerational social mobility impact young people's attitudes regarding the meaning of work? Do future mobility expectations matter for young people's normative attitudes regarding work and welfare? These are the research questions that Bettina Schuck and Jennifer Shore address. Using data from eleven countries, the authors show that the relationship between mobility and an individual's views on work and welfare varies depending on the dimension of mobility (past or future), with expected future mobility exerting a stronger effect on attitudes than past mobility experiences. Self-interest, and not empathy with one's own social origin, is shown to be the primary driver of attitudes toward the meaning of work. The results from this study can inform policymaking to the extent that policy-makers become aware that people's behavior is guided by future expectations of their working life. Short-term measures to promote employment, then, may not suffice to induce changes in attitudes and behavior. What appears to be a more promising policy strategy is to provide a long-term perspective on mobility and give people a credible commitment that they can advance in the future.

These three set of papers, together with the contributions by Kalleberg and Marsden and Kittel et al., allow us to answer our first research question and the first part of the third research question. The contribution by Sümer et al., in particular, demonstrates the important role of parents, whereas Kalleberg and Marsden as well as Schuck and Shore show how important individual traits are. Perceiving parents and parental attitudes and values as a resource (see Kraaykamp et al., this volume), Cemalcilar, Jensen, and Tosun and Kittel et al. show that intergenerational transmission plays an indispensable role in the formation of work attitudes and values in European countries. It is interesting to note that despite differences in the (operationalization of the) outcome variables, the factors influencing work values are rather similar across countries. This can be regarded as a robust finding since the countries analyzed are characterized by marked differences concerning, for example, the role of women in society, the degree to which the countries have a collectivist culture, and the types of political economies and the welfare state regimes in place.

Implications of Work Attitudes and Values

The third set of contributions is marked by a greater diversity in terms of the data sources used, which makes the findings reported more heterogeneous but also very insightful and relevant for different literatures.

Martin Lukeš, Manuel Feldmann, and Federico Vegetti examine how work values impact different forms of labor market participation of young adults in eleven European countries. The authors report a high importance of nonpecuniary benefits among the self-employed, such as independence and creativity, and show that extrinsic values such as job security are more important for employees. Interestingly, the analysis also reveals that work centrality does not differ between the employed and the self-employed. The finding that the self-employed are foremost driven by intrinsic work values is important if we consider that policymakers across Europe and the European Commission have promoted self-employment as a remedy for youth unemployment (Tosun 2017; Tosun, Unt, and Wadensjö 2017; Rapp, Shore, and Tosun 2018). From the perspective of this study, encouraging (young) people without a sufficient level of intrinsic motivation to become self-employed may lead to undesirable outcomes and should not be considered a standard tool for fighting youth unemployment. This does not, however, preclude this pathway for individuals who demonstrate high levels of intrinsic motivation. In other words, rather than considering self-employment as a "one-size-fits-all" model for promoting the labor market participation of young people, it should be considered for those individuals only that have the "right" motivation and mindset about it (see Haynie et al. 2010).

Taking into account the rise in youth unemployment in the wake of the Great Recession (see Tosun, Wetzel, and Zapryanova 2014), Emily Rainsford, William Maloney, and Sebastian Popa examine how experiences of unemployment and low-quality work impact young adults' work values. The latter aspect is a particularly welcome feature of this analysis since research has shown that young people in Europe have faced various nonstandard forms of employment such as "zero-hour" contracts (see Montgomery et al. 2017). Analyzing eleven European countries, this study reports a positive effect on extrinsic work values for one dimension of low-quality work conditions—overqualification. The authors also show that age has a conditioning effect on how unemployment and low-quality work affects work values: the younger the people affected, the greater the impact. These findings underline the general importance of preventing very young people from experiencing unemployment and low-quality working conditions to avoid scarring that might hurt future career paths, which is reflected in recent policies adopted to promote youth employment (see Tosun, Unt, and Wadensjö 2017; Tosun, Treib, and De Francesco 2019).

Mark Visser, Maurice Gesthuizen, and Gerbert Kraaykamp use a particularly rich database with respondents based in thirty-one countries to examine to what extent extrinsic and intrinsic work values are associated with nonelectoral political participation. The results of this analysis show that people who are extrinsically motivated are less politically active, while people who are intrinsically motivated are more politically active, which is a relevant finding for political participation research. However, the relationships between these variables are moderated by the national wealth level: in less affluent countries, the relationships are weaker. Similar to Sümer et al., Visser, Gesthuizen, and Kraaykamp also pay attention to the prevalent cultures in the countries analyzed and reveal that the negative effect of extrinsic work values and the positive effect of intrinsic work values on political participation seem stronger in individualistic countries.

The study by Visser, Gesthuizen, and Kraaykamp aligns with the contribution by Anna Diamantopoulou and Kyriakos Pierrakakis, in which the authors allude to another political consequence of the perception of work attitudes and values. The authors show that work values have the potential to be instrumentalized politically and demonstrate this point by the public and political discourses in the context of the Great Recession, when the Greek government asked for bailouts to prevent state bankruptcy (see Tosun, Wetzel, and Zapryanova 2014). This contribution shows that perceptions of work attitudes and values are relevant to political debate and policy, which is why it is important for political scientists to engage with the topic of work values.

Using a worldwide sample, Anja Van den Broeck, Arne Vanderstukken, Karin Proost, Bert Schreurs, and Maarten Vansteenkiste analyze the predictive power of work values for life satisfaction, happiness, and well-being of young people. Their findings demonstrate that the type of work values held by a young person and the type of values prevailing in his or her environment account for significant variation in a person's perceptions. What is important is that intrinsic work values generally show more positive consequences for people's lives than extrinsic work values.

This set of contributions helps to answer the second research question and the second part of the third research question. First, for all countries under investigation, work values have consequences in various domains of public and private life. Lukeš Feldmann, and Vegetti show how important work values are for determining the different types of labor market participation (employed vs. self-employed) of young people. Rainsford et al. contribute a complementary perspective by showing how negative labor market experiences at a (very) young age affect work values. The political domain is discussed by Visser, Gesthuizen, and Kraaykamp as well as Diamantopoulou and Pierrakakis, whereas Van den Broeck et al. add the individuals' well-being perspective. Visser, Gesthuizen, and Kraaykamp are most explicit in theorizing, highlighting, and discussing the conditioning effects of countries. The other studies do not reveal country-specific effects. In sum, these contributions excel in showing the diverse nature of the implications of work values for different domains and in varying country contexts.

Robustness of the Findings across Countries

We started this article by expressing that using a country-comparative perspective in studying work values is a valuable approach. The collection of studies presented in this special issue shows that the outcome variables vary, but the potential determinants of those variables are relatively similar across countries. Some of the contributions find a conditioning effect of countries or country-level characteristics (e.g., Visser, Gesthuizen, and Kraaykamp, this volume), but altogether the findings reported here are fairly robust across countries. This is a result we initially did not expect to materialize in such a clear manner.

Yet the methodological contribution by Maurice Gesthuizen, Daniel Kovarek, and Carolin Rapp cautions about the validity of the scales used in most country-comparative surveys for drawing cross-country conclusions. While the analysis the authors provide is compelling and will certainly guide future studies employing cross-country survey data, we are confident that the use of many different data sources in this volume increases the level of confidence in the results reported. Indeed, the overall empirical picture still holds true if we vary the data sources that contributors used. The relationships uncovered by the articles are an indication of underlying causal mechanisms, which need to be tested in a systematic fashion by subsequent investigations.

Lessons for Policy Studies and Policymaking

The contributions to this volume of *The ANNALS* embrace a wide range of analytical perspectives in behavioral, political, and social science, with a focus on cross-cultural psychology, comparative politics, political sociology, and sociology. Yet no contribution approaches the volume's theme from the perspective of policy studies. But policy studies have been interested in the characteristics of target groups (Schneider and Ingram 1993), and one of the recent foci of policy studies has been to explore how policy decisions influence the behavior of individuals (e.g. John, Smith, and Stoker 2009; Weaver 2015). This research perspective lies at the heart of the small but growing literature on policy design (e.g., DeLeon 1988; Howlett, Mukherjee, and Woo 2015; Chindarkar, Howlett, and Ramesh 2017; Howlett and Mukherjee 2017), which is linked to questions concerning the implementation and success of public policies. Policy implementation is about putting public policy into practice. Despite this simple definition, the conceptual clarification of policy implementation is not an easy task, as implementation-related activities include a multitude of actors and involve several stages (Tosun and Treib 2018).

Target group behavior is among the different components of the policy implementation process that Winter (2012) and Vancoppenolle, Sætren, and Hupe (2015) identify. It is about the role the policy addressees play in the implementation process, which includes their actions as well their needs. With social benefits, for example, the target group's involvement in the implementation process consists of filing a request and complying with the conditions attached to the granting of the benefits (e.g., regular appointments with case managers; see Shore and Tosun 2019). With other policy types, implementation may entail more substantive changes to the behavior of the target group. Policy success is then the degree to which the behavioral changes attained correspond to those intended—which, however, is not just a matter of objective measurement, but also a matter of presentation and framing (see McConnell 2010). Nonetheless, policies cannot be considered as successful if they fail to bring about any behavioral change.

Despite the omission of the policy perspective from the studies that constitute this issue, our findings on the patterns and determinants of work attitudes and values have important implications for this particular subdiscipline of political science. We demonstrate this point by drawing on the conceptual literature on policy design. For example, Chindarkar, Howlett, and Ramesh (2017) stress the importance of governance capacity and analytical capacity for the quality of policy design. When governance and analytical capacity are high, the authors expect capable design; while in the opposite constellation, where both capacities are low, poor design is expected. When the governance capacity is high, but the analytical capacity low, capable political design is the most likely outcome, which is characterized by a better political quality of the design than quality of the policy content. The complementary scenario (governance capacity low, analytical capacity high) is likely to lead to a poor political design; that is, the quality of the policy is likely to be good, but it may not be politically feasible, and it may result in political conflict, which prevents the policy from being adopted in cabinet and/or parliament.

Attitudes and values appear particularly important for employment policy. When looking at the recent measures taken to promote (youth) employment in Europe, we find that these are supply-side oriented (de la Porte and Jacobsson 2012; Tosun 2017; Tosun, Unt, and Wadensjö 2017; Shore and Tosun 2019; Tosun, Treib, and De Francesco 2019); that is, they aim to increase the employability of jobseekers through improving their skills and qualifications as well as to provide incentive to work rather than to receive welfare benefits (see, e.g., Bonoli 2010; Dinan 2019). The supply-side orientation of employment policies means that state agencies can facilitate measures and programs in which jobseekers participate, but it is in the end the individuals who need to make decisions and engage in the programs provided. If the program offered operates on the wrong premise (e.g., aims to provide a profound and extensive training whereas the jobseeker is interested in short-term, intensive training), it can produce suboptimal policy results. In this context, Tosun and Hörisch (2019) show that active labor market policies provide a good case for contrasting the perceptions of jobseekers with those of policy-makers. Considering the cost of these measures and the negative effects of (long-term) unemployment, taking the jobseekers' attitudes into account is worthwhile.

Education and higher education policy may also rely on misconceptions about young people's work attitudes and values. The German apprenticeship model, for example, has been praised for smoothing out school-to-work transitions, especially in the context of the Great Recession (Protsch and Solga 2017, 387). However, the results of a survey conducted by the Association of German Chambers of Commerce and Industry (DIHK) shows that more than one-third of apprenticeship training positions have not been filled due to a lack of applications (in 2018, 17,000 companies did not receive a single application) or due to a wrong fit between the position and the applicants' skills (DIHK 2018, 3). One of the reasons for the decreasing number of applications is that young people are becoming more interested in higher education, which holds the promise of higher income and more favorable working conditions (e.g., security or working hours).

The increase in higher education participation can be regarded as a policy success, since policy decisions were geared toward stimulating such participation. For many years, Germany was regarded as an exceptional case due to its low participation rates in higher education (see Powell and Solga 2011). From that perspective, striving for changes in young people's work attitudes and values is plausible and even desirable. However, for the German apprenticeship model, it evidently bears a risk, which needs to be addressed by policy-makers. To balance this trade-off, the apprenticeship model may need to become more attractive, for example, in terms of the apprentices' income or working hours. This example shows that a better understanding of attitudes and values on work can indeed help in the design of better policies related to (higher) education and employment. A "better" design means that the intended policy goals can be attained as the intended changes in the individuals' behavior are brought about.

In sum, considering ways to integrate the role of attitudes and values into policy studies, which to date has hardly been endeavored, is promising. Research in public policy has advanced to include the political perspective, but it still concentrates on policy-makers and does not pay (sufficient) attention to policy target groups. In this article, we limited our discussion to the literature on policy design to illustrate the potential for cross-fertilization, but there are other themes in policy studies that are equally worth discussing from the perspective of work values. The "behavioral turn" in public policy that relies on concepts such as *nudges* (e.g., John, Smith, and Stoker 2009) is likely to facilitate the incorporation of attitudes and values as an explanatory factor in policy decisions and their effects.

References

Bonoli, Giuliano. 2010. The political economy of active labor-market policy. *Politics & Society* 38 (4): 435–57.

Cemalcilar, Zeynep, Ekin Secinti, and Nebi Sumer. 2018. Intergenerational transmission of work values: A meta-analytic review. *Journal of Youth and Adolescence* 47 (8): 1559–79.

Chindarkar, Namrata, Michael Howlett, and M. Ramesh. 2017. Introduction to the special issue: Conceptualizing effective social policy design: Design spaces and capacity challenges. *Public Administration and Development* 37 (1): 3–14.

de la Porte, Caroline, and Kerstin Jacobsson. 2012. Social investment or recommodification? Assessing the employment policies of the EU member states. In *Towards a social investment welfare state? Ideas, policies and challenges*, eds. Nathalie Morel, Bruno Palier, and Joakim Palme, 117–52. Bristol: Policy Press.

DeLeon, Peter. 1988. The contextual burdens of policy design. *Policy Studies Journal* 17 (2): 297–309.

DIHK (Association of German Chambers of Commerce and Industry). 2018. Ausbildung 2018: Ergebnisse einer DIHK-Online-Unternehmensbefragung. Available from https://www.dihk.de/ressourcen/downloads/ausbildungsumfrage-2018.pdf.

Dinan, Shannon. 2019. A typology of activation incentives. *Social Policy & Administration* 53 (1): 1–15.

Hansen, Jo-Ida C., and Melanie E. Leuty. 2012. Work values across generations. *Journal of Career Assessment* 20 (1): 34–52.

Haynie, J. Michael, Dean Shepherd, Elaine Mosakowski, and P. Christopher Earley. 2010. A situated metacognitive model of the entrepreneurial mindset. *Journal of Business Venturing* 25 (2): 217–29.

Hofstede, Geert. 1984. *Culture's consequences: International differences in work-related values*. Thousand Oaks, CA: Sage Publications.

Howlett, Michael, and Ishani Mukherjee. 2017. Policy design: From tools to patches. *Canadian Public Administration* 60 (1): 140–45.

Howlett, Michael, Ishani Mukherjee, and Jun J. Woo. 2015. From tools to toolkits in policy design studies: The new design orientation towards policy formulation research. *Policy & Politics* 43 (2): 291–311.

Inglehart, Ronald. 1977. *The silent revolution: Changing values and political styles among western publics*. Princeton, NJ: Princeton University Press.

Inglehart, Ronald, and Christian Welzel. 2005. *Modernization, cultural change, and democracy: The human development sequence*. Cambridge: Cambridge University Press.

John, Peter, Graham Smith, and Gerry Stoker. 2009. Nudge nudge, think think: Two strategies for changing civic behaviour. *Political Quarterly* 80 (3): 361–70.

Lechner, Clemens M., Florencia M. Sortheix, Richard Göllner, and Katariina Salmela-Aro. 2017. The development of work values during the transition to adulthood: A two-country study. *Journal of Vocational Behavior* 99:52–65.

McConnell, Allan. 2010. Policy success, policy failure and grey areas in-between. *Journal of Public Policy* 30 (3): 345–62.

Montgomery, Tom, Micaela Mazzei, Simone Baglioni, and Stephen Sinclair. 2017. Who cares? The social care sector and the future of youth employment. *Policy & Politics* 45 (3): 413–29.

Powell, Justin J. W., and Heike Solga. 2011. Why are higher education participation rates in Germany so low? Institutional barriers to higher education expansion. *Journal of Education and Work* 24 (1–2): 49–68.

Protsch, Paula, and Heike Solga. 2017. Going across Europe for an apprenticeship? A factorial survey experiment on employers' hiring preferences in Germany. *Journal of European Social Policy* 27 (4): 387–99.

Rapp, Carolin, Jennifer Shore, and Jale Tosun. 2018. Not so risky business? How social policies shape the perceived feasibility of self-employment. *Journal of European Social Policy* 28 (2): 143–60.

Schneider, Anne, and Helen Ingram. 1993. Social construction of target populations: Implications for politics and policy. *American Political Science Review* 87 (2): 334–47.

Shore, Jennifer, and Jale Tosun. 2019. Assessing youth labour market services: Young people's perceptions and evaluations of service delivery in Germany. *Public Policy and Administration* 34 (1): 22–41.

Sortheix, Florencia M., Angela Chow, and Katariina Salmela-Aro. 2015. Work values and the transition to work life: A longitudinal study. *Journal of Vocational Behavior* 89:162–71.

Tosun, Jale. 2017. Promoting youth employment through multi-organizational governance. *Public Money & Management* 37 (1): 39–46.

Tosun, Jale, Jose L. Arco-Tirado, Maurizio Caserta, Zeynep Cemalcilar, Markus Freitag, Felix Hörisch, Carsten Jensen, Bernhard Kittel, Levente Littvay, Martin Lukes, et al. 2018. Perceived economic self-sufficiency: A country- and generation-comparative approach. *European Political Science*. doi:10.1057/s41304-018-0186-3.

Tosun, Jale, and Felix Hörisch. 2019. Steering the behaviour of young people: The EU's policy approach to promote employment. In *Handbook of behavioural change and public policy*, eds. Holger Straßheim and Silke Beck. Cheltenham: Edward Elgar.

Tosun, Jale, and Oliver Treib. 2018. Linking policy design and implementation styles. In *The Routledge handbook of policy design*, eds. Michael Howlett and Ishani Mukherjee, 316–30. London: Routledge.

Tosun, Jale, Oliver Treib, and Fabrizio De Francesco. 2019. The impact of the European youth guarantee on active labour market policies: A convergence analysis. *International Journal of Social Welfare*. doi:10.1111/ijsw.12375.

Tosun, Jale, Marge Unt, and Eskil Wadensjö. 2017. Youth-oriented active labour market policies: Explaining policy effort in the Nordic and the Baltic states. *Social Policy & Administration* 51 (4): 598–616.

Tosun, Jale, Anne Wetzel, and Galina Zapryanova. 2014. The EU in crisis: Advancing the debate. *Journal of European Integration* 36 (3): 195–211.

Vancoppenolle, Diederik, Harald Sætren, and Peter Hupe. 2015. The politics of policy design and implementation: A comparative study of two Belgian service voucher programs. *Journal of Comparative Policy Analysis: Research and Practice* 17 (2): 157–73.

Weaver, R. Kent. 2015. Getting people to behave: Research lessons for policy makers. *Public Administration Review* 75 (6): 806–16.

Winter, Søren C. 2012. Implementation. In *Handbook of public administration*, eds. B. Guy Peters and Jon Pierre, 225–63. London: Sage Publications.

THE IMPACT OF THE SOCIAL SCIENCES: How Academics and their Research Make a Difference

Simon Bastow, Patrick Dunleavy, and Jane Tinkler, *all from London School of Economics*

Foreword by Kenneth Prewitt, *Columbia University*

In the modern globalized world, some estimates suggest that around 40 million people now work in jobs that 'translate' or mediate advances in social science research for use in business, government and public agencies, health care systems, and civil society organizations. Many large corporations and organizations across these sectors in the United States are increasingly prioritizing access to social science knowledge. Yet, the impact of university social science continues to be fiercely disputed. This key study demonstrates the essential role of university social science in the 'human-dominated' and 'human-influenced' systems now central to our civilization. It focuses empirically on Britain, the second most influential country for social science research after the US. Using in-depth research, the authors show how the growth of a services economy, and the success of previous scientific interventions, mean that key areas of advance for corporations, public policy-makers, and citizens alike now depend on our ability to understand our complex societies and economies. This is a landmark study in the evidence-based analysis of social science impact.

PAPERBACK ISBN: 978-1-4462-8262-5 • FEBRUARY 2014 • 326 PAGES

LEARN MORE AT SAGEPUB.COM!